The Komnene Dynasty

The Komnene Dynasty

Byzantium's Struggle for Survival
1057–1185

By John C. Carr

Pen & Sword
MILITARY

First published in Great Britain in 2018 by
Pen & Sword Military
an imprint of
Pen & Sword Books Ltd
47 Church Street
Barnsley
South Yorkshire
S70 2AS

ISBN 978 1 52670 229 6

A CIP catalogue record for this book is
available from the British Library.

Printed and bound in England by TJ International, Padstow, Cornwall

Pen & Sword Books Limited incorporates the imprints of Atlas, Archaeology,
Aviation, Discovery, Family History, Fiction, History, Maritime, Military,
Military Classics, Politics, Select, Transport, True Crime, Air World,
Frontline Publishing, Leo Cooper, Remember When, Seaforth Publishing,
The Praetorian Press, Wharncliffe Local History, Wharncliffe Transport,
Wharncliffe True Crime and White Owl.

For a complete list of Pen & Sword titles please contact
PEN & SWORD BOOKS LIMITED
47 Church Street, Barnsley, South Yorkshire, S70 2AS, England
E-mail: enquiries@pen-and-sword.co.uk
Website: www.pen-and-sword.co.uk

Contents

Preface

Let no one be so mad as to believe that there is anything more pleasurable than history.

Niketas Choniates, twelfth-thirteenth century
Byzantine historian

The Byzantine dynasty of the Komnenes lasted from 1057 to 1185, though it effectively can be said to have come into its own in 1081. It followed the dynamic Macedonian dynasty and gave way to the Angeli. The family hailed from the Thracian town of Komne, in what is now the European piece of Turkey. Its extensive landholdings in Anatolia were the basis of the wealth that built it into one of the leading military families of the Byzantine Empire. Komnenes (singular: Komnenos) had distinguished themselves in campaigns under the Macedonians, putting them in a position to seize the Byzantine throne during a particularly weak link in the royal succession.

The Komnenes occupy a particularly sensitive position in the Byzantine era, when the late Roman Empire had endured more than 700 years of domestic and foreign crisis, yet continued to be the great Christian bulwark against the non-Christian East and the aggressive Normans and Latins in the West. The dynasty's predecessors, the Macedonians, had left Byzantium at the height of its reach and prestige; its successors, the Angeli, were merely rearguard fighters against encroaching disaster. In between, it fell to the Komnenes to wage a two-front struggle for Byzantine survival over something more than 100 tumultuous years.

It was under the Komnenes that the Turks first appeared in the Middle East and Eastern Europe. Those redoubtable foes, who were destined to eradicate Byzantium, remain rulers of its heartland to the present day. As if the task of countering Turkish advances was not hard enough, the Normans and acquisitive Italian maritime states in the West—often (but not always) aided and abetted by the popes of Rome—steadily chipped away at the western fringes of the Empire in Greece, the Aegean islands and the Adriatic seaboard. The First and Second Crusades brought the Byzantines into an abrupt and unpleasant contact with the more rapacious elements of the West. Despite their supposedly holy aims, the Crusades and the chronic instability which they caused did their part to undermine Christianity in the entire eastern Mediterranean, with effects that persist until now.

The founder of the Komnenes, Isaac I, gave a foretaste of what was to come by straightening out the Empire's chaotic finances. This brief accomplishment, however, was undone by three unrelated emperors who intervened between Isaac and the next Komnene, Alexios I, who is considered the real solidifier of the dynasty. Under the indefatigable Alexios and his four Komnene successors—John II, Manuel I, the boy-emperor Alexios II and Andronikos I—what might be called the 'management model' of military policy became paramount. This differed from the previous 'patriotic' model in that bottom-line considerations determined the make-up of Byzantine armies and who would command them. The structure of government was in effect militarized, with the emperor at the head of a military aristocracy. The imperial administration was centralized and power removed from the prominent military families in the provinces. This strictly organizational approach encouraged the hiring of mercenaries which, as we will see, removed a vital psychological link between people and military and patriotic sentiment, to the terminal detriment of the Empire.

One key point needs to be borne in mind from the outset: the Byzantines never called themselves by that name. Neither did they call themselves Greeks, though most Byzantine subjects, especially the ruling classes, undoubtedly were. They regarded and referred to themselves proudly as Romans, continuing the long and glorious history of the original Rome, which they considered unbroken from the time of the early republic on the Seven Hills. The founder of what we call the Byzantine Empire, Constantine I (the Great), was simply the emperor, in an unbroken line going back to Augustus, who had taken the momentous step of moving the Empire's capital from Rome to Constantinople in the fourth century, when political and strategic realities in the Mediterranean area had changed hugely since Augustus' day. Many historians, in fact, prefer to call the period between Constantine I and, say, Heraclius, the Late Roman rather than the Byzantine Empire. As we shall see, as late as the twelfth century the royal writer Anna Komnene, who will figure hugely in these pages, could refer to her father Alexios I Komnenos as 'Emperor of the Romans' as a matter of course. The term Byzantine, in fact, only entered general use in 1562. And in modern Greek informal usage to the present day, many Greeks still refer to themselves as *Romii* in a lingering echo of Byzantine times. Thus, in quotes from Byzantine writers referring to 'Romans', we must keep in mind that they mean not Italians but the Byzantine Greeks themselves. The reader will find that I employ the terms 'Byzantine', 'Roman' and 'Greek' interchangeably, especially in the first half of the book. This simply reflects the impossibility of making hard and fast delineations of ethnic and cultural identities in a cosmopolitan Empire, in an era before nationalism came to do the job for us.

The story of the Komnene dynasty encapsulates a point made by Professor Harry Magoulias in the preface to his excellent translation of the *Annals* of Niketas Choniates:

We must never become desensitized to the cutting-edge of the ever-present danger, the threat to life and civilization which was the existential reality of our ancestors, if history is to be more than a story.

The story of the Komnenes may have much to tell us in the early twenty-first century, when the age-old stand-off between East and West, between Christianity and Islam, is again in the forefront of the news.

As in all histories dealing with Byzantium, the reader must put up with a profusion and repetition of names: the Theodoras, the Constantines, the Nikephori and the Alexii, for example, reproduce themselves through generations, and it takes some concentration to keep track of them. Anna Komnene's husband Nikephoros Bryennios, for example, needs to be distinguished from his forebear of the same name who played an important part in the advent to power of the Komnenes. All a historian can do is try and simplify the name tangles as much as is consistent with clarity, and hope that the reader is not derailed too often.

I have decided to dispense with cumbersome chapter notes, which may give a 'scholarly' impression, but for the general reader, and with a subject such as this one, might well be superfluous. They also tend to interrupt the reading flow, more often than not unnecessarily. My sources are outlined in a general bibliographical note at the end.

I extend my sincere thanks to Penelope Wilson Zarganis and her staff at the library of the British School at Athens, without whose help this book could not have been written, my commissioning editor at Pen & Sword, Philip Sidnell, who I hope will be happy to receive 'another exciting Byzantium work', and Nike Morgan and Antigone Kamberou who provided moral support through the tedious months of research. Professor Sergei Karpov of Moscow Lomonosov University, during a chance meeting in Athens, elucidated a few points on the Great Komnenes of Trebizond, on which he is perhaps the world's leading living authority. I would like to have been able to say that some academic or other specialist had read the draft chapters and made valuable corrections, but time pressure did not so permit, and therefore any errors are mine alone.

JCC
Athens
June 2017

Illustrations

1. Michael Psellos and Michael VII (Mount Athos)
2. Joshua of Navi, an emblematic Old Testament figure in twelfth century Byzantine military attire (Hosios Loukas monastery, Greece)
3. Gold coin with the image of Isaac I Komnenos (Numismatic Museum, Athens)
4. Alexios I Komnenos (Hellenic War Museum)
5. Image of Irene Doukaina in St Mark's, Venice (*Der Spiegel/Geschichte*)
6. Anna Komnene in a nun's habit (Greek illustrated youth magazine, c. 1965)
7. Anna Komnene and John II (Greek illustrated youth magazine, c. 1965)
8. Small battleaxe used by the Varangian Guard (Hellenic War Museum)
9. Model of a Greek fire-throwing engine (Hellenic War Museum)
10. Model of a Komnene-era Byzantine siege-tower (Hellenic War Museum)
11. Twelfth century naval battle (Hellenic War Museum)
12. The dromon, a Byzantine warship of the Komnene period (Hellenic War Museum)
13. Period painting of the simultaneous eye-gouging and castration of a conspirator (*Der Spiegel/Geschichte*)
14. John II and Irene (Ekdotike Athenon)
15. Manuel I and his second wife Maria (Ekdotike Athenon)
16. Crown of Nikephoros II Phokas (Ekdotike Athenon)
17. Andronikos I (Hellenic War Museum)
18. John II, Manuel I and Alexios II (Hellenic War Museum)
19. Alexios III Grand Komnenos of Trebizond (Ekdotike Athenon)
20. The monastery of Hosios Loukas, Greece, an example of Komnene-era ecclesiastical architecture (Author's photograph)

Chapter 1

A lady not for turning

One windy day, probably in the autumn of 1106, a sudden strong gust blew down a very old bronze statue in the Forum of Constantine in Constantinople. More than 700 years old, the statue had originally been one of Apollo, but it was said that Constantine the Great, the founder of Constantinople, had it de-paganized and renamed after himself. That formality, like many such formalities, had not stuck and to the people of the capital it was the Anthelion, or 'instead of the sun', a reference to the ancient Apollo who in pagan times was believed to traverse the sky every day in his flaming chariot. So, when the Anthelion unexpectedly succumbed to a blustery southwester, the people were naturally alarmed and, as many still do with such phenomena, attributed a sinister metaphysical significance to it. The commonest interpretation was that the Anthelion's fall portended the imminent death of Emperor Alexios I Komnenos. And the mutterings, of course, reached the emperor's ears.

According to Alexios' daughter Anna, who may well have been present when her father was told of what the fearful people were saying, he laughed it off. 'I am absolutely certain,' he remarked with admirable aplomb, 'that statues blowing over do not induce death.' It is God, he said, who gives and takes away life, and not some sculptor's product. It is a fine and noble reaction, and one worthy of an emperor, yet can we take Anna's assertion at face value? It is impossible to say. Anna Komnene admired her father to the point of sanctification; in her famous memoir, the *Alexiad*, he comes across as a paragon of rulers, near-perfect in body and mind. Yet as she was also one of the most formidable intellects of her time, and not given to self-delusion, we may give her the benefit of the doubt by noting her honesty in an incident that occurred shortly after the statue's fall.

Anna and her three younger sisters one day became aware of an extraordinary commotion coming from the direction of the Agora not far from the palace. Aged about 24 at the time, she was old enough to have known what it was: a conspiracy against her father had just been uncovered, and the ringleaders were being paraded for public ridicule. The girls—probably dressed plainly so as not to stand out in the crowd—slipped out incognito to join the jeering crowds. A jarring scene met their eyes. A group of men, all of them with shaved heads and beards and dressed in sackcloth, were seated sideways on oxen driven through the streets. Their bare heads were decorated with gory sheep's intestines—symbolic 'crowns' for those who would dare to overthrow the emperor. Leading the procession were the equivalent of street wardens, brandishing rods and bawling obscene songs that made fun of the conspirators, all of whom knew what would come next: at the very least, their eyes would be gouged out.

But it was the behaviour of the ringleader that got Anna Komnene's attention. This was Michael Anemas, one of four brothers who had hatched the plot to topple Alexios in league with several noble families and high-ranking army officers. As Anemas was brought into sight of the palace, he was seen to gaze up at the imposing edifice and make a series of gestures. Perhaps he and the other conspirators had been gagged, or simply Anemas could not have been heard above the din of the crowd; but as Anna and her sisters watched transfixed, he raised his hands as if in prayer, and made motions suggesting that he wished his arms and legs and head to be cut off. Whether this was because he truly repented of his acts or wished to die now to escape fearful tortures later, we cannot tell. But Anna seems to have come to the former conclusion—even though Anemas had been convicted of plotting to assassinate her beloved father.

Rushing back to the palace, Anna sought out her mother, the empress Irene Doukaina, who at that moment was in prayer seclusion with Alexios. Irene reluctantly responded to her daughter's frantic gestures and tore herself away from her husband to join Anna at a palace window. Below, Michael Anemas and his accomplices were being led along on their oxen. Anemas' nobility under stress had also impressed the mob, and his captors, noting the swelling signs of public sympathy, appeared reluctant to speed the victims to their fate. A few moments of the spectacle was enough for Irene, who ran back to Alexios begging tearfully for him to reprieve Anemas. 'The truth is,' Anna later wrote, 'we cared for the men for the emperor's sake: it hurt us to think that he was being deprived of such brave men.'

Irene's pleas worked: an official was sent post-haste to halt the grim procession. He was almost too late, for it had arrived at a tall archway known as The Hands. It took its name from a pair of bronze hands on the top; these had been put up years before as a symbolic boundary beyond which a criminal could not hope for a royal pardon. If a condemned man had not yet reached The Hands on his punitive procession, it was always possible for a last-minute pardon to arrive, but once he was through the arch and on the wrong side of The Hands, hope was gone. By Anna's account the imperial official caught up with Anemas right beneath the archway, literally at the last second, and the conspirator, instead of being blinded and possibly put to death, was jailed in a tower—later called the Anemas Tower—near the palace. (We don't know what happened to the other conspirators.)

Anna Komnene's candour and resolve are remarkable for the time. The twelfth century was not an age that exactly encouraged the rise of women in public life. In Europe, from England in the north-west to Byzantium in the south-east, it was kings, statesmen and generals who made things happen. In the concurrent Arab and Islamic world, control by men was even tighter. To be sure, kings and emperors and sultans had wives whose characters and perspicacity sometimes gave them influence in the domestic sphere, or could smooth out the more savage instincts of some leaders. But high-placed women rarely could achieve positions of real political power, which makes the career of Anna Komnene of Byzantium even more remarkable.

Giving her a considerable head start in life was the fact that she had been born (1083) two years into her father's reign, which made her a true *porphyrogennete*, or 'born into the purple'. This was a title given to anyone born while his or her father occupied the Byzantine throne as opposed to, say, being a prince or heir-apparent. Such royal births took place in the famous Purple Chamber of the palace that was set aside for precisely such portentous occasions, hence the designation. In the often-insecure royal environment of Byzantium, where emperors and their families had to spend much of their time and energy fending off rivals, conspirators and coup plots, being a *porphyrogennetos* (the more common masculine form of the term) carried a distinct cachet of legitimacy that could be decisive in keeping a dynasty such as the Komnenes in power.

By many accounts, Anna's looks were a match for her brains. Unfortunately, for Byzantine rulers we have nothing like the startling accuracy of, for example, Hans Holbein's iconic portrait of England's Henry VIII. Any likenesses that have survived are heavily stylized and not to be trusted. The purpose of portraiture in those days, whether through paint or the more elaborate technique of mosaic, was not so much to render a faithful likeness for posterity as to bring out a deeper significance—the impressionistic majesty of what the subject represented rather than what he or she was like externally. Style thus totally dominated substance.

The only hint as to what she actually looked like comes from a contemporary poet and friend of hers, Theodore Prodromos, who wrote that she was dark-haired like her father, of medium height and with large, expressive and playful eyes. And that is pretty much all we have. The adjective 'beautiful' has been carelessly handed down from writer to writer, but without further detail. Anna seems to have also inherited the calm dignity of her mother Irene Doukaina, of the powerful Doukas clan. Anna's own ecstatic description of her mother is rather over the top, and perhaps to be expected from an admiring daughter obsessed with her family's image and power. But keeping this caveat in mind, Irene Doukaina still comes across as an impressive lady. Here is what admirers may have seen while she was still only 15 and betrothed to Alexios:

> She stood upright [Anna wrote] like some young, proud, always blossoming shoot, each limb and her whole body in perfect symmetry... She

> never ceased to fascinate all who saw her... Her face shone with the soft light of the moon... There were rose blossoms on her cheeks, visible a long way off.

Irene's light blue eyes, we are assured, could render speechless anyone who had cause to fear her wrath and her acid tongue, from lazy servants and courtiers to generals and senators. A twelfth century gold *cloisonné* plaque in Saint Mark's in Venice shows Irene as a tall and regal figure, with neat dark hair framing a smallish face and aristocratic mouth. On the other hand, that style was a set standard for Byzantine artists depicting royal or noble women, so we cannot treat it as a lifelike portrait.

Conversely, we have a wealth of information about Anna Komnene's social and intellectual attainments, and character. From an early age, and with the automatic sense of superiority and supreme self-confidence conferred by being a *porphyrogennete*, she considered herself indispensable to the power of the Komnene family and by extension to Byzantium itself. In hindsight, even her physical birth was rather extraordinary; she claimed in all seriousness that her mother endured labour pains for two days more than was necessary, telling her unborn daughter to be patient for a few days so that Alexios could return from a campaign and have Anna enter the world in his presence. The story, though implausible, is not impossible; it also introduces a military element into the beginning of Anna's life in a way that stresses her future loyalty to the Empire and her interest in military and political affairs.

Some historians make the rather disingenuous claim that Anna Komnene, being a woman, could not really have had the breadth of military and political savvy she displayed in the *Alexiad*, on which she began working when she was pushing 60 and by then well out of public life. That claim cannot stand up to scrutiny. Besides the fact that there have been plenty of female political leaders and a few competent military figures through history, Anna's own privileged upbringing and early life steeped her in affairs of state. She was often present when her father the emperor discussed weighty matters with politicians and generals, and was thus able to absorb ideas of how power and influence worked, who were defined as allies and who as enemies, whom to trust and whom not, the insidious traps of human trickery, and above all, the overarching need for the Christian Byzantine state to preserve itself and the ideals of nobility for which it stood.

According to one recent authority, it was this youthful experience that grew and matured into Anna's deep identification of Alexios I with the state itself. In the *Alexiad* 'the Byzantine Empire occupies the centre of the world, and her father occupies centre stage' in 'a cosmic struggle for dominance'. In her eyes, he was almost a second Christ, totally selfless, exerting and sacrificing himself for the greater good. Such a deep and subliminal sense can come only from formative childhood experiences. Of course, Alexios himself was not the near-saint his daughter held him up to be, but her basic notion of the purpose of the state and the military was authentic for its time.

As was *de rigueur* at the time, and has been for royal families until quite recently, Anna was betrothed in infancy. Her selected fiancé was a young noble of her mother's family, Constantine Doukas. In some ways it was an odd match. Nine years older than Anna, Constantine was a son of Michael VII, the previous emperor-but-one, and as such, technically a distant uncle. The betrothal was obviously engineered by Irene to keep the Doukas family in the power loop, as it were. Anna, as the firstborn, was thus expected to become empress regnant (that is, in her own right as opposed to being merely an emperor's consort). It could have been a match made in heaven. Constantine was an almost angelic being, 'blond, with a skin as white as milk, his cheeks suffused with red like some dazzling rose that has just left its calyx'. We are also told that he was, like the typical high-born English boy of a later age, good at sports and games, 'the picture of Eros'. In addition, he, too, was a true-purple *porphyrogennetos*, and at a tender age had the privilege of co-signing palace documents in red ink—an imperial prerogative that only the emperor shared.

The personal vista that spread out before the infant Anna was a glowing one. In time, she would share the throne, as an Augusta, with her handsome husband. But that vista collapsed with startling suddenness. The dynamite that blew it up was the birth of her little brother John on 13 September 1087. At one stroke, her prospects of being crowned in the cathedral of Sancta Sophia were scuppered. Except in extraordinary succession cases, where a male heir could not be rounded up or a male usurper might threaten to step in, any woman's chances of ruling as Augusta in her own right were slim. She was only aged 4 at the time, and probably too young to fully understand what had happened. With the benefit of decades of hindsight, she acknowledged that family and Empire alike rejoiced at John's birth, but there was—literally—a darker side to her memory of the event:

> The child was dark in complexion, his forehead wide and cheeks weak...
> very dark eyes and a sharp character and mind.

Anna's dismay at being pipped to the post of the succession almost certainly accounts for the sniffy and slightly racist tone of her description. True, John may not have approached the fair and angelic Constantine in the appearance stakes, but it was only one, and probably a minor, element in what was to ripen into a bitter and lifelong sibling rivalry.

Not long afterwards, the promising young Constantine Doukas disappeared. Sadly, we don't know any more details, but he may not have been as robust as he looked. The consensus is that he died in the early 1090s, barely out of his teens, from some ailment. Possibly he had been banished after some unsuccessful Doukas plot against Alexios, who would have enough practical motivation for putting Constantine out of the way. If there was foul play, Anna would certainly have revealed it; in her memoir she confesses to 'floods of tears' whenever she thought of him, but makes no accusations. What was painfully obvious from the beginning was that Constantine's demise pushed her yet further down the line of succession.

Knowing now that she would never become commander-in-chief of the Byzantine state and military structure, Anna Komnene grew up determined to make her mark anyway, as befitted a *porphyrogennete*. She was seriously groomed for power. Alexios and Irene provided her with the best education available, from a thorough grounding in the Scriptures to the cream of Greek and Roman literature and thought. Some believe that Alexios discouraged a more rounded education for Anna as unbecoming a woman not expected to play an active role in politics. If that is true, as it may well be, then Anna was able to easily circumvent that restriction by using her prerogative as a princess to gain access to any of the classics she wanted; this way she acquired a facility with classical Greek that few outside the clergy could have attained. She was particularly drawn to the ancient history of Athens and Sparta, which means she would have devoured both the *Histories* of Herodotus and the *Peloponnesian War* of Thucydides, which are the par excellence military histories of the classical period and our main sources for Spartan military prowess in particular. Especially enthralling to her was Homer's hard-slogging, no-holds-barred epic of the last year of the Trojan War, the *Iliad*, a Y chromosome soldier's narrative if ever there was one. And as if that were not enough, she read widely in medicine and metaphysics, and contributed to the corpus of western thought on Aristotle.

With the fleeting young Constantine Doukas out of the picture, the way was free for Anna to acquire a proper functional husband in the person of Nikephoros Bryennios, a member of a military family whose namesake grandfather had been blinded in punishment for an attempt on the throne in 1077. Thus there was no love lost between the Komnenes and the Bryennii; moreover, powerful military families were a constant threat, real or potential, to the throne. The senior Bryennios was under a cloud; though he had fought valiantly in the disastrous Battle of Manzikert six years earlier, sustaining three wounds, he had been unable to prevent the humiliating capture of Emperor Romanos IV Diogenes and the decimation of the Byzantine army at the hands of the Seljuk Turks. Under Alexios, however, the family seems to have been rehabilitated. No doubt Alexios wanted to patch up his differences with the Bryennii in the wider strategic interest, and one way of doing it was to marry off Anna to Nikephoros Bryennios junior, who would be named Kaisar (Caesar), one step beneath the emperor in the court hierarchy, with Anna as his Kaisarissa.

The union was clearly a political one, but Anna very likely found herself genuinely attracted to Nikephoros. Though she would later claim that her true desire was to remain unmarried after losing Constantine Doukas, the record does not support the assertion. By all accounts she had few, if any, qualms about the marriage. To her Nikephoros was 'an extremely handsome man, very intelligent', and indeed 'the most outstanding man of the time'. We may take such lavish praise cautiously, as the product of long hindsight and perhaps unspoken regrets. Also, as in her memories of Constantine Doukas, when in later life she thought of Nikephoros, again there would be 'floods of tears'.

> He was a man surpassing all others... his literary attainments, his multi-faceted political and religious wisdom... What joy suffused his body, that imposing stature, worthy of more than just a royal throne, of something higher and holier.

How seriously should we take such effusions? Separating truth from rosy hindsight is a perilous task. The nearest we can get to doing it is to suppose that, always in her words, the political, regal, military, spiritual and sexual sides of her marriage blend into an intoxicating chemical mix of power. In Anna's mind all those elements constituted the one heady reality of the ruling class.

Anna and Nikephoros were bound in matrimony when she was a mere 15 years of age. That was by no means unusual in Roman and Byzantine times; young people had to grow up fast, without the extended adolescence that only relatively recently has become the norm in our coddled age. In western knightly circles, for example, it was widely believed that if a boy was still at school at 12, he was good for nothing but the priesthood. Even in modern Greece a common saying has lingered that a man should either marry very young or enter a monastery. Developed teenage girls were determinedly pushed into marriage as soon as possible, no doubt to safely channel sexual urges whose free use could destabilize society and fuel crime. Whether Byzantine morals in general were indeed improved by this custom, however, is debatable.

Anna bore the personable Bryennios no fewer than eight children, of whom just four survived infancy. Few personal details are available, but in her exhaustive memoir she hints that her life was never free from some kind of problem, mostly to do with envy of her exalted position. Her character, moreover, was not one to brook opposition of any kind, and perhaps that helped bring on some of what she terms her 'continual misfortunes, some from without, some from within'. She also appears to have had not much of a sense of humour or the ability to philosophize life's reverses. The world weighed heavily on her keen mind. For the next two decades she lived in the very nexus of the ebb and flow of domestic and foreign policy, taking it all very seriously as befitted a Kaisarissa. It is almost inconceivable that, given the extraordinary agility and absorptive capacity of her mind, during this period she did not acquire a familiarity with military affairs. Almost certainly her husband, himself a man with literary leanings, coached her extensively on the subject. Yet all the while she was tormented by a slow burn over the fact that her younger brother John would one day succeed his father as emperor, keeping her in the political shade. In the end, she decided to act. She would not have long to wait.

In 1118, worn out by arduous campaigning and the cares of office, Alexios I died after months of what appears to be worsening congestive heart failure. Here's where Anna's memoir ends, and as a result, her record becomes murky. According to hostile later writers she made a bid to place her husband on the vacant throne, with herself as empress, only to be forestalled by John who (she claimed) surreptitiously removed and palmed her father's ring of office as he was bending in sympathy over the dying emperor. Alexios must have long known the machinations that were going on in view of his imminent demise.

His wife Irene Doukaina had made no secret of her desire to see Anna and Nikephoros in blissful union on the throne, and according to the later writer Niketas Choniates, the emperor retorted, in one of his last recorded statements, that 'the whole Roman realm will laugh if I place that Macedonian [Bryennios] on the throne instead of my own son'.

This was too much for Irene, who shot back: 'All through your life you have done nothing but cunning deeds, and your words have done nothing but mask your thoughts. You're the same as always, even on your deathbed!' This outburst may not be taken too seriously; it could well have been the product of fatigue and despair over her husband's terminal illness and the cares of office. But a great part of those cares was precisely the ongoing worry whether her revered daughter would indeed wear the royal diadem she deserved. But there was a point beyond which Irene would not go to push Anna to the top. Not so Anna herself, apparently. Choniates is one of several writers who claim that Anna Komnene seriously considered putting her brother John out of the way when it became clear he was the successor, and most historians agree that an assassination plot at some point was on the cards, though just how serious it was we cannot say.

The threat would explain John's reaction and Anna's swift exclusion from the circle of power and banishment to a convent. Interestingly, Nikephoros Bryennios remained untainted by the affair, as we see him riding on campaign by the side of John II, before his own death in 1138. This, of course, raises the question of what Bryennios' relations with Anna were after her fall from grace. We know that they were not always harmonious. She herself asserted that as a nun she did not receive a single visitor in thirty years, a claim we may attribute more to her own wounded pride than to any basis in fact. When she was forced into monastic obscurity, the marriage was already over.

Despite Kaisarissa Anna's outwardly impeccable dedication to her husband and the wider royal family, she nursed a deep streak of frustration that Nikephoros Bryennios did not have the assertiveness that she would have liked to see in a man. She wished there were some way around the strict conventional ban on women leading armies; in one memorable moment of fury captured by a chronicler during her attempt to derail her brother John, she cried that she 'wished she had the penis' in her marriage rather than Bryennios—a sentiment that speaks volumes more than any more delicate paraphrase. She saw herself as the necessarily figurative soldier of her layer of the family, prevented only from taking up the sword by her unfortunate and unmerited lack of male genitalia.

Partly for this reason, Anna Komnene has been dragged into that murky corner of academia known as 'gender studies'. Practitioners of this school have claimed, with a touch of triumphalism, that she was the consummate feminist of her time. She was quite definitely not. Far from supporting and fighting for the rights of her sex, as a true feminist would, she deprecated the vast majority of women as weak and emotion-driven. Her ideal for other noble women, including her mother, reveals curiously masculine criteria: an hourglass figure, modesty, devotion to motherhood and family and all-round agreeability—and demurely veiled on their infrequent ventures out of doors. These are not attributes a diehard feminist would hold up for emulation. And Anna Komnene, despite what she put down on paper in later and wiser years, cannot be imagined as herself conforming to that stereotype. She was one of nature's fighters, if not with a man's weapons, then with a woman's wit.

Though a powerful presence at court, she was not necessarily widely liked, but strong and persistent in her views, and eager to absorb military matters. Certainly, her *Alexiad*, like the *Iliad* on which it was consciously modelled, bursts with well-described military events that betray a not inconsiderable knowledge of strategy and tactics from the outset. But was it all her own work? We know that Bryennios made extensive notes of his own about Alexios' campaigns at the express request of Irene Doukaina, and almost certainly Anna drew on these. But that, of course, is no failing in a military historian, and indeed indicates a degree of care and conscientiousness. In the final analysis Anna alone was the driving mind behind the organization and writing of the *Alexiad*, a task that consumed at least ten years.

Another academic sub-discipline with much to say about Anna's character (as it has come down to us) is psychoanalysis. To begin with, she gives the distinct impression of being what the French would later call *une femme aux hommes*, a woman who feels comfortable around men and seeks their company, not only from an erotic standpoint but also out of a desire to identify with male power. The snappy remark to her husband that she wished she had his genital equipment would appear to support this view. Then there are the incessantly glowing descriptions of her father, bordering on star-struck adulation, which have led some to wonder whether he represented the vicarious penis-power that she subconsciously wished for. Or perhaps it was a subconscious cover for a love-hate relationship. Correspondingly, she despised eunuchs, of which there were many in the Byzantine court, and gives them merely passing mention in her memoir. In another famous passage from the *Alexiad* which often has been picked over for pointers to Anna's character, she casts a most appreciative eye over the tall blond Norman leader Bohemond Guiscard:

> He was slender of waist and flanks, with broad shoulders and chest, strong in the arms; overall he was neither too slender, nor too heavily built and fleshy, but perfectly proportioned... His hair was light-coloured and did not go down to his shoulders as it does with other barbarians... His eyes were light blue and gave some hint of the man's spirit and dignity.

John II Komnenos was well aware of his pushy and strong-willed Kaisarissa sister's attempts to sideline him, even perhaps to the point of murder. He must have known that at his birth, Anna had disparaged his darkish colouring, so unlike the fair and rosy complexion of the young blonde Constantine to whom she had been betrothed as an infant. And that was probably just the most egregious of her prejudices towards her brother. But as far as is known, he took no punitive measures against her apart from confiscating her property assets—and that was just temporary. She retired, humiliated, to the convent of Theotokos Kecharitomene (Mother of God Full of Grace), which had been built by her mother and which, conveniently, had separate sleeping quarters for distinguished members of what was otherwise an austere commune. Here she had plenty of time to ruminate and reflect, and gradually build up the grand nostalgic notion of her father as a being only slightly less than divine. In the words of a modern scholar:

> The Byzantine Empire occupies the centre of her world, and her father occupies centre stage. [There is] a cosmic struggle for dominance, in which the empire is pitted against its many foes. Her father is the defender of the state... a Christ-like figure, who devoted his great talents to the defence and enlargement of the state.

This is indeed the impression one gets from ploughing through the *Alexiad*, which Anna began about 1143, after she had been in voluntary monastic confinement for at least twenty years. But is it an accurate one? Most commentators assume that the work is an obvious, if sophisticated, hagiography of her father, and by extension the best years of the Komnene dynasty. However, Anna herself was quite explicit in her claim that she did not intend her work to be anything but a straight and objective record of events, and she would not shy away from controversial material. Therefore the historical verdict must remain open.

Anna Komnene's inner frustrations may have boosted her eager descriptions of battles and campaigns that, writes one scholar, 'give no hint of a female sensibility, but rather a joy of male bravery, clever strategies and toughness'. It is admittedly hard to reconcile this style with a woman who is closeted away from the turmoil of the world. A nun, we feel, ought not to write like a battle-hardened war veteran. But she was such a remarkable woman that we feel no incongruity in this. Had she been able to ride into battle, she would likely have been a veritable Boudicca. Besides, in Byzantium, as in later papal Rome, military prowess and religious devotion coexisted quite happily, the one complementing the other.

Anna Komnene's religious convictions were unswayable, firm and fully Orthodox. She set her jaw in approval when a heretical priest of the Bulgarian Bogomil sect—one of those periodic European movements trying to hark back to 'basic' Christianity that included the Albigenses of France—was burned at the stake in the Hippodrome in view of the palace. When it came to preserving the religious foundations of the Byzantine state, she was as tough as they come. Along with her religious beliefs came a firm adherence to the principle of eugenics—the theory that noble families are far likelier to produce all-round achieving men (and women) than other social classes. For her the ideal man would be nobly-born, tall, of athletic physique, handsome of features, aggressive and courageous in battle, yet also temperate, intelligent, cultured and gentle and courteous to women—an ideal, one might add, that precious few women over the ages have ever had the pleasure of knowing.

Why she waited so long to begin writing—or, by some accounts, to begin dictating to a sister-scribe—is a mystery. Very likely she jotted down random thoughts and memories in the intervals between her religious devotions, putting them into literary shape only later. She may have spent time revising and correcting and editing. There is a hint in the opening paragraphs of her memoir that she deliberately waited a long time before putting pen to paper for fear that if she did it too soon, 'someone might conclude that in composing the history of my father I am glorifying myself.' Whatever the reasons for the delay, it is clear that time had not dimmed the intensity of her emotions. 'Floods of tears fill my eyes,' she writes, 'when I think of Rome's [i.e. Byzantium's] great loss,' referring to her revered father. During the day and in the evenings by candlelight, she worked on her memoir, fighting off fatigue. 'As I wield my pen at lamp-lighting time, I feel my words to be slipping away as I doze a bit over my writing.' Then, the great work finally at an end, there is no sign that the writing has eased her soul. 'God has indeed visited me with great calamities... Let this be the end of my history, then, lest as I write of these sad events [i.e. the deaths of her father and husband] I become even more resentful.'

As the very last word of the *Alexiad* (in its English translation, at least), that 'resentful' shows that Anna Komnene could never in the end come to terms with the unpredictable ebb and flow of power relationships that in her view diluted the Komnene nucleus and set the stage for dynastic decline. Her work has been characterized as better literature than history, more an attempt to imitate Homer and Plato than to provide an impartial historical narrative of the mediaeval court to which she belonged. On the other hand, it has been argued that the *Alexiad* belongs to the paradigm of 'feminine history', which is purported to be much more subjective and feeling-laden, and with sharper insights into character, than strictly factual 'man-written' works. Whatever the merits of such arguments, until her death, in or about 1153, aged around 70, Kaisarissa Anna remained a true Komnene, flintily devoted to royal family and Empire, and confident to the end, despite her many disappointments, that her dynasty was the pinnacle of all realms. She will loom large in the pages to come.

Chapter 2

Constantine's Legacy

To conquer, one must rely upon the allegiance of a group animated with one corporate spirit and end. Such a union of hearts and wills can operate only through divine power and religious support... When men give their hearts and passions to a desire for worldly goods, they become jealous of one another, and fall into discord... If, however, they reject the world and its vanities for the love of God... their union makes them stronger; the good cause makes rapid progress, and culminates in the formation of a great and powerful empire.

Ibn Khaldun (fourteenth century)

It is one of the many ironies of history that the best case for Byzantine military policy through the centuries was made by an Arab philosopher-historian owing allegiance to those who would in the end destroy Byzantium. Ibn Khaldun has perhaps never been equalled, even in the West, for the cogency of his observations on human nature and historical processes. When he wrote, the Byzantine Empire was fast expiring, and perhaps because of that he didn't expend too much thought on the Greeks and Romans. Yet the passage quoted above, taken from his ambitiously-titled *Muqaddama al-Alamat* (Introduction to the Universe), shows up the ideological and religious basis of theories of statehood common to both the Christian Byzantines and their Muslim rivals.

When in the late winter of 1081 Alexios Komnenos strode confidently into the palace, aged just 24, to take his place as Byzantium's seventy-sixth emperor, he was well aware that he was continuing an unbroken tradition lasting more than 700 years—or, if we include all of Roman imperial history, around 1,100 years. One of the more remarkable yet least-remarked phenomena of history is the longevity and cultural unity of the East Roman or Byzantine Empire. Since its formal opening for business on Monday morning, 11 May 330, the Empire maintained a remarkable political, spiritual and cultural consistency. Nowhere near the same can be said of any of the present nations of East or West. To take a similar time span, the difference between, say, the England of the tenth century and the Great Britain of the twenty-first is enormous, and not just because of overwhelming social and technological change. The very concept of the state and what it is for have been altered far beyond what was believed in the time of King Alfred of Wessex. Similarly, the France and Germany of today bear little resemblance to their embryos of eleven centuries ago. The European Union's attempt in the late twentieth and early twenty-first centuries to revive something like a multinational Empire already seems to be fraying at the seams. In Byzantium on the contrary, from the day when Constantine I (the Great) inaugurated his Rome-replacement Constantinople on the twin foundations of the power of Late Rome and the Christian faith, the template was set and proved amazingly durable.

This is not to say that Byzantium did not have its serious threats and crises that might have felled less well-founded regimes. The supreme position of emperor, in fact, was a curiously precarious one. In only a minority of cases did the eldest son of an emperor inherit the throne. Of Alexios' seventy-five predecessors, about half died while reigning, mostly from some ailment, chronic or sudden (few, if any, passed on peacefully from pure old age). Thirteen were assassinated, sometimes in horrific fashion. Eleven were deposed, six abdicated (usually going to a monastery, voluntarily or not), four fell in battle, and two perished in hunting accidents. There are question marks over the ends of several emperors, as some fatal ailments could well have been the result of poisoning by relatives or rivals, and history abounds with examples of how the innocent-sounding term 'hunting accident' can cover many sins. The turnover, consequently, was on the high side, averaging more than ten emperors over any calendar century.

Yet in the middle of the eleventh century those Byzantine Greco-Romans of a thoughtful and educated bent could feel pretty proud of themselves. For more than 700 years their Empire had seen off foe after foe. More than once Constantinople had been in deadly danger, but always its soldiers and faith had pulled it through. While France and England, for example, had mutated from feudal ex-Roman backwaters to royal nation-states, and while the once-insignificant and scattered Arabs had been welded into a formidable power by the new creed of Islam, Byzantium had stood steady as a rock, absorbing the repercussions from both sides while maintaining stability in the east Mediterranean, the world's most important trade basin.

There were few times when the Byzantines could sit back and fully enjoy the fruits of peace. There always seemed to be someone to fight off, whether it was the Muslims in the east or pagan tribes in the north and west, and even Christian foes such as the Normans in the Mediterranean. But two things had sustained the Byzantine state through all that turmoil: the Orthodox Christian faith and the personal stake that every Roman subject had in the preservation of the capital Constantinople and the emperor who, as the vicegerent of the Almighty, was revered as the supreme symbol and protector of his (and occasionally her) people. (An analogy of sorts can be seen in modern Britain which since around 1300 has been a virtually constant majority-backed monarchy and for most of its history has had to defend itself against threatening continental powers.) The dynasty of the Komnenes can be better understood if we review previous Roman-Byzantine history to see how the solid state tradition was built up, and what the Komnene fought to uphold.

The most striking aspect of the epochal decision by Emperor Constantine I to transfer the Empire's capital from Rome to Constantinople in the early fourth century is the sheer willpower and energy with which he threw himself into that colossal task. If we are to believe Constantine's biographer Eusebius of Caesarea (and there is no overt reason why we should not), the emperor personally and on foot traced with his spear-point the perimeter of what was to become the inner core of Constantinople, hitherto the Greek trading town of Byzantion. According to Eusebius, those officials accompanying Constantine soon became exhausted, but he carried on remorselessly, saying he would stop 'only when He who is ahead' of him told him to. From Edward Gibbon onwards, this legend has been all but dismissed as religious propaganda. But even if we choose to take that stance, the story is a powerful reminder that Christian determinism provided the entire ideological and intellectual foundation for the subsequent Empire which, from beginning to end, fought to uphold that all-encompassing principle.

Constantine I himself, as is well known, was Rome's first Christian emperor, whose late-in-the-day conversion was the first decisive move towards making Christianity the state religion. Again, the latter-day revisionists have been busily at work here, claiming that Constantine's conversion was a political tactic only, and that he himself could well have secretly remained a pagan. As evidence, they point to the fact that he converted only when he was clearly dying, which implies a lifetime of doubt and a timid 'taking out spiritual insurance' when the end was nigh. From what we know of Constantine, such conduct would be completely out of character. The undoubted fact is that Constantine's policies did entrench Christianity and its propagation as the basic domestic and foreign policy tenets of the Empire. If we are to (as many do) take at face value Constantine's claim to have seen a bright cross in the sky with the Greek words 'By this conquer' (En touto nika) before advancing on Rome to defeat his pagan rival Maxentius in 312, then there can be no doubt that the Christian ideological foundation of what was to grow into the Byzantine Empire was firmly set in place before even the founding of Constantinople. Indeed, Constantine gave himself the additional title of Isapostolos, or equal to the apostles, to stress the unquestioning respect that he was due. Every Byzantine emperor who followed him continued that tradition.

It's worth lingering a little over Constantine I, as he was the one who inherited more than three centuries of Roman imperial practice and adapted it almost seamlessly to serve a Christian instead of a pagan polity. It may be hard for someone

brought up in a secular democratic tradition to completely understand the ratio-
nale behind what is commonly (but wrongly) considered 'divine-right' rule and
how it was accepted as more or less 'natural' for many centuries. It is as if classical
Athens' famous experiment in democracy in the fifth century BC had been completely forgotten. In fact, democracy had not so much been forgotten as rejected
as unworkable in the complex and turbulent Mediterranean at the start of the
Christian era, when Rome's dominions stretched from Britain in the north to
Palestine in the south and east, encompassing peoples of radically different eth-
nicity and culture.

Democracy is hard work, and requires political maturity on the part of a great
many citizens and political leaders, not to mention a degree of economic stability
and peace. When domestic or foreign crisis strikes, the public, weary of deliber-
ation and debate, cries for action and leadership, caring little for what form that
leadership will take. When people are afraid and insecure, liberties take a back
seat. And so it was in the last few decades before Christ. There was no way the
equitable mechanisms of the Roman Republic, designed for a homogeneous Italian
population, could have handled the huge administrative burden that Rome had
assumed. The pressures had triggered unstable and violent politics in Rome. In 44
BC Julius Caesar was assassinated two months after he was voted *dictator perpetuus*
in recognition of the fact that Rome had become too big to be handled by anything
less than a strong man at the helm. And few complained, or were in a position to
do anything about it, when seventeen years later Octavian took the name Augustus
and became *Imperator*, inaugurating the long line of Roman emperors of whom
Constantine was the fifty-fifth.

Constantine was acclaimed emperor in Britain by the Roman contingents stationed there on the death of his father, the Caesar Constantius Chlorus, in York
in 305. Thus at the outset he had the instrument that had become vital to anyone
hoping to secure supreme power—the army. It was largely thanks to the enthusiastic support of his soldiers, plus his own steady and courageous character, that
eventually led him to Rome to eliminate Maxentius at the Battle of the Milvian
Bridge. But the army was just one of the two pillars of strength that an emperor
needed to retain his hold on power; the other was religion, which, by Constantine's
day, had essentially come to mean Christianity.

Whether Constantine indeed gazed on a shining cross in the sky north of
Rome is a disputed issue, according to the ideological or religious outlook of
each writer, and cannot be dealt with here. Suffice it to say that in that age such
supernatural phenomena were considered quite normal, and indeed were much
sought-after by ambitious men as signs, real or imagined, of divine favour.
The Roman army already enjoyed a long tradition of pagan piety centring on
the notion of the emperor as *invictus* (invincible, or unconquered) by dint of

divine protection embodied in the concept of *felicitas*, or good fortune. But the emperor as a man was distinguished from his godlike aura called the *numinus*. Every Roman military camp had its shrine where this 'blurring of the distinction between patron gods and client emperors', in the words of Constantine's biographer Paul Stephenson, was revered. If all this sounds vague and inconclusive to a mind of today, it may be that we haven't enough concrete evidence with which to paint a sharper picture. The point to be made here is that Constantine, thanks to a devoted military establishment, his momentous decision to apply his power to the fight for Christianity and not least his own dynamic personality, struck at precisely the right historical moment to set the pattern for what was to morph into the Byzantine Empire, the greatest Christian power of its time, and perhaps for all time.

Constantine finally became sole and unquestioned ruler of the Empire after defeating his eastern rival Licinius in battle in 324. His first biographer, Eusebius of Caesarea, places the encounter in its standard religious ideological context:

> One side [that of Licinius] advanced confident in the great throng of gods and with a large military force, protected by the shapes of dead people in lifeless images. The other [that of Constantine], girt with the armour of true religion, set up against the multitude of his enemies the saving and life-giving sign as a scarer and repellent of evils.

The sign Eusebius refers to is the *chi-rho*, a superimposition of the Greek letters Χ and Ρ, the first letters of ΧΡΙΣΤΟΣ, or Christ. It was the sign that Constantine's soldiers had carried to victory after victory since the Milvian Bridge, and encapsulated in one potent symbol the new direction politics and war were taking. By the time he had overcome his internal rivals, Constantine's method of warfare, in Stephenson's words, 'transform[ed] how Christians viewed war, and allowed the transformation of a Roman army into a Christian army'. It was a transformation that would last right up until the Komnenes and beyond.

The greatest change from previous Roman imperial practice may not at first have been apparent. Whereas Roman emperors until now had demanded worship as gods—that is, recruiting religious practice to prop up the head of state—Constantine stood that on its head. The state was now pledged to prop up religion by the full force of its political and military instruments, and that is how it remained until the fall of Constantinople more than a millennium later.

It would be a mistake to consider the founding of the new capital of Constantinople as a conscious break with the old Roman past. In fact, it was precisely the opposite: a reinvigoration and reinvention of the Rome-based Empire, designed overtly to enable the continuation of the Augustan tradition that so recently had fallen into discredit. The day of inauguration was commemorated by a monument on which the following was inscribed:

> To Thee, Christ, King and overseer of the world, I bestow the city your servant, with its sceptre and the entire Roman state; preserve her and save her from all harm.

The new capital on the Bosporus was, in fact, officially named New Rome (*Nova Roma*), and the official language continued to be Latin, though Constantinople lay well inside Greek-speaking territory. Most important of all, even after centuries had passed and the Greek character of the Byzantine Empire had become dominant, the emperors always called themselves and their subjects Romans (a term which echoes in Greek colloquial parlance to this day).

This template received its first and most serious test very quickly. Constantine's successors—his quarrelling sons Constantine II, Constantius and Constans (to the confusion of generations of students)—were by no means up to the task their larger-than-life father had bequeathed to them. Their stages of rule are a depressing chronicle of nearly a quarter of a century of intrigue and murder; when the survivor of this maelstrom, Constantius, died of a fever on campaign in 361, an intriguing figure was waiting in the wings to take his place – and, if possible, upend the whole ideological and religious basis of the Empire that Constantine I had laid down. This was Julian, a bookish and eccentric young man who had been untouched by Constantius' bloody purges of potential rivals to the throne largely because no one thought he could be a serious player in politics. These experiences of what he had been told was Christian statecraft, plus a thorough classical education in Athens where paganism still ran strong, were enough for him to jettison Christianity altogether and try and restore the pagan divinities.

Before assuming the Byzantine throne, Julian had grown up fast. His appointment as a general in Gaul had caused him, against all expectations, to abandon his nerdy ways and become a skilled and courageous military commander. To the general acclaim of his soldiers, he marched on Constantinople and was crowned emperor. But when he tried to change the state religion back to paganism, conspicuously performing sacrifices and divinations with more than ordinary zeal, that soldierly support soured quickly. The clergy and the vast bulk of the population had never warmed to the new emperor, so when a Persian spear fatally pierced his abdomen in a battle on the Tigris River in the summer of 363 (a persistent rumour claimed that a Christian officer in his own army cast the fateful weapon), he was far from universally mourned. Indeed, Julian has ever since been saddled with the epithet Apostate, to fix for all time his sin of trying to turn back a tide that was proving to be unstoppable.

As if to compensate for the deviation under Julian, and the few confused reigns that followed him, it fell to Theodosius I (379–395) to restore yet more thoroughly the Christian model of the state and foreign and military policy. A Spaniard given to flashes of murderous temper, Theodosius pursued a cautious foreign policy, preferring to concentrate on home affairs, in particular the eradication of all remaining pagan traces in the Greek and Roman world, including the Olympic Games, which had continued uninterrupted for more than 1,000 years. (More than 1,500 years would pass before the Games were resurrected in their modern form.) It is often wrongly assumed that Constantine the Great established Christianity as the official religion of the Late Roman Empire; in fact, he and his rival Licinius merely legalized Christianity along with any other belief that people might choose to adhere to. It was Theodosius who firmly put the official stamp on the faith of Christ, allowing no other to pollute the ideology of the state and possibly aid Constantinople's foes.

Theodosius was as devout as they come. While on campaign against the last pagan pretender to the throne, his army suffered reverses. We are told by the chronicler Orosius that just before the Battle of Cold River in northern Italy he lay prostrate on the ground all night in tearful penitence and prayer, asking himself why the fight against the pagan was going so badly. The next day, writes Orosius, a violent wind turned the enemy's arrows back and inspired the emperor's army to win a signal victory. Under Theodosius, army camps resembled travelling churches, with soldiers required to engage in mass prayer before every march. The old Roman military oath to serve the emperor was expanded and modified to place the Trinity at the top of the chain of command: 'By God, Christ, and the Holy Spirit, and by the majesty of the emperor, which second to God is to be loved and worshipped by the human race.'

Were the remnants of paganism really as serious a threat to the Empire as Theodosius supposed? The answer may be given in military-strategic terms. Julian had fallen in battle against the Persians, a power that had never ceased to be a strategic threat to Greek and Roman power in the east Mediterranean ever since Darius landed his seaborne army at Marathon in 490 BC. When the Roman republic mutated into Empire, the Parthians had occupied what had been, and what would again become, the Persian Empire, and arduous indeed was Rome's effort to subdue them to keep the eastern fringes of its own Empire secure. It is generally accepted that the Parthians were an intermediate stage in Persian history between the Achaemenid dynasty that features in the Persian Wars of the ancient Greeks and the Sasanids who took over the running of Persian power in AD 224. During their tenure, however, the Parthians had developed sophisticated combat techniques from which the Romans, and later the Byzantines, could learn much.

Beneath the inevitable rivalry for territory along the Empire's eastern borders, there ran a deeper religious and ideological battle. The Persians were Manichaeans, adhering to a creed which the official Roman–Byzantine church found repugnant and a threat to the loyalty of the populations in the border regions. The church itself was having to deal with heresies springing up here and there like weeds in a ploughed field, moving Theodosius soon after his accession to firmly uphold Catholic Christianity (seemingly the first-ever appearance of the term 'Catholic', meaning all-encompassing) as the state faith, threatening everything else as worthy of 'visitation by divine vengeance, and... the stroke of our own authority'. Thus, even if the Persians had not presented a strategic threat, the very fact of their non-Christian religion would very likely have moved the Roman armies against them anyway.

Before his death Theodosius had divided the Empire between his two sons Honorius and Arcadius, assigned to rule the West and East respectively. Neither proved competent, with the result that the Italian Rome was sacked by Alaric's Goths in 410. That catastrophe, the first time that the Eternal City ever succumbed to external invasion, set the seal on its decline, lending even more legitimacy to the claim of Constantinople to being the real, surviving Rome. The Goths at this time were just one of several marauding East European peoples ranging across Europe and making life insecure, further boosting the importance of Byzantium as the most stable and enlightened power in the continent.

It was this vision that stimulated one of Byzantium's most illustrious emperors, Justinian I (527–565), to take personal charge of defending the Empire against pagan attacks and reuniting East and West in a renewed Roman realm. Large parts of Italy were still technically under Byzantine control—though somewhat shaky in places—and Justinian was not about to let these regions slip into barbarism simply by default. This emperor, who devoted much of his time to updating and codifying the great corpus of Roman law, took seriously his descent from the great Augusti of old. Small wonder, then, that he fought strenuously to bring the original Rome and all Italy back into the fold. Thanks to his brilliant general, Belisarius, he succeeded for a while. But simultaneous strategic problems in the East and political problems at home prevented him from bringing the full force of the Roman military to the reconquest of Italy. Yet the dream remained. Whatever travails and mortal threats the Empire might undergo, wrote Kosmas Indikopleustes at the time, 'the Roman state is not dissoluble, will remain unstained through the ages, as the first to believe in the Lord Christ.' By 'Roman state' he clearly meant whatever Rome had conquered, ranging from Britain to Syria and Egypt. The vision, in fact, was even wider: as God and Christ were for all mankind, so the whole physical globe was theoretically subject to the Christian Empire. This mindset pervaded the Empire for its entire career. (It's a supreme historical irony that the Byzantine Empire was fated to be eclipsed by another religion, some of whose adherents today take precisely the same uncompromising universalist view.)

The third emperor after Justinian, General Maurikios (582–602, usually called Maurice in older histories), rose to the throne on the laurels of successfully ending a twenty-year war with Persia and securing the Danube River as the Empire's north-west frontier. Maurikios was one of those soldier-emperors who thought deeply about the relationship between strategy and politics, and put his thoughts down for posterity in the form of the *Taktika kai Strategika* that is the first western treatise on military science. The work starts out by firmly stating the philosophical and spiritual basis of all military activity:

> Over all our thoughts and actions let there be the Holy Trinity, our God and Saviour, our secure divine hope, He Who plans great and worthy things, before any favourable outcome.

This opening paragraph is no mere ritualistic invocation. All foreign and military policy was based on the basic task of breaking down all barriers to the expansion of Christianity. 'Wars had only one aim,' writes Guerdan, 'to find a way to the heart, to make an opening through which the divine light could enter.'

Byzantine generals and politicians knew as well as anyone that at the outset of every endeavour, the outcome is uncertain, that the best-laid plans can and do go very wrong. In many such cases blame cannot be clearly laid at anyone's door; concatenations of events are carried along by their own logic. In our secular age we try, often vainly, to dig for 'rational' causes of such upsets. In Byzantium the answer was already there: there is something bigger than human authority and rationality, and that something, or Someone, ultimately drives events. As long as that basic fact of life was kept in mind, emperors and generals could plan their battles and campaigns but be able to accept the result philosophically if they went wrong—of course, assuming no one specifically messed up, in which case, well, the Almighty had His own purposes. A general was likened to a good sea captain who, despite his skills, is often defeated by the weather.

When Maurikios took power, the Roman military had been allowed to languish. He was quite disappointed in the senior officer corps:

> Our military affairs have been neglected for a long time, covered over completely by forgetfulness; and as long as the generals are ignorant even of obvious matters, many are the unhappy events that occur, both because soldiers are untrained and the generals inexperienced.

It's astonishing to read such an account just a few decades after the masterful campaigns of Belisarius and Justinian's efficient war management. Maurikios was very sensitive to the psychological aspects of generalship, implying that too much strictness, far from stiffening an army, could easily demoralize it.

> We advise the general above all to love God and seek justice, and hasten
> to secure God's favour, which he will obtain, unless it is not His will...
> He must be gentle and calm to others, austere and frugal in his life and
> appearance, and not haughty or difficult to his escort.

We see here the ideal Roman military officer, a man of authority yet considerate to his subordinates, avoiding displays of superiority in his private and professional life, and above all a devout Christian because it was Christianity that ultimately he was called on to fight for. Some men met Maurikios' lofty criteria, but most probably didn't; yet few doubted the ultimate spiritual foundation and significance of the Byzantine state.

It fell to Heraclius (610–641) to fulfil the fighting part of the duties of a Byzantine emperor. By the time of his accession—after dethroning the blood-thirsty tyrant Phokas and having his remains, by some accounts, turned into dog food—the Empire continued to be Roman in name only. Its official language had become Greek, along with its wider literary and spiritual culture. The change had its effect on the imperial ideology, which became even more intensely Christian and turned Heraclius into the first crusader. Whereas Justinian had been content to manage strategy from the palace in Constantinople, Heraclius as a true soldier took the field in person. He was also aided, it was claimed, by an extraordinary intervention of divine power in the twenty-sixth year of his reign when he was away fighting the Persians.

The Avars, an East European people of Mongol origin, had originally been allies of Byzantium, but perceiving that the Empire was under strain from the Persian campaigns in the east they had begun raiding imperial territory. In 617 they surged to the very walls of Constantinople, unnerving even Heraclius but not the steely Patriarch of the Church, Sergios, who sold off tons of ecclesiastical gold, silver and jewels to pay for a new army and navy. Some of the money also went to bribe the Avars to withdraw. But they returned with a vengeance nine years later, again while Heraclius was away campaigning in the east. This time they made a direct assault on the city. Patriarch Sergios was the heart of the resistance, walking fearlessly atop the walls carrying a large icon of the Virgin Mary and exhorting the defenders to stead-fastness. Facing the spirited defence, the Avars believed there were more troops in the city than there actually were. They pulled back when the Roman navy the Church wealth had paid for defeated the Avars offshore. In thanks for what was universally believed to be the Virgin Mary's decisive contribution, the famous Orthodox hymn *Te Hypermacho* (also known as the *Akathistos Hymnos*, or Standing Hymn) was penned by an unknown genius. It remains a key liturgical text of the Orthodox Church today.

In the West Heraclius is best known for his conquest of Jerusalem, which had been in Persian hands for many decades. The term Crusader (*Staurophoros*) was actually given him by one of his propagandists, at least four centuries before anyone in the West embraced the concept. In a grand scene in 630 Heraclius rode triumphant into Jerusalem bearing the True Cross which had been carried off by the Persians and which he had personally retrieved after torching the Persian capital of Ctesiphon. He also appropriated the now-defunct Persian title of Great King, which in Greek is *basileus*, a term which the Byzantines themselves were henceforth to apply to all emperors. The seizure of Jerusalem raised Heraclius to superhero status in the eyes of his people; to not a few, his very name suggested that he could even be a descendant of Herakles, the legendary strongman of Greek mythology.

In the military sphere Heraclius radically reorganized the entire army structure, dividing the Empire into sixteen military districts, termed themes, which were responsible for recruitment and defence. Heading each theme was a general, who also had a decisive say in civil matters such as finances and justice. The decentralization represented by the themes would prove durable through subsequent centuries, up to Komnenes and beyond.

Yet Heraclius' reign ended badly. A new and frightening foe was surging out of the deserts of Arabia; Muhammad the Prophet had just sown the seeds of Islam, and fired by this new faith, fanatical Muslim armies were steamrollering everything in their path. In 636 their General Khalid ibn al-Walid mowed down a Byzantine army at Yarmuk in Syria. Three years later Amr ibn al-As trounced another at Ayn Shams in Egypt, and a year later Alexandria fell. Heraclius, alarmed, raced to Jerusalem to rescue the True Cross just before that city fell to the Arabs. But he was already a dying man. For some time he had been afflicted by a strange depressive illness made worse by news of the military defeats. It got to the point where strange phobias paralysed him. Add to that an obscure genital ailment and dropsy, and no one was surprised when he succumbed in 641, as the Muslims gobbled up his easternmost provinces one by one.

The appearance of Islam did not have the effect on Christian Byzantium that we might imagine in hindsight. Muhammad's teachings were only very vaguely known outside the Arab world, and to many Byzantines they seemed just another obscure heresy of the kind that the official church had been battling for as long as anyone could remember. The new adherents did, after all, believe in God, and as such they were better regarded than the pagan Persians. In fact, there were not a few churchmen in Constantinople who were quite prepared to argue that this new sect was a punishment for neglect of the official creed in the eastern provinces, and that a simple reassertion of imperial authority there would solve the problem. It may have been a reason why Heraclius (apart from his illness) did not see fit to take the field against the Muslims in person. Hardly anyone realized that what the Empire was dealing with was not just another heresy but pure, steel-tipped jihad that would strike, jab and hammer persistently and patiently over no fewer than eight centuries, until the Roman/Byzantine Empire was brought to its knees.

Islamic influence, in fact, may have had a hand in a severe religious controversy that plunged the Empire into crisis in the eighth century. This was the infamous iconoclast controversy, pitting the traditional icon-venerating church against a new wave of puritan believers who had no use for graven images of any kind. Among the adherents of the latter were several emperors, led by Leo III, who may have wanted to placate the religiously unreliable populations of the frontier regions who might absorb Muslim and Jewish influence. Much violence and domestic conflict ensued before the iconoclasts were defeated and official church doctrine reaffirmed in 787.

Leo III, the tough-minded founder of the Isaurian dynasty, took over at a most crucial moment in 717, when Constantinople was under siege by some 80,000 Arab soldiers by land and 1,800 Arab ships by sea. The siege lasted a year, during which the Byzantines deployed their secret devastating weapon. What became known as Greek Fire (or, to the Byzantines, *hygron pyr*, liquid fire) was invented by a Greek chemist. The exact components and proportions of this fearsome compound are still not fully known. It was largely a mixture of sulphur, tartar, Persian gum, pitch, Mesopotamian surface petroleum and pine resin. When the stuff was ignited, nothing could stop it. It was most effective at sea, where ship crews squirted it through rudimentary flame-throwing nozzles onto the Arabs. Water was useless against it, as the Arab sailors found out the hard way; only urine and sand, it was said, could douse the blaze. To their credit, the Arabs fought bravely against this firestorm, but in the end they had to pull back. This encounter, plus the repulse of Arab invaders at the other end of Europe by France's Charles Martel at Tours in 732, is credited with saving Europe from Islamic conquest. 'The faith of countless millions was determined by the chances of war,' writes Will Durant, echoing Gibbon. To this day the Greek Orthodox Church honours Leo III as a 'saviour of Christendom'.

Hardly was the Arab threat dealt with than a new one appeared—the Bulgars, who had formed a durable kingdom in what is now still Bulgaria and were intent on seizing Constantinople for themselves. Leo's son and successor Constantine V had to personally take the field nine times over the next twenty years to bring the Bulgars to heel; but they rose anew under Krum, who in 811 defeated Byzantine emperor, Nikephoros I, and scraped out his skull to use as a drinking-cup. There followed several bloodstained decades in which emperors were deposed and murdered until in 829 Theophilos inaugurated a period of relative stability. Theophilos is best known for his elaborate throne flanked by mechanical roaring lions and topped by a tree with mechanical singing birds in its boughs—all made of the purest gold. He used it to awe a good many official visitors from East and West. His successor Michael III was erratic, displaying periods of ability and resolve between longer periods of indolence, insecurity and partying, including what would be the Byzantine equivalent of nocturnal pub-crawling. The resulting internal disorganization paved the way for the dynasty immediately preceding the Komnenes and in a way preparing the ground for them. These were the Macedonians.

Chapter 3

A hard act to follow: The Macedonians

When Isaac I Komnenos inaugurated the Komnene dynasty in 1057—though it would take twenty-four more years for the dynasty to substantially kick in—he was as well aware as anyone in the Empire that he needed to be at least as good as the dynasty that had preceded him, the Macedonians, who had occupied the Roman throne for 190 years and who in scholarly hindsight can be said to have presided over the high period of Byzantine politics, culture and power.

The origin of this dynasty took the most unprepossessing form of a rough and unlettered Armenian peasant named Basil. His family had been relocated from Armenia to Thrace in Europe, then captured by the Bulgars and transported to what is present-day Romania. There, probably because a lot of Macedonians had also been transferred to that place, he assumed that identity. Basil might easily have been classed among those describable as all brawn and no brain. He was immensely strong and had an uncanny way with horses. Until the end of his life he remained illiterate, but made up in cunning and quick-wittedness for what he lacked in book-learning, though he could never shake off a thick Armenian accent which grated on the ears of the upper-crust Greeks.

Yet his biggest admirer was the most upper-crust Greek of all—Emperor Michael III, who found in Basil the ideal roustabout companion. Basil, like many determined yet low-born young men of the Balkans, had somehow found his way to Constantinople in search of the good life. At first he slept in doorways. A rather improbable story, written years later and with an obvious propaganda flavour, tells how, on Basil's first night in the big city, he huddled in the doorway of a monastery near the Golden Gate, the main western city entrance for anyone coming from Macedonia or Greece. The abbot was awakened during the night by a disembodied voice commanding him to get out of bed and go and 'open the door to the emperor'. The abbot opened the gate to find a most un-imperial ragged vagrant huddled there, so he went back to bed. Thereupon the mysterious voice sounded a second time with the same command; the abbot went to the gate again and viewed the same sorry-looking figure, and returned to his bed again, no doubt rather disgruntled. The third time he heard the command he felt a sharp blow in the ribs. 'Bring in the man who lies before the door,' the voice ordered. 'He is the emperor.'

As with most such stories, our rationalist minds are inclined to dismiss it out of hand. But something rather extraordinary must have occurred, as we next find the ragged and penniless Basil—after being taken into the monastery, washed and given a new set of clothes—holding down a respectable job in Michael III's court and indeed rising to the post of High Chamberlain. How an illiterate and rough Armenian peasant achieved this remains an intriguing mystery, especially if we consider that the post of High Chamberlain was until then always given to a eunuch—and Basil was very far from being such a thing—and that the job involved literally sleeping next to the emperor as his closest and most reliable security detail. Some of the emperor's trust in him may have been cultivated when, according to another more probable story, Basil tamed a magnificent but uncontrollable horse that Michael had received as a present. Or when he engaged in a wrestling match with a huge Bulgar and hurled him across the room—presumably with the emperor watching.

This sudden and close relationship raised many eyebrows. Some suspected a homosexual tie, but that cannot be proven. Perhaps it was more complicated, as Michael ordered Basil to divorce his wife and marry the emperor's half-Swedish mistress Eudokia Ingerina. It was an ingenious way of helping Ingerina gain formal access to the palace, which she could never do if she remained Michael's illicit paramour. Thus the marriage to Basil was very likely a pure formality. We cannot discount the possibility that permutations of straight and gay relationships were often combined in the same people at or near the pinnacle of power that enabled them to get away with what the lower orders could not. And there was more: when Ingerina fell pregnant, it was widely believed that the child was in fact the emperor's. All Constantinople gossiped about this titillating palace soap opera that did not bode well for the future, as experience had shown that the royal stepsons and half-brothers who emerged from careless liaisons were a chronic source of dynastic instability. And one influential man was alarmed enough to try to do something about it.

Bardas Kaisar was an uncle of the emperor who in 855 had helped the emperor rid himself of his strong-willed mother who had acted as regent during his minority. As Michael III was just 15 when he seized the reins himself, he relied hugely on the older and far more capable Bardas, who in Lord Norwich's words turned out to be 'a brilliant administrator possessed both of farsighted statesmanship and boundless physical energy'. While the young emperor enjoyed life with his half-Swedish girlfriend, Bardas sent his brother Petronas with an army deep into what is now east Turkey to attack Muslim positions and take a host of prisoners. Over the next few years Roman arms scored more victories at the Euphrates and in Egypt; the former campaign was led by Michael himself. In 863 Petronas marched along the south coast of the Black Sea with 50,000 men (and the emperor as high-level observer) to attack the Muslim Emir Umar ibn Abdullah who was threatening the north-east provinces. At Poson the forces clashed; Umar fell, along with the greater portion of his force, which had included Christian heretics. Another successful battle shortly afterwards disposed of other Muslim foes. Well might the Empire rejoice and hope that a new era of greatness was at hand.

Bardas, justifiably, believed he could take credit for helping Michael mature, as it were. So his chagrin can be imagined when Basil, the muscular Armenian lout, appeared practically out of nowhere to worm himself with astounding ease into the very heart of the imperial entourage. At first he regarded Basil as little more than a temporary irritant, but he soon realized that the newcomer was potentially far more dangerous than that. Basil was, of course, well aware of this and played his own clever cards. Suspicions were sown in Michael's mind: might not Bardas be scheming to do away with his nephew and grab the throne for himself? It was a reasonable question, and may well have had substance behind it. There was certainly plenty of precedent. Back when he was 15, did not Michael boldly dismiss his regent mother when she became too dominant? Sure, Bardas in the meantime had become a key figure of benefit to the Empire—but that was just the point. Roman-Byzantine history was bursting with examples of key figures of benefit to the Empire turning against their rulers and seizing the throne. It probably never occurred to Michael that Basil himself aimed to be precisely one of them.

Bardas must have known what was afoot, because he pulled out of a planned expedition to Crete that was aiming to retrieve the island from Arab control. A combat situation, he knew, would be fraught with possibilities for doing away with him. He confronted Michael and Basil, who solemnly swore—we are told, with the actual blood of Jesus Christ kept in a small vial in the cathedral of Sancta Sophia—they had nothing against him. Sacred blood or no, Michael and Basil had no intention of keeping their promise, as Bardas even now suspected. The unholy charade ended while the army was encamped near the old city of Miletos on the Asia Minor coast. When during a staff meeting in the emperor's tent Basil thought he saw Bardas make some secret signal, he felled him with a mighty sword blow. This was no mere self-defence, as Basil and the emperor tried to make out; almost certainly the crime was long in the plotting. Basil's route to supreme power was now open.

The influential and strong-willed church patriarch, Photios, was perfectly well aware of what had really happened and begged Michael to abandon the Crete campaign and return at once to Constantinople. This he was only too happy to do, with his chief rival now out of the way; even happier was High Chamberlain Basil, who on Whit Sunday 866 saw his intrigues and murders rewarded with his coronation as co-emperor in the Sancta Sophia cathedral. As worshippers listened, and Michael and Basil sat on their gilded thrones, the solemn chant of a court secretary echoed beneath the vast dome, telling the world that the schemer Bardas had 'brought his death upon himself' and that Basil the faithful, Basil the loyal, would henceforth be 'manager and guardian of [Michael's] empire'. It had taken just nine years for the rough stable-hand to rise to wear the imperial purple and golden diadem.

The question easily arises: did Michael, knowing the character of his new co-emperor, feel any qualms about installing him in the palace? He probably did, but at the same time may have felt he had little choice. Michael himself was an unwilling sovereign, quite content to live a dissipated and immoral life and leave the necessary tough and dirty work of actual leadership to Basil, who appears willing enough to accede to the arrangement. But as Michael delved deeper into drunkenness, corruption and association with the underworld of Constantinople, and the people lost whatever respect they may have originally had for him, Basil had to act. On the night of 24 September 867 the emperor, Basil and Eudokia Ingerina (still in the curious position of being Basil's wife and Michael's mistress) dined at the palace. Michael hit the wine to an extraordinary degree and, blind drunk, lurched off to his bedchamber. Unknown to him, however, Basil had tampered with the door bolt so that the door couldn't be locked from the inside. Once Michael was in bed and snoring, a band of conspirators burst in and slaughtered him where he slept. We can imagine Basil nodding in satisfaction when the news was brought to him. On the following day Michael's bloody remains were quietly buried and the Byzantine populace—it must be said with a degree of relief—accepted Basil I as their sole sovereign, the founder of the Macedonian dynasty.

At this bloodstained point we may take a look at the time-honoured divine-substitute principle of the late Roman and Byzantine emperors that had been firmly in place as the state ideology since Constantine the Great. Michael III was not the first emperor to be hacked to death—there was the even more gruesome precedent of Phokas in 610—and neither would he be the last. What, then, did such acts do to the idea that the emperor was Christ's deputy on earth? If legally and substantially he was, then wasn't regicide really equivalent to the far greater crime of deicide, *lèse majesté* of the highest order? The issue was, in fact, rather more complicated, and had to do with the place of the church in the scheme of things.

By the ninth century Byzantium rested on two solid pillars: the state, headed by the emperor; and the church, headed by the patriarch. As Helene Ahrweiler has pointed out in her many studies on Byzantium, this was not what has often mistakenly been called a theocracy. The emperor's job was to protect the Christian realm from external enemies and keep the domestic administration in place, while the patriarch's job was to maintain the people's faith and keep the Empire on a straight spiritual course. Of course, political and social tremors often knocked these two pillars against each other; but even though cracked and chipped, they stayed pretty much separate. Whereas the emperor had his regional governors and generals, the patriarch had his metropolitans and bishops.

The emperor, in fact, was not an absolute ruler, because the presumed divine right to rule came with an important and often overlooked safety valve. The divine right applied to the *figure* of the monarch, not to his individual personality as such. It was the institution rather than the imperfect man who was theoretically God-sanctioned. The real ruler of Byzantium, in fact, was considered to be Christ Himself. Writes Guerdan:

> The palaces in which [the emperor] lived were not homes, but theatrical sets reminiscent, naturally, of a church. Chapels outnumbered apartments and relics were hung on the walls, such as the Rod of Moses and the True Cross, and, on a background of gold, enormous images of Christ and the Theotokos, the Mother of God. Every month came processions of icons to renew the sanctity of the atmosphere.

It followed, then, that any emperor who sullied his rule either through cruelty or incompetence or both was considered to have forfeited God's grace and be fair game for toppling, peacefully or otherwise. Hence the sometimes-extreme violence with which some emperors were removed; having held God's responsibility and then grievously abused it, they were considered to have deserved what they got.

Doctrinal issues were especially salient in the 860s, as Pope Nicholas II in Rome was asserting a troubling independence of Constantinople, still the seat of the one true church. Photios, the strong-minded patriarch, was determined to thwart Nicholas' plans, but before he could act, Basil I sacked him. The last thing the new emperor needed at this stage was a schism with Rome, especially as the Holy Roman Empire in Europe, created by Charlemagne, was setting itself up, worryingly, as the supposedly *real* Roman Empire. The old late Roman dream of clawing back Italy and the West had never died, and if Basil hoped to accomplish what even the great Justinian had failed to, he needed the pope's backing. Two months after Basil's accession, Nicholas conveniently left this world, to be replaced by the more accommodating Pope Hadrian II.

Basil I, the rough and unlettered stable-hand, and in the eyes of many little more than a thug, proved to be an expert in the assessment and handling of political power. His lack of intellect, in fact, gave him a distinct advantage over the endless debating and procrastination of the overeducated secular and ecclesiastical elites; he knew where and when to strike instinctively, without expending too much mental energy over it. Nearly 200 years later the intellectual and polished writer Michael Psellos would marvel at how the Macedonian dynasty, criminally 'born of murder and bloodshed... took root and sent out such mighty shoots'.

Within a dozen years Basil had brought the Bulgars into the Orthodox fold, plus a band of pagan Greeks who had held out in the mountains south of Sparta. The imperial navy under Niketas Oöryphas cleared Arab and Slav privateers out of the Adriatic Sea and the Gulf of Corinth. In the east, several times Basil personally took the field against the Saracens and a group of heretics called the Paulicians, taking advantage of their feuds to claim back lost Byzantine territory in Syria. At home he rebuilt the royal palaces and the main public buildings in Constantinople, giving the city a glitter it had never seen before and has never seen since. (As Lord Norwich sadly notes, 'there now survives of his work not one stone resting on another.')

Although he had set up his dynasty by methods which would not quite conform to the morals of a present-day secular democracy, Basil I had a certain right to be proud of himself. And of course, the founder of any dynasty requires above all a competent heir to carry on the next stage. Basil had one in his eldest son Constantine, whom he adored, who had been familiarized with battle conditions at his father's side, and who showed great promise. But in one of history's frustrating mysteries, young Constantine died in 879. Accident, illness, palace intrigue— we simply don't know what happened. Most likely foul play was not involved, as we don't find Basil—though beside himself with grief—inaugurating any bloody witch-hunt, as he would have if he had suspected anyone of engineering the death of his favourite son.

Basil spent the remaining seven years of his reign declining physically and mentally. One day in the summer of 886 he rode out for a hunt that was to prove fatal. The only account of his death that we have seems so unlikely that many historians dismiss it as a fanciful tale. We are told that the emperor, riding alone in front of the rest of the party, came on a stag drinking at a stream and charged it. The animal, far from fleeing, charged its attacker and got its antlers hooked under Basil's belt. The emperor, unhorsed, was dragged along by the running stag. Eventually the rest of the party found him still hooked to the antlers, grievously injured, and cut him loose. (The stag got away.) Nine days later Basil succumbed to internal bleeding. A likelier theory, more probable precisely because it would have been hushed up anyway, was that a member of his hunting party put him out of the way.

But who would have wished such a murder? One person in particular had everything to gain by it, for both emotional and practical reasons. This was his second son Leo. To the degree that Basil had doted on the unlucky Constantine, he loathed Leo, and the feeling was mutual. Why this was so can be inferred from the prince's first act after he was crowned Leo VI: he ordered that the remains of Basil's predecessor, the murdered Michael III, be transferred to a more prestigious resting place. Some chroniclers take this as a strong indication that Leo was in fact Michael's son, not Basil's, and in view of the confused marital relations prevailing at court in Michael's time, it's quite plausible. It would also explain why Basil hated him. For Leo VI, just 20 when he was crowned, showed definite abilities that would earn him his place in history as Leo the Wise. He was as learned as his father had been illiterate; he studied and wrote constantly, and delivered his own sermons from the pulpit of Sancta Sophia. And thanks to his detailed concern for the law and legal expertise in general, he gave the Macedonian dynasty a bedrock of stability.

In foreign policy, however, Leo was less sure-footed. Neighbouring Bulgaria, newly converted to Christianity, was on its way to becoming a reliable ally of Byzantium. But Leo derailed that process by approving an ill-conceived plan to divert the Bulgars' main trade route to Constantinople and put it in Greek hands. The new Bulgarian tsar, Symeon, turned on the Byzantines and inflicted a stinging defeat on them in 896. Leo eventually bought off further Bulgar hostility by agreeing to pay them tribute. This strategy, though of short-term tactical benefit, was overused by the Byzantines to their detriment, as it simply encouraged other powers to blackmail the Empire with threats of war. It was to set an ultimately fatal precedent.

The Arabs, meanwhile, were also on the march. Despite the fact that the celebrated Abbasid caliphate was long past the peak of its prestige and power, the Muslim world's outlying sections were vigorously carving out their own spheres, at the expense of both the figurehead caliphs and the Christian world. The emirate of Egypt, for example, following Morocco and Tunis, declared its independence in 868, just after Basil I had got rid of Michael III. This news could not but be of concern to those Byzantine traders handling vital grain shipments from North Africa, especially after Egypt annexed Syria in 877. As long as the Saracens confined themselves to the southern shores of the Mediterranean, not much harm was done. But their presence in Europe, namely Crete, Sicily and southern Italy, was another matter altogether. Taormina, Byzantium's last outpost in Sicily, fell to the Arabs in 902. Shortly afterwards a Saracen fleet penetrated into the Sea of Marmara and was repulsed, but in revenge fell on the city of Thessalonike which suffered a week of fearful slaughter and was left a smoking ruin.

In the face of these threats Leo cuts a curiously inconsistent figure. He knew his military science but seems to have let defence policy languish. Too often, as in the case of the Bulgars and Saracens, he reacted defensively to hostile acts rather than taking the tactical initiative. Perhaps this is typical of intellectual leaders who tend to think too much and often prefer to take events as they come rather than plan specific offensives. To be fair, serious domestic issues weighed heavily on Leo's mind and absorbed his attention, such as the overriding imperative to have an heir that took him through four controversial marriages, over which the fussy Church gave him endless trouble. Only in 908, after more than two decades on the throne, did Leo feel strong enough to attempt an overseas campaign, sending a fleet to clear the Saracens out of the Syrian port of Laodikeia (now Latakia). The operation was successful, encouraging the emperor to attempt to retake Crete from the Arabs three years later. The attempt was a disaster. For six months the Byzantines threw everything they had at the powerful Saracen defences, but eventually had to give up. On the way back to Constantinople the fleet was ambushed by a Saracen force and almost completely sunk. The shock of the news was too much for Leo, already in very poor health and bedridden. On hearing it, he is said to have turned his face to the wall and passed away.

The succession passed to his younger brother Alexander, who turned out to be one of the worst characters ever to occupy the Byzantine throne, and whose mad and dissipated rule fortunately lasted just a little over a year. But that short period was enough to alienate the Bulgars, who had made overtures for a peace treaty and whose envoys had been dismissed in a shower of drunken insults from the emperor. No one was thus sorry when Alexander perished, probably of a stroke brought on by his insanely pleasure-seeking lifestyle. It was the signal for Leo's widow Zoe to push her 7-year-old son Constantine to the throne, which was accomplished in 915 only after months of often violent intrigues over who would be the boy's regent until he came of age.

At this point many scripture-reading Byzantines may well have recalled the dark warning in Ecclesiastes 10: 'Woe to thee, O land, when thy king is a child.' They need not have worried overmuch. Constantine VII was a genuine *porphyrogennetos*, a rare enough being to warrant that title as part of his official designation. In his long reign of forty-four years he demonstrated the supreme art of political survival, especially when he was forced to share the throne with Romanos I Lekapenos, a general, for more than half of those years. Thanks partly to an insecure and grief-filled childhood aggravated by unstable politics, Constantine Porphyrogennetos learned early how to hedge his bets and not rock the boat. Dismissed by many as an ineffectual figurehead, he was nonetheless intelligent and popular, surviving on the throne simply by not being a threat to anyone's ambitions. He wisely left the risky conduct of foreign military operations to Romanos, who duly came to grief in 944 after a period of misrule at home and thus left the 36-year-old Constantine in full control.

He cut an impressive physical figure, tall and well-built, with a full black beard and penetrating blue eyes. Later he had a tendency to gain weight, thanks to a propensity for the good life. Known as the Scholar Emperor, Constantine preferred books and philosophy over fighting and politicking, and with good reason. He put his thoughts on statecraft into a book known by its Latin title *De Administrando Imperio*, which he wrote for the benefit of his son, the future Romanos II. In his years of observing his Empire, he became familiar with every cog of its vast workings. Genial, generous, fond of company and of food and drink, an unstinting patron of the arts and literature, Constantine Porphyrogennetos was the personification of what has been called the Macedonian Renaissance of Byzantium.

It was in the middle of Constantine VII's reign that a development occurred that would prove momentous for the subsequent history of the world. This was the emergence of the Russians as a power to be reckoned with in east Europe. As early as 860 this new people, the Rus—led probably by Norsemen—had sailed in strange long ships across the Black Sea and into the Bosporus, burning and looting as they went. This was the first of many drives by the Russians to force an outlet to the warm and trade-filled Mediterranean Sea—a drive that is still a prime aim of Russian policy. Before Constantinople the raiders had lingered, assessing the city's defences, and finding them too strong, withdrew. To the people, it was one more sign of divine intervention. But in 941 the Rus were back, and in much greater force, with many hundreds of ships sent by Prince Igor of Kiev. What stalled the Russians this time was not prayer—though that will have helped—but the trusty Greek Fire, which was squirted through primitive flame-throwers on the prows of ships. With the front line of ships in flames and their personnel burned alive, the rest of the Russian fleet beat a hasty retreat.

Perhaps it was the shock of encountering Greek Fire that set Byzantium's relations with the Russians on a much better course soon afterwards. In 989 Vladimir, the fifth Grand Duke of Kiev, converted to Christianity, abandoned his free and licentious love life and married a Byzantine princess to whom he remained a faithful husband and made Kiev (to be followed later by all Russia) into a steadfast ally of the Byzantine Empire. Russian monarchs adopted the divine-right ideology of the Byzantine emperors and continued it unchanged through the long line of tsars, right through the Communist era (1917–1990) to our own time; though no one, to be sure, invests Russia's present heads of state with divine sanction, the mindset still prevails in the practice of Russian rule which differs significantly from the ideals of the West but nonetheless seems to be accepted as lending a measure of security to the majority of the Russian people.

When Constantine Porphyrogennetos died aged 54 after a lingering illness, his son and successor Romanos II inherited a glittering realm, and most people expected him to handle it as well as his father did. But instead he fell head over heels for a Greek innkeeper's bewitching daughter named Theophano who at 18 found herself elevated to empress. While Theophano became the ruthless arbiter of domestic policy, her husband scored a single foreign success by sending his general Nikephoros Phokas to recapture Crete from the Saracens, which he accomplished in March 961 after a general massacre of them in Candia (modern Heraklion).

But the young Romanos did not enjoy his reign for long. Just four years after his accession he was dead—poisoned, many believed, by the unscrupulous Theophano, though that story is still disputed. Whatever the truth, as the empress, and expecting her third child, she needed a male protector. Her eldest son Basil was only 6. There seemed to be only one trustworthy man to take over until Basil attained his majority, and that was the victor of Crete, Nikephoros Phokas, who at the time was on his way back from retaking Aleppo from the Arabs. Hastening to Constantinople in response to an urgent message from Theophano, he rode into the city in the grand style of an ancient Roman emperor, bearing before him the ragged robe worn by John the Baptist. The public acclaimed him as 'the White Death of the Saracens', and the way to the palace seemed clear. But Theophano's opponents threw obstacle after obstacle in the general's way, forcing him to retire to Kappadokia until the political knot could be untangled. There his senior officers raised him on a shield to proclaim him emperor in the old, time-honoured Roman manner. In mid-August 963, after demonstrations in his favour in Constantinople, he was rowed across the Bosporus in a *dromon* warship, seated on a silver throne with an ornate golden canopy. Ashore he donned a magnificent outfit, mounted a white horse and rode in triumph to Sancta Sophia, to be crowned Nikephoros II.

What followed would provide rich material for any soap opera. To start with, Nikephoros as emperor was obliged to marry Theophano and protect her sons. But if ever there was a case of beauty and the beast, this was it. A visiting Italian cleric, Liutprand of Cremona, has left the following unflattering description of Nikepohoros:

> [A] monstrosity of a man, a dwarf, with a broad, flat head and tiny eyes like a mole... [with] a short, thick, grizzled beard; disgraced by a neck scarcely an inch long, piglike by reason of the close bristles on his head... a big belly.

Probably because he was aware he was not the best-looking of men, Nikephoros Phokas had never particularly cared for female company, devoting his life to the military. In many ways he was more a monk than a general, and even as emperor he took little or no care over his outward apparel. Liutprand sniffed at his linen robe, 'old, foul-smelling and discoloured by age'.

We may therefore take at face value Nikephoros' avowal, when accused by the Church of illegally marrying a previously-married woman, that he had never had sex with her. Yet he would undoubtedly have liked to, for he was genuinely smitten with Theophano who was less than half his age. He was honest and religiously devout enough to respect her unwillingness to sleep with him, but insisted that his marriage was nonetheless valid. In time the Church had to give in. But given the personal trouble he had been put through, it was something of a relief when he took the field against the Arabs and seized back Cyprus from them in 965. To fight and to simultaneously serve the cause of Christ—that was his mission in life.

The rough-edged Nikephoros was no diplomat, and under his rule relations with Byzantium's neighbours worsened. He insulted Bulgar emissaries, calling them 'hideous and filthy beggars'. Italy was overrun by Otto the Saxon who was crowned Holy Roman Emperor (a title which the Byzantines always dismissed as illegal and contemptible), largely because Otto nursed a series of old grievances against Constantinople. Pope John XIII, who had crowned Otto, was dismissed as 'a blockhead'. Unsurprisingly, Byzantium found itself at war on three fronts: the Saracens, the Bulgars and Otto the Saxon in Italy. To pay for these conflicts the emperor had to tax the people heavily, while a string of poor harvests sent the price of bread skyrocketing. The unrest came to a head in a major riot in the Hippodrome on Easter Sunday of 967, where many people were crushed to death. The sight of Nikephoros sitting in the imperial seat watching it all impassively did nothing for what remained of his popularity.

As for Theophano, she was already mapping out her future. Still just 28, she had been casting about for a suitable consort and found one in John Tzimiskes, a handsome Armenian general who was recalled from an eastern campaign but confined to the Asian side of the Bosporus. If Nikephoros thought that this would keep him out of the arms of Theophano, he was mistaken. Tzimiskes would furtively row across the strait at night and slip into Theophano's rooms in the palace. There, in between their lovemaking, they would plot how to rid themselves of the monkish emperor. Their chance came one stormy night in December 969, when Tzimiskes and a band of conspirators sneaked into Nikephoros' spartan bedroom, woke him up, savagely beat him and then hacked him to death. Such was the grisly end of the one who only a few short years before was acclaimed the White Death of the Saracens.

While the emperor's bloody head was held up in a window for all to see, and the rest of him dumped in the snow, the city rejoiced as the news spread. Tzimiskes lost no time in hastening to the throne room, where he donned imperial garb and had himself proclaimed John I. Seated proudly with him were Theophano and her two sons, Basil and Constantine. While not exactly a match made in heaven, it seemed to hold promise—but not where the Church was concerned. The patriarch, the strong-willed Polyeuktos, would not legitimize John's reign until he had put away Theophano with whom he had had illicit relations; this would also serve as an atonement for the gruesome assassination of his predecessor. John didn't hesitate; the Empire, in his view, was more important than sex, and a shocked Theophano found herself without warning packed off to an island in the Sea of Marmara. Some months later she somehow slipped back to Constantinople to confront John and shower him with insults before being dragged away to a more distant exile in Armenia.

We mention these events—which a later age would call 'headline-producing'—to show how even the most sordid scandals surrounding the palace and the state leadership of Byzantium did not even dent the solid ideological position that the emperor was God's ordained chief on earth. We may be quite sure that the affair between John Tzimiskes and Theophano and the brutal elimination of Nikephoros Phokas, to name just two scandals, were known in detail to the ever-alert people of Constantinople and the influential classes elsewhere in the Empire. Yet there is in the records no sign of the kind of public indignation that would dominate the news, say, in our own era of 'democratically-elected' governments. To the best of our knowledge there were no strident calls for an abolition of the monarchy or a socialist insurrection. The Byzantine people took such human ups and downs in the highest places in their stride. Individual writers could, and did, severely censure the conduct of public figures, but their writings rarely cast doubt on the underlying validity of the state set-up.

John I Tzimiskes, despite the bloody ruthlessness with which he came to power, turned out to be a considerate and capable ruler. If the chroniclers of the time are to be believed, he was possessed of just about every physical and moral virtue: fair-haired and blue-eyed, well-proportioned (if a little on the short side), irresistibly charming (a quality that the ill-starred Theophano no doubt appreciated), and fun-loving, but also an excellent horseman and archer. We are told that his concern for the disadvantaged extended to regularly visiting a leper hospital and personally washing the inmates' leprous sores.

John was fortunate to inherit an army that had been boosted and honed to a fine cutting edge by his predecessor. He would need it, for in 969 Prince Svyatoslav and an army of some 50,000 Russians were descending on the Empire through Bulgaria. About 12,000 Romans under Bardas Skleros barred Svyatoslav's way at Arkadiopolis and decisively smashed him. Two years later John took the field against Svyatoslav in person, and found him encamped near the Bulgarian capital of Preslav. There the emperor fell on the Russians like a whirlwind, slaughtering and burning great numbers. After Svyatoslav was forced to agree to a humiliating peace, he was murdered on his way home. And, of course, the Muslims in the east were an ever-present threat. In 975, in a daring campaign John recovered most of Syria from Arab rule and seemed on the point of recovering Jerusalem when a political rival in his entourage spiked his drink with a slow-acting poison. Either because of that or of some illness contracted in the unhealthy Middle East, he returned to Constantinople a dying man. The sandals that purportedly belonged to Jesus Christ, which he had brought back with him, did not stop him from succumbing in January 976. He was 51.

While John Tzimiskes was ruling, Theophano's elder son Basil was growing up in his court. When John died Basil, 18, took his rightful place on the throne as Basil II. As a teenager he had shown a penchant for seriousness and achievement. He could not be more unlike his younger brother Constantine, who was content to live a life of apathetic indolence and luxury and more than willing to give up any role in the affairs of state. Basil was not a particularly impressive-looking young man, being short and inclined to portliness and sporting full, untrimmed facial hair. He consciously refused to dress the part of an emperor, preferring rough workmen's attire that often went a long time without a wash. In short, Basil preferred substance to style, and work to display.

From the outset he was ringed by deadly domestic foes. Hardly had he been crowned than Bardas Skleros, the victor of Arkadiopolis, attempted a *coup d'état* on the grounds that he had been unfairly passed over for the succession to John I. Another Bardas, by the surname of Phokas, helped Basil fend off that threat, but staged an attempted coup of his own shortly afterwards. Basil personally rode out to face him in battle in Anatolia along with his supposedly feckless brother Constantine (the future Constantine VIII). In April 989 at Abydos, when the opposing forces were drawn up, the pretender Bardas Phokas mounted his horse and thundered towards the young emperor, who sat firmly on his own horse, clutching an icon of the Virgin Mary in one hand and his sword in the other. But before Phokas could reach Basil he was seen to sway in the saddle and then topple to the ground, where the pleasure-loving Constantine earned his place in military history by despatching him with a spear-thrust. Phokas could have been the victim of a stroke or of one of those notorious Byzantine slow-acting poisons that ooze evilly through the whole history of the Empire. Another version of the event says Phokas was felled by a rain of javelins, but the most prominent chronicler of the era, Michael Psellos (of whom we will hear much more later) heaps all the credit on the icon of the Virgin Mary in Basil's hand. This interpretation reinforces the already ironclad ideology of the office of emperor (as distinct, it must be remembered, from the actual person wearing the crown) as being under divine authority. But the actual experience left Basil himself with a scarred psyche. In Psellos' words, 'he became suspicious of everyone, haughty and secretive, ill-tempered and irate with those who failed to carry out his orders.'

It might be said that Basil from then on took his job over-seriously. Still shunning all attire except the plainest, and abolishing useless ceremonials, he made sure his word was law, and if anyone dared to cross him or break the law, 'terrible was the vengeance he took on the miscreant.' While Constantine reverted to his life of ease and pleasure, Basil untiringly rode out to the frontiers to make sure they were secure. It was during his reign that Prince Vladimir of Kiev accepted Christianity and made the Russians into allies of Byzantium. On the home front, the ageing

Bardas Skleros was pensioned off. It was against the ever-troublesome Bulgars that Basil exercised his most fearful wrath, earning him a cognomen that rings ominously down the centuries—the Bulgar-slayer.

Basil's first encounter with the Bulgars had been an unfortunate one. In 986 Tsar Samuel had invaded large parts of Greece; when the still-inexperienced Basil moved against him, the Roman army was shattered in the Battle of Trajan's Gate. Fuming, he spent the next dozen years plotting the utter destruction of the Bulgars. His chance came in 1000, when he began systematically retaking Thessalonike and north-east Greece, thanks partly to an army organized to peak efficiency. The resulting guerrilla war in the Balkans dragged on for more than ten years, until in the Kleidion defile in 1014 Basil virtually annihilated Samuel's army. The emperor is said to have dealt with his several thousand prisoners in a uniquely horrific manner by blinding them all except every hundredth man who was left with one eye to lead the hapless rest of them home. Some doubt hovers over this terrible tale. It is not mentioned by Psellos, who penned an admiring life of Basil and could well have hushed it up. Edward Gibbon is the one who gave wide currency to it, followed by most in the West, to whom the sensation value has proved irresistible. Yet Basil II among the Greeks is proudly remembered as the Bulgar-slayer, with many streets in modern Greek cities bearing his name and sinister sobriquet.

At the time of his greatest triumph Basil was 56, apparently retaining much of his youthful stamina. He was active at home as well as abroad, suppressing those nobles who 'enriched themselves at the expense of the poor'. His wider aim was to break up the large noble estates that had spawned serious rivals such as Bardas Skleros and Bardas Phokas. A free peasantry, he believed, was the backbone of the army, and that belief paid off in decisive battles such as Kleidion. After that he ruled for eleven more years, until in December 1025 he passed away, worn out by constant campaigning in the east. In all his long reign he appears single-handedly to have maintained the state. In Lord Norwich's judgement, 'no lonelier man ever occupied the Byzantine throne.'

Basil left the Empire at the height of its prestige. According to E.R.A. Sewter, a noted translator of Byzantine writers,

> Everywhere the might of Roman arms was respected and feared. The treasury was full to overflowing with the plunder of Basil's campaigns. Even the lamp of learning, despite the emperor's known indifference, was burning still... The lot of ordinary folk in Constantinople must have been pleasant enough. For most of them life was colourful, and if the city's defensive fortifications were at some points in disrepair they had no cause to dread attacks.

After Basil II the Macedonian house began its downhill course, and our survey of the post-Bulgar-slayer rulers will be brief. Basil's brother, the easy-living

Constantine, found himself emperor in his mid-sixties, and it's fair to say the position terrified him. In between gourmet cooking and watching live porn shows in the palace, he consigned anyone he saw as a threat to the torture chambers. Three years into his reign he fell ill and died. He had no sons but three daughters, the middle one of whom was given in marriage to an elderly senator named Romanos Argyros, who became Romanos III. This man refused to sleep with his wife Zoe, who as a remedy took a lover one-third her age. The situation appeared tailor-made for a plot to get Romanos out of the way. Sure enough, six years after being crowned the emperor, he was drowned in his swimming pool, most likely by conspirators under Zoe's orders. Without any sign of mourning she duly elevated her boyfriend Michael the Paphlagonian to the throne as Michael IV.

Despite his youth and sexual precocity, however, Michael was not in the best of health himself. An epileptic, he was later stricken with dropsy. His physical relationship with the blonde and bubbly 50-something Zoe soon petered out, and to ease his conscience he devoted himself to good works and gestures of abject and prostrate divine worship. In 1041, barely able to stand or ride, he nevertheless by sheer force of will campaigned against the Bulgars and defeated them outside Thessalonike; he lived just long enough to enjoy a triumphal entry into Constantinople, after which he wasted away to his demise. He was not yet 30.

A new emperor had to be found, and one was procured in Michael Kalaphates, whose father had been a shipyard worker (the word *kalaphates* means caulker) and had risen rather quickly to social prominence. Distantly related to the late emperor, the teenaged Michael Kalaphates had been formally adopted by Zoe while Michael IV was still alive. His character was not a good one. When he became Michael V he ruled as a petty tyrant, banishing Zoe from the palace, ordering her hair cut off and exiling her to Prinkipo Island in the Sea of Marmara. This was too much for the people and clergy of Constantinople, who stormed the palace and came close to razing it completely. Zoe was recalled, and the terrified Michael was seized and his eyes jabbed out in front of the mob; the man in charge of this ugly deed could well have been a young Norwegian prince, Harald Hardrada, a veteran of several years' service to Byzantium (more on whom will be told in Chapter 8). Blind and bleeding, Michael was deposed and packed off to a monastery.

With Michael the Caulker out of the picture, the way was free for the ageing Zoe to rule as empress in her own right, along with her so-far neglected younger sister Theodora, who had been spending her life quietly in a convent and was most reluctant to leave it. But the two sisters, as unlike in appearance as they were in character, could not get on, and this inability was reflected in state mismanagement. Zoe realized that a male consort was necessary for political stability and she embarked on her third marriage, to a wealthy member of the noble Monomachos family. In June 1042 Zoe and Constantine Monomachos, who became Constantine

IX, were married in Sancta Sophia. It was not long before Constantine admitted to a long-standing affair with a much younger woman; had he been a strong ruler, that could have been forgiven. Instead, he neglected the army and had the humiliation of witnessing the most portentous historical event of his reign—the final traumatic schism between the Greek Orthodox and the Roman Catholic churches in 1054. The late Roman Empire could expect no more aid or sympathy from the old Rome.

Months after the schism, Constantine IX died after lingering too long in his bath in chilly weather. By this time Zoe, too, had passed away, leaving Theodora to resume the place on the throne where she and her sister had left off thirteen years before. At 77 years of age Theodora was capable enough, but after a year and half of rule she succumbed to a devastating intestinal malady. Thus did the great dynasty of the Macedonians slide to its end. The date was 31 August 1056.

Chapter 4

1057: Isaac the Founder

By the summer of 1057 the average Roman-Byzantine at all aware of political affairs would have been heartily sick at the spectacle of the Empire's leadership apparently disintegrating. In the thirty-two years since the death of the great Basil the Bulgar-slayer, eight emperors and empresses had come and gone in a maelstrom of intrigue, chicanery and scandal that would have taxed the abilities even of seasoned palace hands to keep the state mechanism on an even keel. One of these was a highly talented administrator, diplomat and writer named Michael Psellos. Nearly 40, Psellos had seen a lot in his career so far, and was not easily impressed or fazed. But what he witnessed on 1 September 1057 stunned even him:

> All the populace of [Constantinople] poured out... There was dancing and rejoicing everywhere... I have taken my part in many imperial processions, but in all my life I have never seen such splendour.

The cause of the festive atmosphere was the arrival of a crusty general who had become the latest people's favourite. His name was Isaac Komnenos, destined that same day to be the founder of the dynasty of the Komnenes.

To be fair, at that point the people of Byzantium would have accepted almost anyone on the throne with the promise of some staying power. When Theodora was on her deathbed she had summoned the strength to name Michael Bringas, an elderly senior civil servant, as her successor. This man ruled for a year as Michael VI, appropriately called Michael the Codger by the mass of people. He made himself highly unpopular, especially with the army, which he seems to have despised. At Easter four generals, led by Isaac Komnenos, had sought an audience with the emperor to complain about rampant favouritism in the civil administration and the corresponding neglect of the army. Psellos was there, as Michael's private secretary, and expected the emperor to do the proper thing and address some good words—even if insincere—to the men who were defending his Empire's borders. Instead, Michael peremptorily ordered Komnenos to stand before him and heaped abuse on him for supposedly mismanaging the eastern campaign and helping himself to public money—all of which was quite untrue. The other officers tried to get a word in edgewise, but the Codger forbade it. Komnenos, stunned, appears to have been given no chance to rebut the charges, and Michael dismissed them all from his presence. In doing so, he assured his own overthrow.

That night Isaac Komnenos and the others gathered secretly in the great echoing space of Sancta Sophia, aided by the sympathetic patriarch who opened the doors for them. In the flickering candlelight they debated who should lead the coup against the Codger. Komnenos himself, with his senior rank and commanding presence, was the choice of most. In Psellos' description, 'one look at the man was to inspire respect.' At first he refused the honour. Perhaps he'd had enough of the whole sordid political business and wished only to retire to his quiet estates in Paphlagonia, in what is now north Turkey on the Black Sea coast. But the others insisted, and eventually he gave in.

To make sure that the first meeting with the emperor was not just a result of a temporary bad mood, the generals were granted another brief audience, which seems to have simply confirmed the conspirators in their aim. For the next few weeks Isaac Komnenos, from his Paphlagonian estate, built up and coordinated the conspiracy. Word spread like a brushfire. Disaffected officers and their units flocked to his standard from all points of the compass. 'Without the least hesitation,' writes Psellos, 'recruits poured in, every man, like a runner, trying to get there before his comrades.'

Isaac appears to have had his secret doubts. From what we know, he was not a power-hungry individual and viewed with inner distaste the task of moving on the man who, after all, was the legitimate sovereign and setting in motion a civil war. But the army leadership collectively had no such qualms; it had long been the secret desire of the generals to supplant civilian emperors (who, it was whispered in the camps, were ruled by their eunuchs) with men of their own, to give the Empire some additional backbone to deal with the incessant threats from east and west, and—who knows?—revive the old dream of reclaiming Italy and Old Rome. So when the time came to move in July, a month after being proclaimed emperor by the army, Isaac Komnenos proceeded with exquisite caution. Staging a coup was a serious, life-risking business and as little as possible had to be left to chance.

Isaac's troops, the majority of whom seem to have been junior officers and enlisted men, were enthusiastic at the prospect of one of their own on the throne. But their loyalty could not be taken for granted in the longer term—unless they were rewarded for their exertions. For this purpose he set up roadblocks at all the thoroughfares leading out of Constantinople, allowing only the most restricted movement through them, probably to prevent wealth from fleeing the city. The civil service seems already to have been a shambles, as Psellos informs us that Isaac had little difficulty in drawing up reliable taxpayer lists and appointing his own collectors so that when he was master of the capital the state coffers could be full.

With that groundwork laid, the military side of the operation could commence. At his new base at Nikaia (Nicaea) across the Bosporus, Isaac formed his soldiers into units, into each of which he placed a core of hardened veterans and men known to stay cool under fire to stiffen the unit. This way he tried to mitigate the phenomenon of entire units breaking in battle, a frequent cause of major military defeats in the past. The braver and more able men were promoted to field officer rank. Discipline and order were strictly enforced, both on the march and in encampment. Delinquent soldiers only needed to be confronted with Isaac's terrifying scowl for any corporal punishment to be unnecessary. The mediaeval equivalent of radio silence was to be kept at all times. In camp, while the troops rested, Isaac and his retinue that included members of his Komnenos family stayed up at night considering his next moves.

In the court circle at Constantinople, Psellos was becoming anxious. The emperor appeared all but oblivious of the mortal threat gathering across the Bosporus. The attitude was all the more inexplicable as Michael had a loyal army to fight with. At length the emperor was persuaded to use some of the ample funds available to beef up his forces. Psellos and other courtiers had been arguing this course until they were blue in the face. In a conference Psellos advised Michael to get the patriarch on side, and send a mission to Isaac's camp urging a compromise and promising the rebel general money and a promotion if he gave up his rebellion. This would give the Codger time to assemble the western armies and whatever foreign forces were willing to join them. A strong loyalist force under Isaac's Bulgarian brother-in-law, Prince Aaron, and a Theodoros, a eunuch who held the rank of Domestikos Scholai (or regional commander) of the East, crossed the Bosporus and encamped within sight of the rebels.

The loyalists were impeded from the start by questionable morale—there were daily desertions to the rebel camp—and the irresolution of Theodoros. Nonetheless, the imperial force destroyed the bridges over the Sangarios (now the Sakarya) River to cut off access to Isaac from the Komnenos estates and their manpower. On 20 August, at Petroe about two miles north of Nikaia, the emperor's men commenced battle with a spirited charge on Isaac's left flank. The location was a plain called Haidos (in later accounts transformed into the sinister-sounding Hades), where Isaac commanded the defending centre, with Romanos Skleros in command of the right wing and Katakalon Kekaumenos the left. In the imperial camp Theodoros occupied the centre, with Basil Tarchaniotes on the right and the Bulgarian Aaron on the left. Araon's wing overran Skleros, who was captured; Isaac Komnenos was at first swept away by the imperial onrush, but when Theodoros seemed to have victory in his grasp Aaron halted, unsure of what to do next.

It was a fatal halt, as it gave Isaac enough time to find out about the success on his own right, where Kekaumenos had smashed the imperial charge and launched a counter-attack on Tarchaniotes' Macedonians. The counter-attack swept through the imperial camp, where two of the emperor's generals were killed. News of this reverse paralysed Aaron further, which enabled Isaac to stay put in the centre, defying all attempts to budge him. Heavy iron spears hurled at him failed to find their mark. Four burly Russians from the division of Radulph the Frank almost overcame him, but failed. Isaac's rocklike steadiness heartened his army, which stopped running and assembled for a counter-attack, which worked better than even he could have expected. We are told that Radulph gallantly stopped running and turned to challenge Isaac's general Nikephoros Botaneiates to single combat. The deadly encounter ended when Radulph's sword broke and the fetters of captivity were placed on him. Theodoros' force was smashed to bits and nothing now stood between Isaac and the capital.

When news of the Battle of Petroe (known also, probably wrongly, as the Battle of Hades) reached Michael, he was stunned and his whole entourage (including Psellos) with him. There was nothing he could immediately do. Psellos for one suspected that Theodoros had been secretly in league with Isaac all along, a charge which may well be true. Adding weight to this charge is the fact that Theodoros refused to countenance another attempt against Isaac. With a military move thus ruled out, Psellos was given the task of heading a mission to Isaac's camp, and with his talent for diplomacy work out a deal. To Psellos the command was 'a bolt from the blue'. He was by no means certain he would survive this hazardous task, and moreover had no real confidence that he would get anywhere; Isaac was on a winning streak, and why should he listen to the entreaties of an emperor on the ropes?

When Psellos told Michael this, the emperor shook his head sadly. Of what use was Psellos' great learning, he said, when in the hour of need he shirked his duty? 'When your friends suffer misfortune, or rather your *masters*... you care not a jot how you may give them assistance.' In somewhat melodramatic terms Michael reminded his listener of the great friendship shown to him in the past and the base ingratitude that Psellos was now displaying in return. Michael ended with an effective salvo of emotional blackmail:

> Never mind, I will go along the path that destiny has prepared for me, and, as for you, be sure that some day someone will bring on you censure and reproach for having betrayed your master and friend.

Of course, the speech had its desired effect. Psellos was quick to insist that it was not cowardice that deterred him from the mission but its impracticality. He suggested that he be accompanied by a senator, and Michael agreed at once. In the end, the mission to Isaac was composed of three people—Psellos and two senators, Theodore Alopos and Constantine Leichoudes, a noted intellectual. The trio bore a specific proposal that Isaac was to assume the title of Kaisar under the emperor, in the unspoken assumption that he would in due course succeed to the throne. A short sail brought them to Isaac's camp where, just four days after the Battle of Petroe, they were received with surprising honours. Rebel officers told them they abhorred shedding their countrymen's blood and longed for an end to the conflict. They were accompanied to Isaac's tent, and told to dismount and wait outside. When Isaac was ready the party was shown in.

Psellos found the rebel leader 'seated on a high throne, with a small bodyguard in attendance... dressed not so much as an emperor as a general'. Some small talk ensued, drinks were passed around, and then Isaac brought the meeting to a close without a word of negotiation having yet passed between them. It was a considerate gesture from Isaac, who allowed the envoys to rest and get some sleep. Before dawn the next morning they were awake and discussing how to present the imperial case. When the sun was well up, the three were summoned to Isaac's presence. This time the setting was grander—and more intimidating. Isaac was in a bigger tent, 'big enough for an army,' ringed with concentric circles of soldiers. All stood stiffly to attention, all were armed with either swords or lances or the hooked iron *romphaia*, and all were totally silent.

Standing at the entrance to the tent was Isaac's brother John Komnenos, the captain of the bodyguard. When Psellos and the others approached, John entered the tent momentarily, and when he came out he threw open the door; at the same instant the troops outside raised their voices in a deafening rolling roar that went through the serried ranks until culminating in one thunderous united shout. Trying to recover from that shock, the envoys stepped gingerly inside the tent. The spectacle that met their eyes was fantastic. Isaac was seated high on a gold cloth-covered couch, clad in a gorgeous robe, his feet on a stool. As the envoys approached he held up his head haughtily and puffed out his chest (which the waspish Psellos noted made his face red with the effort). In a small circle in front of him were members of the nobility. In front of them were the senior commanders and other distinguished soldiers, and on the flanks was a formidable display of light-armed troops from all parts of the realm:

> There were Italians, and Scyths from Taurus, men of fearful appearance, dressed in fearful garb, both alike glaring fiercely about them. They were not alike in other respects, for while the one tribe painted themselves and plucked out their eyebrows, the other preserved their natural colour.

This was political theatre of the first order.

Barely moving his hand, Isaac Komnenos motioned his visitors to his left. When they were near enough to be addressed, he asked for one of their number to give him the imperial letter and state the imperial business for all to hear. Not surprisingly, no one wanted that dubious honour. But Psellos, flattered by the others as a 'philosopher', was talked into it. His heart was pounding as he stepped forward into the forest of foes, handed Isaac the letter and turned to speak. He had carefully rehearsed his speech beforehand, but roars and shouts from the assembled troops often interrupted him. Cleverly, he avoided any hostile words and instead showered Isaac with compliments, yet reminded his hearers that Michael VI remained the true sovereign. Some hecklers loudly disputed this, soon to be joined by the rest of the troops. Psellos fell silent and waited 'until they had bawled their heads off' and resumed his speech, delicately pointing out that many emperors had been kaisares before their elevation to supreme office, and there was no reason why it should be any different with Isaac.

'But Isaac has power already!' came a shout from the ranks.

'But he's not the emperor yet!' Psellos shot back, adding that as rebels they had no legal position at all. (That was a risky statement to make, but he got away with it.) Then he addressed Isaac directly: 'Give up the title of emperor and your accession to the throne will have the sanction of legality.' This clever bit of rhetoric threw the assembly into some confusion, which Psellos exploited by appealing directly to Isaac's sense of justice.

> Now suppose that you were emperor [and] the commander-in-chief of the army entered into a conspiracy... engineering a plot to dethrone yourself and at the same time excusing himself with a recital of all his sufferings and a description of the indignity with which he had been treated— would the pretexts put forward justify the plot in your eyes?

Isaac was put on the spot. These were the precise circumstances in which he had rebelled against Michael VI. And he truthfully had to answer 'No'. He appeared to be coming round to Psellos' arguments when a great and menacing cry resounded through the huge tent. Was their leader about to cave in to the slick diplomatic verbiage of the emperor's emissary? Swords were drawn, and for a moment it appeared that Psellos' life was in danger, but Isaac calmed the unruly men down.

According to his own account, Psellos resolutely confronted the threat, and Isaac, fearing a clash, dismissed the assembly. When the soldiers had gone Isaac took Psellos and his two fellow envoys aside for a most extraordinary confession:

> Do you really believe that this imperial robe has been put on me with my approval? Do you think that if it were possible for me to run away I would refuse to escape? Of course not. They [probably meaning his troops] persuaded me to take this course in the first place, and now I am in their power, hemmed in on all sides... For the present I do not covet supreme

power. I am satisfied with the position of Kaisar. Let the emperor therefore send me fresh dispatches, to the effect that when he dies he will
bequeath the Empire to nobody but myself.

Isaac may have been familiar with the passage in Plato's *Republic* where the philosopher says that reluctant leaders tend to make the best leaders. But more likely his
own temperament shrank before the awesome task of occupying what was likely
the most powerful throne in the world at that time. His original aim had been to
get rid of the boorish and unmilitary Michael VI rather than snatch supreme power
for himself. But his army—and the military aristocracy that backed it up—had no
such qualms; he knew that all those soldiers out there who were ready to give their
lives for him would be satisfied with nothing less than seeing the imperial diadem
on his head. Caught between two fires, he had recourse to secret diplomacy. He
sent Psellos back to Constantinople under oath to convey to Michael his proposals,
promising, if they were accepted, to go 'without delay and pay him the honour due
to an emperor and a father'.

The utmost secrecy was essential. If just one rebel soldier got wind of what was
afoot, the whole deal would be off and Isaac himself compromised. The scheme was
worked out that evening at dinner. At dawn the following morning Isaac arranged
for his official reply to the emperor to be distributed among the soldiery; it was an
innocuous document, designed to calm any suspicion that he might be going behind
the soldiers' backs. The *real* message to the emperor was memorized by Psellos and
the other envoys, who at once sailed the short distance to Constantinople, arriving
at the palace before noon. When the emperor heard Isaac's proposals he appeared
willing to grant almost all of them. 'He can even wear a crown if he wants, though it
would be unusual for a Kaisar.' One thing Michael did insist upon was that the two
would share power equally. Other than that, he was willing to pardon all the rebel
officers and soldiers. Psellos and his fellow envoys were ordered to return to Isaac
with that promise, though Michael asked for some time in which to think up some
excuse to the people and clergy for what he was about to do.

On 31 August Psellos reached Isaac's camp to find the rebel leader rather shab-
bily dressed, even though seated on his throne of honour and surrounded by his
retinue. On receiving the emperor's message on shared powers he had it read
aloud, to general approval. The army was satisfied because Isaac's presence in the
palace was assured, and perhaps more importantly, there would be no reprisals.
Then, in private, Psellos delivered the real, and secret, message to the effect that
Isaac would be welcome in Constantinople 'in a few days'. Overjoyed, Isaac sent
his men home on extended leave and prepared to pack his bags. That same day
news arrived that Michael had abdicated and fled for sanctuary to Sancta Sophia;
to Psellos it seemed too good to be true, but a succession of other messengers

appeared to confirm the story, adding that the clergy and large numbers of people were on the verge of popular revolt in favour of Isaac.

The rebel leader himself was inclined to disbelieve the news as highly exaggerated. But as he was mulling it over, yet another runner loped up to his tent, gasping that Michael had indeed stepped down and that an imperial galley, replete with a torch-bearing escort, was being readied to bring Isaac in triumph. The exhausted messenger swore that he had personally witnessed Michael dressed humbly in a monk's habit—the obvious outward sign that he had abdicated. Even then Isaac remained sceptical, until yet more news-bearers arrived, all confirming the same thing.

Now what would become of Psellos and the other envoys? They were the emperor's men, and the emperor had fallen. In Isaac's camp they were the equivalent of prisoners-of-war. Psellos says he spent that night in dread, unable to sleep with the expectation that his throat would be slit in the morning. But is that really true? There is evidence to suggest that Psellos was deliberately distorting this part of the story, mainly because he may well have been secretly in league with Isaac all along. It would certainly not be beyond the capacity of this wily diplomat and scholar. In fact, at this point it is worth taking a brief look at this extraordinary man who played such a spotlighted part in Byzantine history.

Constantine Psellos was born in 1018 to an upper-class but by no means wealthy family which, despite its lack of resources, ensured that young Constantine would have the best possible, if interrupted, education, from the earliest possible age. We are told that at age 10 he could memorize Homer's entire *Iliad* in the original. Classes at the University of Constantinople were free to anyone of proven intellectual ability, regardless of class or background, so there was no social or economic barrier to his achieving the utmost in academic qualifications. By the time he was 25 he had absorbed all he could of law, philosophy, mathematics, science and theology, enabling him to earn a professorship of rhetoric. His sheer ability gave him an *entreé* to the court of Michael V, where he progressed rapidly upwards. There the lure of power politics seized him. Constantine IX Monomachos and Michael VI the Codger both doted on him. In 1054 he took holy orders and the name of Michael, by which he is known to history. By the time of his mission to Isaac he had achieved the rank of the equivalent of prime minister, all before he was 40 years old. He was described as tall, with attractive eyes and a pleasant personality.

Historians agree that he was a most complex man. According to Basil Markesinis, 'his sense of where power was shifting was almost unerring.' He was the Byzantine equivalent of a Borgia, of the Italian humanists of a later era who questioned the traditional powers and privileges of the old aristocracy who were beginning to be upstaged by a new aristocracy of commerce and wealth. Psellos represented the latter, a powerful force for change in late Roman society. He can be described as not only like a Borgia but also a Machiavelli, a largely unscrupulous realist whose dedication to the state welfare was absolute, an unhesitating schemer when he believed it was warranted. To him, the eternal truths were to be found only in divinity and family values; anything else was transient and worthy of manipulation in the overriding interests of the Empire. And it is this attitude that doubtless helped him weather situations that could have defeated a more rigidly principled man.

At this point, prompted by the remarkable narrative of couriers bringing constantly updated news to Isaac, it would also be pertinent to briefly look at what a much later age would call the 'information flow' in eleventh century Byzantium. In a society without newspapers or magazines, radio or television, internet or social media, important news did get around. The people of Constantinople, for example, were somehow kept well aware of what was happening, especially in the halls of power. As in all societies there were individuals with access to information—in this case priests who broadcast from the pulpits, travelling merchants coming through the gates, or soldiers on leave—who would inform small social groups which would then disseminate the information to larger groups, and so on. As in the case of Psellos' final mission to Isaac, there appear to have been couriers whose specific job was to carry state news to where it was needed.

On 1 September Michael Psellos, somewhat surprised to find his neck still intact, mounted his horse to follow Isaac Komnenos' triumphal progress to Constantinople. At first he rode in the rear but in due course Isaac invited him up to the head of the column to ask his advice on various matters, reassuring the envoy that he was *persona* quite *grata* after all. The sun was well up when Isaac entered Chrysopolis, the main town on the Asian side of the Bosporus, to a tumultuous welcome. Roadside crowds, cheering and dancing, sprinkled perfume over him as he passed. Psellos was amazed at what he saw:

> It was not merely the people of the city, nor the Senate, nor the host of farmers and merchants, that made up the happy throng: there were students of the theological colleges there, and dwellers on the mountain-tops, and hermits who had left their communal homes in the rock-tombs...

Even that strange class of holy men called stylites, from their practice of living for years on the top of marble pillars, unprotected from the elements ('living in mid-air', according to Psellos), came down from their perches to witness the big event.

If Isaac himself kept a sombre expression through all the adulation, he had good reason to. He simply couldn't really believe his good fortune, and would well be wondering if he was stepping from a frying pan into a fire. As the crowds roared he turned to Psellos: 'Philosopher,' he said, using his favourite term for the man, 'I'm not sure this is going to end well.' Psellos tried to reassure him that his foreboding had no real foundation, and that he should in the end trust to God, who after all had brought him to where he was now. Psellos' words were a confirmation of the ideology that God in the end was responsible for placing emperors on the throne, and if they proved unworthy, removing them. Isaac, the grizzled military aristocrat, revealed that he had not thought in those terms before. His eyes filled with tears of disappointment, as it sounded as if Psellos was flattering him just as any shallow courtier would. 'I appreciated your tongue when it spoke in insolence more than now, when it flatters and praises.' By now the glittering Bosporus was in sight, with the imperial galley ready. 'In fact,' Isaac continued, 'I regard you as first among my friends.' Later that day, under the vast echoing dome of Sancta Sophia, Isaac Komnenos was crowned Isaac I. The dynasty of the Komnenes had begun.

The year of grace 1057 still had a few months to run—only to the Byzantines it was the year 6565, as their calendar dated from the putative creation of the world according to the theology of the time. While the East Roman Empire had been churning through its succession of rulers to end up with Isaac I, the rest of Europe and Middle East were going through historical processes that would impinge ever more closely on Byzantium and its fortunes. And for Byzantium itself the future was beckoning in the Komnenos household in the tiny form of a 1-year-old and probably highly precocious infant born to Isaac's brother John. His name: Alexios.

Western Europe was about to embark on what is conventionally known as the High Middle Ages, when feudalism as an economic system attainted its apex. It was a time of awakening intellectual and cultural growth, thanks in great part to the vital Byzantine link in trade with the Muslim domains. The popes of Rome were engaged in a mighty tussle for power with secular-minded rulers in the Holy Roman Empire. Universities grew and flourished. The Christian church, as in Byzantium, reigned supreme over rulers and ruled alike. 'Above all,' writes Professor Wallace Ferguson, 'it was the great age of the *Respublica Christiana*, when all nations of Western Europe formed parts of the commonwealth of united Christendom.'

In 1057 Holy Roman Emperor (a title, as we have seen, never recognized by Byzantium) Henry IV, just 7, had been reigning for a year. But because he was so young, Germany was roiled by anarchy; dukes, lords, bishops and abbots carved out their own autocratic domains. The same was more or less true in Italy, leaving the papacy poised to assert a renewed power after the great schism with the Greeks three years before had freed it from concerns in the East. Already in that year an ambitious young German Catholic monk named Hildebrand was making a name for himself in the papal *curia* strengthening the institution against the power of the Roman nobles and the bumptious German rulers—in less than twenty years, under the name Pope Gregory VII, Hildebrand would bring his iron will to bear against a mature and equally stubborn Henry IV in one of the epochal political conflicts of history. The great power struggle between the popes and the German emperors that would last well into the thirteenth century illustrated the very different approach in the West to the perennial issue of how to reconcile the spiritual with the secular power. Byzantium, as we have seen, had solved the problem a long time before by placing Christ at the true headship of state and emperor and patriarch beneath that figurehead. Failure to do so in the West resulted in much needless political and military conflict.

The former Roman-Byzantine possessions in south Italy and Sicily had fallen under the sway of the Normans, who had discovered the pleasant climate in 1016 and since then had poured into the region in great numbers. In 1057 they were led by the ruthless and virtually indestructible Robert Guiscard, who two years later received lands formally from Pope Nicholas II. By sheer force of will and arms, Guiscard extended his sway over much of Greece, adding a new and formidable member to Byzantium's roster of enemies. He will figure largely in the story to come.

France had as king the weak Henry I, who proved unable to control the powerful nobles who preyed upon travellers and were responsible for widespread social insecurity. It would be three more years before Philip I ascended the French throne to begin to claw back some of the royal prerogatives, and in the process help make France a power to be reckoned with—even as far as Byzantium, which within a few decades would soon feel that power on its doorstep. England was in the last stages of its Saxon monarchy. In 1042, at about the time Empress Theodora passed away to make way for Constantine IX Monomachus in Constantinople, Edward the Confessor had become king in England, displacing the Danish-line monarchs; but his marked Norman sympathies and pious nature made him, in the eyes of many of his Anglo-Saxon subjects, the wrong man for the crown. Edward's death in 1066 would move his distant cousin, Duke William of Normandy, to stage the famous Norman conquest and alter the entire course of English and European history.

In 1057 a 17-year-old Spanish boy was growing up to be one of his country's most renowned *caballeros*, or knight-errant mercenary warriors. Named Rodrigo Diaz, he was born in the reign of Fernando I of Castile who united neighbouring Leon and Galicia and created the nucleus of a Spanish state that would soon revive to cast out the Muslims occupying the south of the Iberian Peninsula. Diaz later became known and revered as El Cid, and his marginal importance to this story is that his campaigns against the Muslim Moors began what is known as the *Reconquista*, or 'reconquest' of south Spain for Christianity—a more or less exact parallel of what the Byzantine Empire was doing at the other end of the Mediterranean.

In 1057 the once-magnificent Abbasid caliphate of Baghdad was at its last gasp. The decline had begun two centuries before, after the twenty-year rule of the celebrated al-Ma'mun. It was a time when the Arab poet Anwari could exult:

Blessed be the site of Baghdad, seat of learning and art;
None can point in the world to a city her equal...
The gardens filled with lovely nymphs equal Kashmir;
And thousands of gondolas on the water
Dance and sparkle like sunbeams in the air.

Al-Ma'mun had surrounded himself with a 4,000-strong bodyguard of Turkish troops who acted as a praetorian guard and after his death became uncontrollable. His successor al-Mu'tasim actually fled the anarchy of Baghdad, his successors taxed the people heavily to pay for sumptuous palaces, and from then on it was all downhill. The last Abbasid caliph, the ineffectual al-Qa'im, invited the Seljuk Turks to Baghdad to oust the clique that was oppressing him but was in turn oppressed by the redoubtable Seljuk Turkish chieftain Tughrul Bey who formally ended the Abbasid dynasty in 1058. From now it would be the Seljuk Turks who would be Byzantium's most formidable Muslim foes.

The East Roman Empire had spent four centuries holding back the Islamic tide that had been surging up from the Middle East ever since the Prophet Muhammad's early followers embarked on their zealous conquests. The first big shock for Byzantium had come at Yarmuk in Syria in 634, where General Khalid ibn al-Walid destroyed Emperor Heraclius' army and gathered all Syria into the Muslim domain. Jerusalem had fallen into Khalid's lap four years later. In 717 the Umayyad caliph Suleiman butted his head fruitlessly against Constantinople, and 'solaced himself with good food and bad women'. The Abbasids, who took power in 750, were helpless to stop the Byzantines from clawing back much of what they had lost in Asia Minor, but the young caliph-in-waiting Harun al-Rashid took the fight back to the very walls of Constantinople, only to be bought off by Empress Irene.

Arriving at the shores of the Mediterranean, the Arabs quickly learned the ways of the sea and almost from the outset the Byzantine navy found its hands full. Cyprus and Rhodes were the first Greek islands to fall to the Muslims, to be followed in later centuries by Crete, as well as Sardinia, Corsica, Malta and finally Sicily. Now known to all as the Saracens (from the Arabic *sharq*, or east), the invaders rolled up south Italy and reached the very walls of Rome in 846; twice they tried to seize the Eternal City, but were finally driven off by an Italian fleet organized by Pope Leo IV (the battle is commemorated in a canvas by Raphael now in the Stanze of the Vatican). Sicily was a Saracen possession until the advent of the Norman Robert Guiscard and 'Saracen cities, castles, and palaces built with marvellous art' were razed.

Egypt in 1057 was relatively prosperous under the rule of the Muslim Fatimid dynasty, the least aggressive of the Muslim houses and the one most inclined to trade with the Christian powers and get along with them diplomatically. The Fatimid caliph at the time was Mustansir, a devotee of the good life which he is said to have considered a better deal than the rigorous Muslim practice of 'staring at the Black Stone [in the Kaaba in Mecca] and drinking impure water [from the Zamzam well in the same city].' Trade with Byzantium especially in vital grain and textiles, flourished. Cairo prospered mightily; a traveller reported a metropolis of multistorey brick homes and thousands of shops 'so filled with gold, jewellery, embroideries and satins that there was no room to sit down'. Mustansir's tolerance of other faiths was reciprocated by a fabulously wealthy Christian merchant who fed the whole population of Cairo at his own expense during a five-year famine. This, then, was the international scene that Isaac I Komnenos was called on to deal with.

The Komnenes traced their descent to the town of Komne in east Thrace (now the European portion of Turkey). It's not clear how they acquired their wealth; we must assume it was through trade and amassing landholdings. They are recorded as having extensive estates in Paphlagonia (now north-west Turkey), an area rich in olives, vineyards and livestock. The family itself sought a noble pedigree commensurate with its economic power; the story was put about that its distant ancestors arrived from Rome with Constantine the Great, a tradition that is of course impossible to verify. There was, however, enough of an accumulated lineage to enable Isaac to marry Princess Aikaterine of Bulgaria while he was still a military man. That marriage set the seal on the position of the Komnenes among the top layer of East Roman aristocracy.

Among this aristocracy there was a noted differentiation, with the eastern considered superior to the western. This could explain the Komnenes' preference for a base in Paphlagonia rather than Thrace, which may have been too associated with Bulgar 'barbarism' and other presumably undesirable Balkan influences. The family thus joined other noble military houses such as the Doukas and Skleros families, who were collectively known as the *theia gene*, or divine clans. The Komnene and Doukai in particular were closely allied. Modern researcher Constantine Varzos well reproduces their importance in the Byzantine mind:

> Two heroic bloodlines, they produced the best descendants, who did not boast of obscure god-ancestors as the ancient kings and heroes did, but were well-built and endowed by nature with strategic knowledge and great-mindedness.

Contemporary admirers (probably seeking political favours) praised the Komnene as 'divine from the womb'. They were seen as civilizing any aliens with whom they intermarried, such as the Bulgar Princess Aikaterine. There is a tantalizing hint in the poetry of the time that some adventurous Komnenes might have sailed past Gibraltar and into the Atlantic Ocean. Varzos cites a verse by an unknown poet:

> The surge of the Atlantic gives me strength...
> The Komnenes, generations of rulers
> Who ply the seas of the trophy-winners
> Where not even strong Herakles could pass.

In Constantinople the Komnenes perhaps wisely kept themselves behind thick-walled mansions with a minimum of outward ostentation, in order to distinguish themselves from the flashier nouveaux riches. Inside those walls laboured armies of servants and unpaid slaves for the more menial tasks. Some members of the family, however, seem to have fallen foul of the system and descended into poverty.

The first Komnenos of whom we have more than the flimsiest knowledge is Manuel Komnenos Erotikos, whose mother was the sister of Cyprus-born General Theophilos Erotikos. This officer staged an unsuccessful mutiny against Constantine IX Monomachos and was punished by being dressed up in a woman's clothing, seated on a donkey and paraded before jeering crowds in the Hippodrome. Manuel's brother Nikephoros Komnenos had been named military governor of Asprakama, in what is now Armenia. He is reported to have ordered his men to pledge allegiance to himself to the point of 'dying alongside' him. Such ambition triggered imperial suspicions, which included whisperings that he was plotting to set up his own independent kingdom in Georgia; he was recalled to Constantinople and had his eyes put out.

Isaac, the firstborn son of Manuel Komnenos Erotikos, was probably about 40 years old when his father was humiliated in the Hippodrome. At the outset of Constantine IX's reign he held the office of Domestikos of the East, with command over all the armies east of the Bosporus. In 1054 Empress Theodora, possibly because he was considered too close to the patriarch who had split from Rome, sacked him. We have already described his public humiliation by Michael VI, which led directly to his reluctant but well-planned rebellion. But as many a usurper before him found out, seizing control of an Empire and actually running it were two quite different things.

Isaac I had hardly set foot in the palace when he set to work feverishly putting the whole imperial house in order. Psellos tells us that he didn't even pause to change his battle-soiled clothes or take a bath. When night came he didn't retire to the royal bedchamber that no doubt had been carefully prepared for him, but sat up by lamplight poring over state business. Outside the palace walls, he knew, the soldiers who had followed him from the provinces into battle were roaming the taverns and brothels of Constantinople, and like restless soldiers everywhere, could easily slip into brawls. To ward off that possibility Isaac issued swift orders for them to disband and go back to their homes, after giving them fulsome praise (and spresumably their pay); the more valorous men were decorated. Soon the streets were calm again, to the relief of many, including Psellos, who could never be sure how the victorious troops would treat him after he defied them in Isaac's camp.

After this, great things were expected of the new Komnenos ruler. The mass of people, who could not know him closely, entertained an image of some superman. Those diplomats and officials who dealt with Isaac personally, however, came away with a more complex impression. Dispensing state business and receiving envoys, he invariably came across as cold and hard, especially when in the habit of uttering blood-curdling threats against potential enemies. He honed his throne manner into a veritable art of political theatre. Seated majestically on the gold cloth, with his senators grouped submissively on either side, he would set his face into a thunder-browed mask while maintaining a complete silence that unnerved the senators, who 'stood rooted to the spot, as if they had been hit by lightning'. Their pulse rates would rise in fear whenever Isaac refused a petition or a request. In fact, he spoke little but well, choosing his words with care, and often meaning more by what was unsaid. A small, barely-noticeable motion of his head was often enough to get an order carried out. He was intolerant of opposition, distrusting silver-tongued orators and refusing to listen to them. However, in his private and relaxed moments, says Psellos, he was pleasant and tolerant.

Like any self-respecting Byzantine emperor and vicegerent of God on earth, Isaac placed great value on appearances whenever dealing with foreign ambassadors. For these occasions he donned his richest, most dazzling robes. In many cases it worked, for example, with envoys from Egypt and Parthia, who were suitably impressed. He would also abandon his usual laconic style for the foreigners, flooding them with rhetoric that could be either flattering or menacing, as the occasion demanded. He probably was influenced here by his legal scholars, though he refused to admit it. He was also canny enough not to waste state money on futile campaigns; moreover, he never had much use for the 'barbarian' generals in his army, believing most of them to be incompetent and timid.

In his administration Isaac can be fairly described as an obsessive workaholic. He was single-mindedly intent on clearing away decades of waste, inefficiency and corruption as quickly as possible, before age or political rivals could stay his hand. Psellos vividly likened the Roman state structure at the time to 'a monstrous body with a multitude of heads... hands so many as to be beyond counting... its entrails festering and diseased... here afflicted with dropsy, there diminishing with consumption'—and he certainly was in a position to know. Much of this corruption had grown up under the powerful court eunuchs, which was ironic because castrated public servants of senior rank were believed (at least theoretically) to be less corrupt than others simply because they had no offspring on behalf of whom to intrigue. The eunuchs were always a considerable power and enjoyed high status. Many a father willingly consented to his son's castration so that he might rise to a position of prominence and influence as a 'beardless official'—an ambassador, general or governor of a province. There could also have been another, deeper, reason for what we would regard as a monstrous practice: Guerdan suggests that a castrated official was regarded as the earthly equivalent of a sexless angel; as the angels surrounded the throne of God, so the sexless eunuchs surrounded the imperial throne, in a replica of heavenly realities. In fact, they had their own anthem beginning with the words, 'We the cherubim...'

By Isaac's time the earthbound 'cherubim' had assumed near-total control over imperial appointments and policy. It is also worth considering whether the average court eunuch, a person of some ability and talent, might nurse a subliminal envy and resentment of men whose genital capacities and testosterone remained intact and were used. Isaac himself may well have thought so, as one of his first acts was to strip the eunuchs of their more conspicuous powers and let everyone know that at last a real soldier was at the helm. To symbolize this change, he had coins minted depicting him with a drawn sword instead of the usual *labaron*, or imperial standard, that accompanied images of previous rulers.

But with that symbolic drawn sword, Isaac tried to cut out too much too fast. Decrees and laws enacted by his predecessor Michael VI were annulled or changed without the consequences being properly thought out. The emperor was like a battlefield surgeon, for whom every case was an emergency. If a problem couldn't be solved in a single day, he fretted. And once he began cutting, he couldn't stop. Noble families were taxed mercilessly, followed by the monasteries and the Church itself, which complained bitterly. But Isaac defended all his exactions as being in the public interest. As an old-style military aristocrat he had no use for wealth or display, just unrelenting public discipline at warp speed. Neither wise counsels nor concern over the public reaction could hold him back once he had an idea in his head. Again, we turn to Psellos for a keen judgement:

> Had some rein kept him under control, he would have overrun the whole inhabited world, country by country. He would have won glory on every battlefield... But lack of restraint, refusal to accept reason as his guide, they were the ruin of his noble character.

The diplomat's assessment of Isaac's character may owe something to classical Greek psychology as expressed in the great Athenian tragic plays, where mythical heroes such as Achilleus, Orestes and Oedipus could have had the universe at their feet were it not for the 'tragic flaw' in their personalities that in the end brings them down.

Partly because of his iron conviction that he was always right, Isaac soon found himself in conflict with the strong-minded Patriarch Michael Keroularios who had backed his seizure of the throne and had actually crowned him. Keroularios had played a leading role in the acrimonious schism with Rome in 1054, and that alone ought to have tempered the emperor's relations with him as someone not to be taken lightly. But however much the patriarch may have opposed the popes, he took a rather large page out of their book by insisting on the primacy of the spiritual over the secular power. There seemed to be no way he could overtly do this in the Byzantine system, where the emperor retained the headship of everything; therefore he had recourse to symbolic gestures of defiance such as wearing footwear dyed in the special shade of red reserved only for the emperor himself. This was too much for Isaac, who packed Keroularios off to exile on Prokonnesos, an island in the Sea of Marmara, where he died shortly afterwards. Replacing him was one of Psellos' fellow envoys to Isaac's camp, the learned and influential Constantine Leichoudes.

Isaac had dealt with the troublesome issue of the patriarchate just in time for him to turn his attention to an invasion of the Pechenegs (also known as Patzinaks), a pugnacious and nomadic tribe originating in south Russia but living in what is now Romania. In autumn 1059 a Pecheneg force crossed the frozen Danube into Byzantine territory, seeking new homes after being displaced by other nomads. Their advance rang alarm bells in Constantinople, as it was well known that though they were neither disciplined nor ordered, and carried no arms or armour except a spear, and knew little and cared less about battle tactics, they were merciless and vicious fighters. Any Roman army sent against them had to steel itself against their fanatical mass attacks. Even in defeat the Pechenegs were known to be able to re-form apparently out of nowhere. No one expected them to respect any agreement or treaty.

The emperor was aware of all this as he set out in September at the head of an army to stem the Pechenegs' advance. His fame went before him, as Psellos reports that the enemy's morale plummeted at the news of his approach. To them he was the 'wielder of thunderbolts', a veritable Zeus in the flesh. But being Pechenegs they could not shrink from the coming fight; they decided to attack the mass of Roman shields in front of them piecemeal, in howling detachments. The aim was probably to wear down the army by these nuisance attacks and save the mass charge for later. Whatever the tactical purpose, it didn't work. The Byzantine ranks were too tight and disciplined, and all assaults just bounced off them. At this the Pecheneg commanders broke off the engagement and challenged Isaac to a renewal of the fight in three days' time. But being Pechenegs, they of course had no intention of sticking to what they said, and used the time to flee into the Bulgarian hinterlands. When the three days were up Isaac advanced to the enemy camp but found only old people and infants—those who couldn't travel fast—left behind by the invaders. Unsure of whether this was one more Pecheneg trick and fearing an ambush, Isaac determined that the campaign was a success and turned back, laden with booty. On the return march a violent storm caused some casualties, but Isaac entered his capital in triumph for the second time.

Perhaps no event in Constantinople was more elaborate, more flamboyant, than a triumphal entry by a victorious emperor. The processions staged by the old Roman emperors paled by comparison. It taxed the emperor's own energies to the utmost, which was why he would usually spend between one and seven days preserving his strength, either on the Asian shore of the Bosporus (if he was coming from the east) or outside the gates to the west of the city. In Guerdan's description, once rested, the emperor would board his galley or mount his horse, to be met outside the city by richly-apparelled senators and other nobles who would praise him to high heaven and receive his ritual response: 'How are you, my eminent children? How are your wives, my daughters?' Then he would proceed slowly onwards, stopping several times to pray at various churches or monasteries and change his clothes each time. At one monastery he would don a golden robe and fasten on a new sword. Delegations were constantly offering him crowns, which he was obliged to try on. In front of him, at some distance, rode the imperial horse guard; behind stretched a procession of eunuchs and other officials. And that was before he even entered the city.

At the traditional triumphal entrance, the Golden Gate, the emperor would dismount and personally open the golden centre portal which was always kept closed except for occasions such as this. Once through, he faced ecstatic crowds lining the route to the palace; children tossed flowers in his path; officials held out laurel wreaths and bejewelled armlets for him. The procession reached its climax in the Mese, the main central thoroughfare. Colourful tapestries and bowers of flowers hung from every balcony. The street had been swept carefully beforehand and sprinkled with rose water. At the Augusteion next to Sancta Sophia, the patriarch would come out to greet the emperor, who had to dismount and change his clothes once more in a small chapel. Inside the great cathedral he had to endure a whole string of ceremonials before arriving at the main gate of the palace.

There he would see a throne, a golden organ and the True Cross set up in the open air. He would walk up to the throne and sit in it, whereupon a crowd gathered by the notorious political clubs of Constantinople, the Blues and the Greens, would cry in unison: 'Only one is holy!' More golden bracelets appeared, which the emperor had to put on. This was the signal for the crowd to keep quiet and listen to the emperor's set speech. It was usually a plain, unadorned account of his battles, victories, booty and number of captives. As the crowd applauded, he would remount and ride across the Hippodrome to the palace proper. There he was met by his Augusta, who would remain on her knees until the emperor got down from his horse and raised her up. As if all that were not demanding enough, palace festivities would be in order until the small hours, after which the exhausted emperor could finally get some rest.

After the Pecheneg campaign a change came over Isaac. He became more haughty and autocratic than ever; he compelled even his brother John to follow strict palace protocol like any other Byzantine subject. It would appear that only Isaac's Bulgarian wife, the Augusta Aikaterine, preserved the human touch in the palace environs. The couple's relationship appears to have been stable enough. When her husband was on campaign she prayed for him. With her royal bearing she made a favourable impression on all who met her, and no doubt helped smooth any ruffled feelings left by her husband's brusque manner. Isaac himself devoted more hours to his favourite pastime, hunting. We read how he hallooed loudly, encouraging his hunting dogs to ever greater speed. His favourite quarry was the crane, which he was expert at picking off with a spear-throw in mid-flight (or so the chronicles say), and he would take exceptional pleasure in watching as the stricken bird 'danced the dance of death, turning over and over, now on its back, now on its belly'.

The emperor had a special lodge built outside the walls of Constantinople, where he would spend whole days, hunting from dawn to dusk. One story has it that he narrowly escaped being struck by lightning while leaning against a tree, an experience that shook him considerably. One day in November he felt a pain in his side, which he thought was a muscle sprain brought on by his constant activity with the spear. The following day this symptom of overexertion was compounded by a chill and a fever. Psellos rode out to the lodge to find Isaac in bed. As he was himself a medical man in addition to a scholar and diplomat, he felt the emperor's pulse. Then the royal physician intervened. 'The fever isn't serious,' he told Psellos in what the minister thought was an overconfident tone. 'It should pass in a few days.' The doctor was right, though as soon as Isaac began to eat solid food, a worse fever racked his body. Presently he was transported back to Blachernai Palace, where he appeared to recover, joking and bantering into the night. The next morning Psellos went to the palace to find the emperor prostrate in bed again, scarcely able to breathe and with a stabbing pain in his side. Isaac lay there mutely looking up at his chief minister, wordlessly wondering if the end was near. The palace physician reported that the emperor's pulse had become weak and irregular. Psellos himself observed the arrhythmically pulsating wrist artery and quietly decided that the end was near.

The news had gone through the palace and soon the Augusta Aikaterine and her daughter, the gold-red-haired Maria, the emperor's brother John and a nephew, gathered round Isaac. In tears, they all urged him to make the effort to move to the Great Palace and put the imperial affairs in order. At this, he got out of bed and walked unsupported out of the room; 'like some towering cypress being violently shaken by the wind, he tottered as he walked forward.' Somehow, again unaided, he mounted his horse. By the time he reached the Great Palace Isaac was barely conscious, which is how Psellos received him. Inside, in the classic Greek tradition, the Augusta and other female members of the royal family chanted formulaic dirges of sorrow, Aikaterine leading and the other tearful women following. It was all very solemn and tragic, in keeping with the belief that the man in the bed was about to breathe his last. Then Isaac muttered that he would like to be received into the bosom of the Church. What followed was a most unseemly scene.

Aikaterine suddenly stopped grieving and turned on Psellos. 'What a fine way to show your gratitude, philosopher,' she snapped, 'by planning to convert your emperor to the life of a monk!' Psellos at once vigorously denied ever having had such an intention, and turned to the emperor to ask him who, if anyone, had advised him to retire to holy orders. Isaac replied weakly but probably truthfully that it had been his own decision, and here he must have gestured to his wife. 'This lady,' he said, 'true to her womanly instincts... blames everyone else for a suggestion I make myself.' At this, Aikaterine poured out all the bitterness that had been accumulating in her breast through the years:

> I take on my own shoulders all the sins you ever committed... I will answer for the wrongs you have done... The deepest darkness can cover me, the outer fire can burn every bit of me—I would welcome it. And you—have you no pity now for us in our desolation? What sort of feeling have you, to take away yourself from the palace, and leave me behind, condemned to a widowhood full of sorrow, and your daughter, a wretched orphan?

As her emotions surged, her dramatic rhetoric became more doom-laden:

> Hands, maybe not even friendly hands, will carry us to far-away places of exile. They may decide on some worse fate. It may be some pitiless fellow will shed the blood of your dear ones. No doubt you will live on after you enter the Church, or perhaps you will die nobly, but what will be left for us? A life worse than death!

The Augusta's outburst, as recorded by eyewitness Psellos—and there is no reason to doubt his veracity—is revealing. First, it sounds like a masterpiece of emotional blackmail. Second, and more important, it shows that the fate of the Komnene house and her own family rather than her husband's life was uppermost in her mind. Was then her conspicuous and loud lamenting just a show? It is hard to avoid the conclusion that she actually had considerable hopes for Isaac's recovery. Third, life in the royal chambers must not have been as harmonious as was officially made out. Aikaterine was tired of being the emperor's buffer zone, absorbing all manner of political blows on his behalf, playing the 'good lady of the house'. His intention to flee to a cloister in case he recovered from his illness seemed to her the basest ingratitude for her support of him all these years.

But Isaac was adamant. Beaten, Aikaterine asked her husband at least to name a worthy successor, a 'man who serves you with the greatest loyalty and devotion'. The emperor seemed to perk up at this, and named the president of the Senate, Constantine Doukas. As we have seen, the Komnenes and the Doukai shared membership in the highest layers of Byzantine aristocracy, and Isaac's choice seemed designed to ensure a smooth transition. Constantine Doukas himself was an unassuming man, not letting his presidency of the Senate swell his head. He cared little for display and outward honours, sometimes going about in rough farmer's apparel. When called to the palace, he was seen to be extremely shy and modest, and stood respectfully before the imperial bed. In a brief speech which Psellos recorded, Isaac told Constantine Doukas that he had had him in mind for the succession for some time, hinting that he considered Doukas a more capable man for the throne than his own brother John. Applause mingled with sobs as Isaac stopped speaking. Doukas, overawed by what he had just been appointed to, seems to have uttered not a word in response.

As to what happened next, we have only a vague outline. The precise date and cause of Isaac's death remains disputed. Psellos, for all his value as an eyewitness to events, cannot quite be trusted here. We do know that after naming Doukas as his successor Isaac was carried to the nearby Stoudion monastery overlooking the Sea of Marmara not far from the Golden Gate. There, far from being at death's door, he is believed to have lived as a humble monk for two more years, doing menial jobs and writing learned commentaries on Homer. This narrative would reinforce suspicions that Isaac was not really as ill as Psellos claimed, and many others present believed. There is also a good deal of circumstantial evidence to suggest the whole 'deathbed' scene of nominating Constantine Doukas could have been staged by the Machiavellian Psellos as a way of smoothing out his own career, as he and Doukas were the best of friends. Consequently, Psellos could now wield more influence over the throne than he ever could under Isaac I.

Chapter 5

Interregnum: Diogenes' disaster

When Isaac got better, Psellos writes, he regretted what he had done. But he could not break his solemn promise to Doukas. As a tough soldier, he had tried to apply military-type discipline to the affairs of the Roman state, mercilessly slashing costs, building up the army and enforcing his will with the iron fist of a battlefield commander, uncaring of how unpopular he might become. Constantine X Doukas (1059–1067) was a man of a very different stamp, a bookish, pen-pushing bureaucrat like his crony Psellos. Far more at home in the halls of law and diplomacy than in the field, he was a typical Doukas, in whose family veins ran the blood of a governing class. (The name is a direct derivative of the Latin dux, or duke.) In elevating one of their number to the throne, the family achieved an ambition going back centuries. But despite the Doukai's renown as an aristocratic military family, Constantine conspicuously shunned military affairs. Psellos was more than happy to help him along that direction, as he had always resented the army's influence over Isaac. The result was a vast and mushrooming bureaucracy that drank up public funds that should—given the constant threats butting against the Empire's borders—have better gone for defence.

Constantine X's first moments as emperor were shaky ones. After Isaac had given his blessing to the succession, in front of everyone Psellos took the imperial robes and placed them on Constantine, seated the new ruler on the throne and slipped the imperial red sandals on his feet. That done, the Senate and a body of magistrates came forward and did obeisance, the final sign of the transfer of power. When the throne-curtain was drawn and Constantine was alone with Psellos, the new emperor could not keep back his tears, raising his arms above his head in thanks to God. When the curtain was pulled back he addressed the assembled dignitaries on the subject of 'justice, mercy and righteous dealing'. No doubt he meant what he said, and reaped considerable popularity because of it. But was it what the Empire needed at that juncture?

Psellos continues his gripping *Chronographia* with an account of Constantine X's reign, but here the tone changes. He introduces and describes the new emperor—'in very truth appointed by God'—in cloyingly worshipful terms more suited to crude political propaganda than objective history. Small wonder, for Psellos as prime minister was very much the court favourite, sometimes wielding more actual power than his sovereign. There is little doubt that Constantine was a good-natured ruler and cared for the state. Psellos claims there were no executions in his seven-year reign, even when in 1060 some city officials plotted an attempt on his life. Before becoming emperor Constantine had married twice, his first wife having succumbed to illness. The second wife, the well-to-do Eudokia Makrembolitissa, gave him three sons and two daughters. The Komnenes, for their part, were given due consideration. Isaac's brother John Komnenos was given command of the western army; at the time, he had been married for fifteen years to Anna Dalassene, the daughter of a renowned general. They had several children, among them three boys, Isaac, Adrian and Alexios; this last-named was destined to turn the fortunes of the Komnenes around in no small way.

If we may risk a bold generalization, Constantine X believed in conciliation rather than confrontation. He abhorred violence, refusing to inflict floggings or blindings where it was his privilege to decree them. At home he was a beloved family man, fond of playing with his children. His daughter Zoe, in her teens, was betrothed to Adrian Komnenos in order to keep the Komnenes in favour. Constantine's youngest son, also named Constantine, had been born after the accession, and therefore was a true *porphyrogennetos*. Yet the emperor seems to have been unwilling to wait until the child grew up, especially as his eldest son Michael was already on the verge of manhood and displayed qualities which his father believed fitted him for the throne.

Though Constantine knew little and cared less about military affairs, security problems pressed in on him anyway. At some point in his reign several high-placed officials hatched a plot to assassinate him by sinking his galley while he was being ferried up the Golden Horn to the Blachernai Palace. The plot was foiled, and the conspirators were lucky to be merely sent into exile when ordinarily they would have been beheaded. Even then the emperor confessed to feeling sorry for them, weeping during a private dinner with Psellos over how they must be suffering away from their homes while he was banqueting. However, it would be a mistake to assume that Constantine was a fainteheart. He was not one to run from battle if it were forced on him, as when at one point two western barbarian tribes joined forces to attack the Empire. Feeling the call of duty, Constantine rode off to fight; he had once remarked to someone who had sworn to shield him with his own body: 'Good! Don't forget to deal me a blow yourself, when I have fallen.' In some way—we are not told how—Psellos brought him back to the capital. Obviously the prime minister didn't trust the emperor's lack of military ability. The tribes anyway withdrew after being defeated by a small Roman force.

In October 1066 Constantine became ill. For the next six months he got steadily worse, and when it was apparent that he would not recover, Psellos felt he had to step in to preserve the comfortable status quo for himself that Constantine's close friendship had provided. The minister may have had a hand in persuading the dying emperor to make his wife Eudokia swear that she would never marry again—to eliminate the possibility of an outsider gaining the throne—and to make sure the succession would go to the emperor's own Doukas offspring. In May 1067 Constantine died, to be succeeded officially by Eudokia as empress regnant. She at once took the full reins of power, brushing aside her eldest son Michael, who by now must have been in his twenties and quite capable of ruling. Yet he appeared to acquiesce in his mother's coup. Psellos excuses Eudokia's dominance as designed to protect her sons rather than exalt herself. As proof he cites an exchange with her in a church, when Psellos, in an outburst of courtier flattery, wished aloud that she would rule for the rest of her life. Far from being flattered, the empress turned on him. 'I hope it will not be my fate to enjoy power for so long,' she snapped. And as the year 1067 progressed, it became apparent to her that she could not withstand the brutal pressures of rule unaided, and began to cast about for a second husband.

This, of course, presented a peculiar problem, as she had solemnly promised her dying husband never to re-marry, and the powerful senior clergy was ever-ready to remind her of it. Therefore she did her researches in great secrecy, not even telling Psellos, although it was common knowledge throughout the court. She won over the Senate by arguing that the vow she had made was basically unfair in that it was detrimental to the welfare of the state, hence morally invalid. With that hurdle overcome, she eventually picked a distinguished military aristocrat named Romanos Diogenes, described by contemporaries as 'exceptionally good-looking, with broad shoulders and bright, flashing eyes'. At the time he was languishing in exile for some conspiratorial act. Brought to the palace, he was taken before Eudokia who, it is said, wept for joy when she saw him.

Yet one more problem remained for the empress: how to break the news of her intended re-marriage to her son, the heir-apparent Michael. There is some mystery here; was Michael still so immature that his mother didn't trust him on the throne, though he was a full adult? If so, what was Michael's own attitude? And there was Psellos, who had been hoping that Eudokia would keep her promise, and the throne in the hands of the Doukai, instead of handing her body and realm over to a stranger. He did not take the news at all well, and was the first to accost Eudokia about what her son might think. 'Let's go up to him,' she replied airily, 'and explain how things are.'

Feeling sick with dread, Psellos followed her up the stairs to Michael's bed-chamber. Eudokia gently shook Michael awake, calling him 'my emperor' and other such endearments. 'Rise and receive your step-father. Although he takes the place of your father, he will be a subject, not a ruler.' In view of later events, this was clearly a piece of fiction calculated to allay Michael's unease. The young man, still half-asleep, glanced about him confusedly—Psellos says suspiciously— and followed his mother downstairs, where Romanos Diogenes was waiting.

The two men embraced, though Psellos observed that Michael was totally expressionless and without any apparent feeling. There was little that Michael, faced with a fait accompli, could have done anyway. Romanos IV Diogenes was duly crowned on the first day of 1068, and Psellos found someone whom he could very willingly despise. Yet in a short time Romanos, Psellos and the rest of the Empire would find themselves almost overwhelmed by a new foe from out of the east, a foe that would eventually see off the Empire, still occupies the Byzantine heartland and remains a force to be reckoned with in the Middle East. These were the Turks.

The Turks originated in central Asia between the Altai Mountains and the Caspian Sea. Related to the Mongols, they typified the highly patriarchal nomadic tribes of those regions whose social systems favoured the periodic rise of powerful leader figures. The southern branch of the Turks, who did not share the conspicuous Mongol features of their northern brethren, clashed with the Chinese in the sixth and seventh centuries. The earliest indication of Turkish speech dates from about 731 in Mongolia, with a script borrowed from Aramaic. The Turks were led by a *khagan*, who ruled over a layer of lesser *khans*, who in turn dominated a submissive populace. Their religion was shamanistic, heavily dependent on a variety of nature spirits, both good and evil.

The western Turks had penetrated into the Arab world quite early, making themselves useful to Muslim and Christian ruler alike thanks to their endurance and warlike qualities. These had come in very useful during the waning years of the Abbasid caliphate in Baghdad, where Turkish praetorian guards wielded power over their puppet caliphs and became the chief means of extending Muslim power at the expense of Byzantium. Two years before Isaac Komnenos' accession to the throne in Constantinople, a Turkish chieftain of the Oghuz tribe named Tughrul Bey formally assumed supreme power in Baghdad. Tughrul was the first sultan of what was soon, under his nephew and successor Alp Arslan, to become the Seljuk Turkish state. Alp Arslan (meaning Lion-hearted Hero) was a competent and just ruler as well as an intellectual, 'devoted to the study of history, listening with great pleasure and interest to chronicles of former kings'. On his becoming sultan in 1063 he used his new Saracen armies to seize Herat, Armenia, Georgia and Syria from the Byzantine sphere.

For these reverses the Byzantine state was very much to blame. Armenia, with its high mountain plateaus and Christian population, was a valuable eastern buffer for Byzantium. But Constantine X, apparently blind to those advantages, had abruptly raised taxes on the Armenian people while depriving them of a local militia and for good measure persecuting them for their brand of Christian belief which differed from the official Orthodox dogma. With Armenian enmity to the capital well and truly stoked, Alp Arslan found the country relatively easy to swallow up. Lord

Norwich echoes much sound historical opinion when he writes that the Armenians 'found themselves wondering whether even conquest by the Turks would prove appreciably worse than their present subjection to the Greeks'.

They need not have wondered. Tughrul Bey, none too gentle in his incursions, had massacred thousands of city-dwellers on at least one occasion. Alp Arslan, who is said to have sported a moustache 'so long that he used to tie up the ends' while on a hunt and to have worn a hat nearly 6ft tall, took out his aggression on the Armenian city of Ani, which held out against his Seljuks for twenty-five days but in the end was overrun. An Arab chronicler who is believed to have been present, Sibt ibn al-Gawzi, reported that he couldn't walk the streets without stepping on heaps of bodies. It wasn't just the Seljuks' ardour that caused the fall of Ani; the Armenians themselves were demoralized by Byzantine misrule and could not get up enough spirit to fight back effectively. By the end of 1067, when Constantine X died, Alp Arslan had penetrated right to the Anatolian heartland, sacking Kaisareia (now Kayseri) and slaughtering its inhabitants. Naturally, this incursion had thrown the Byzantine government into a state of high alarm. It was perhaps the main reason Eudokia had chosen to marry the glamorous and impressive Romanos Diogenes, who at once perceived the scale of the threat, as his family owned large estates in Kappadokia that now lay under the shadow of the advancing Turks.

Romanos IV Diogenes was about 40 when the crown was placed on his head and Eudokia became his wife. He was already married at the time, but given the exigencies of state, there was probably little trouble in annulling that status. He was in the prime of life and action, and no doubt thanked his lucky stars for his good fortune, as not so long before he had been sentenced to death for some vague conspiracy he had allegedly been part of. The sentence had been commuted to exile, perhaps because of his good record on campaign against the Pechenegs, and Eudokia's call had found him languishing in a remote location. Psellos had known him for some time, and was not impressed. The cashiered general struck him as an abject favour-seeker often running to him for some help. But here we must allow for some bias, as Romanos' accession was a victory for the military party which Psellos' 'courtier party' had constantly tried to keep at bay. When Romanos became emperor, Psellos saw (or imagined he saw) that he pretended to be loyal to Eudokia for a few days, after which he could barely conceal his resentment as being the junior partner in the palace arrangement. 'To begin with, he growled inwardly, but as time passed his disgust became obvious to everyone.'

Romanos approached Psellos for advice on what to do about the Seljuks. The courtier advised him to make his preparations slowly and carefully before commencing war. The emperor, it seems, either took no notice or was sidelined by other advisers, with the result that he rushed to prepare himself. In the palace he tried on his armour, brandishing a spear in one hand and a shield in the other, boasting of what he intended to do to the enemy. While some of those present clapped and cheered, Psellos felt a foreboding. Something wasn't quite right here. Such displays of vainglory, the prime minister felt, ill-suited someone who would be ultimately responsible for a sustained and difficult campaign. As for Romanos, he almost certainly yearned to emerge from Eudokia's shadow and make a manly name for himself. Psellos, however, would surely have agreed with the dictum of a much later age that war was too important to be left to the generals. Nonetheless, in the autumn of 1068 Romanos set out with a mixed force of Macedonians, Franks, Kappadokians and others to try and beard the Seljuk lion wherever he could be brought to bay.

If that was Romanos' strategy, it proved beyond him. Wherever he marched through Syria and west Persia he was outmanoeuvred and outwitted by Alp Arslan's mobile detachments that could strike anywhere. The emperor's campaign was limited to seizing strategic heights and then coming down from them when the enemy refused open battle; he saw his men decimated when he was incautious enough to march them through narrow vulnerable defiles. The imperial army was not of the best; it had suffered years of neglect under Constantine X Doukas, to be inherited by Romanos as a second-rate agglomeration of foreign mercenaries led by senior officers of doubtful reliability. Romanos himself fought bravely on this initial campaign, saving many of his men, but in the end he was forced to withdraw.

Back in Constantinople, Romanos shrugged off the debacle and took on the manner of a stern ruler. Having proved his manhood in combat, regardless of how the battles had turned out, he finally had the coveted psychological authority to bypass his wife and lay down the law. To Psellos, who never liked him from the beginning, he was displaying all the symptoms of incipient tyranny. Romanos would contemptuously brush aside all advice, though Psellos claims he often tried to turn the emperor from his stubborn course. Romanos' relations with Eudokia worsened, as he appeared to forget the great distinction she had bestowed on him and would often treat her insultingly.

In the spring of 1069 the Turks renewed their offensives in Asia Minor, wiping out any temporary advantage the Byzantines might have gained the previous year. Romanos duly set out a second time, insisting that Psellos go with him. Possibly the emperor was reluctant to leave his chief minister in Constantinople for fear that he and Eudokia might plot to overthrow him. During the march Romanos, perhaps out of an inferiority complex, tried to prove to Psellos that he was quite as knowledgeable and expert in military science as his prime minister was in philosophy and science in general. The debates between the two were long and lively. But when it came to actual military science in combat conditions, the emperor could not quite put his money where his mouth was. Psellos reports that whenever the enemy was encountered, 'our men fell in the tens of thousands, while a mere handful of our adversaries were taken prisoner.' The Roman army, for all its faults, put up a creditable fight, but inevitably in the end had to pull back. Writes Psellos waspishly:

> The result of it all was that Romanos became more proud and more insolent than ever, because, forsooth, he had twice commanded an army. He lost respect for everything and—worse still—the evil counsellors to whom he listened led him completely astray.

Among those he completely lost respect for was Eudokia, whom he reportedly treated 'like a captive taken in war'.

The result of Romanos Diogenes' two expeditions so far was to further stir up the Turks' hostility and render further conflict inevitable. When in 1070 they began raiding Byzantine territory, the fighting on the frontiers was almost constant. The senior commander there was a nephew of the late Isaac I, Manuel Komnenos, who was captured but by subtle diplomacy won his Saracen captor over to the Roman side and therefore was able to return home. There followed a truce between the emperor and Alp Arslan, enabling Romanos to spend some time in the capital where Psellos and the Doukas family were ever ready to plot against him and he needed to be continually on his guard. He also used the interval to rest and rebuild the army and plan his third—and what he hoped would be the decisive—campaign against the Seljuks. With an army of about 70,000 men—rather more devoted to him than Psellos would have us believe—he crossed the Bosporus in March 1071 to finally settle accounts with the Turkish conqueror.

Whether Romanos had a coherent strategy to deal with his elusive foe is hard to fathom. Psellos claims he had nothing of the sort and that he essentially blundered into the campaign. A rather different opinion is held by one of the emperor's field staff, Michael Attaleiates, who in a much-read account credits Romanos with not only undoubted physical courage but also determination and foresight. Yet the final verdict on Romanos' military expertise must tilt towards Psellos' negative image, even when we take into account the minister's loathing of the emperor that drips from every page of the *Chronographia*. On the march eastwards, the emperor's character flaws became more pronounced, to the consternation of his officers, including the otherwise admiring Attaleiates. He kept himself aloof from his staff and soldiery while his temper became progressively fouler. His disposition was not improved by a fire that killed some of his best horses and destroyed many of his possessions. He saw sinister portents everywhere, and when a soldier was brought before him accused of stealing a donkey he had the man's nose chopped off—ignoring the victim's anguished appeal to the icon of the Virgin that an emperor always carried into battle. Attaleiates saw this as a harbinger of divine wrath on the army, and he turned out not to be wrong.

In his pursuit of the enemy, Romanos had a choice either of carrying the war into Seljuk territory to eliminate Alp Arslan or playing a defensive game and beefing up the fortifications and other strong points around the Byzantine provinces, scorching the earth in front to prevent the Seljuks from gathering supplies. After some debate Romanos decided that the second course would carry unacceptable risks, as the garrisons needed to man the strong points would be vulnerable to constant attack and the possibility of encirclement. Therefore the order was given to advance. But that raised the issue of where the army would be able to anchor itself as a forward base of operations. One place suggested itself: Khelat, a castle held by the Seljuks north of Lake Van, which General Joseph Tarchaniotes and the greater part of the army had orders to capture, while the emperor and his other divisional general, Nikephoros Bryennios, Grand Domestikos of the West, made for the smaller fortress at nearby Manzikert (sometimes called Malasgird), which was seized without a struggle.

Romanos Diogenes' move caught Alp Arslan by surprise. Believing he could trust in the truce he made with the Byzantines, the Turkish leader was heading south to Egypt, aiming to neutralize the Fatimid dynasty there, long a thorn in the side of the Seljuk sultans. He received the news while besieging Edessa (now Urfa), plus an offer from Romanos proposing a territory swap that would give Manzikert to the Byzantines. Alp Arslan might have agreed, had it not been for the aggressive tone of the message, which made him double back at top speed, raising emergency levies among the Kurds and in Azerbaijan; he was in such a hurry to cross the Euphrates River that many horses were drowned.

At his camp at Theodosiopolis (now the east Turkish city of Erzurum) Romanos had faulty intelligence of where he adversary actually was. He was not helped by the quality of his commanders, whom he could never quite rely on for unquestioned loyalty, as the perennial political tussle between the military and the courtier factions divided the senior ranks as well as the administration in the capital. The officer corps seethed with mutual distrust that enervated any morale that might have remained at high level. For example, there was Andronikos Doukas, Grand Domestikos of the East and a nephew of the late Constantine X, who occupied a senior staff position despite his uncompromising opposition to Romanos, and had been appointed to replace yet another of the emperor's truculent generals, Nikephoros Botaneiates, who had been removed for insubordination. Both Bryennios (who was either the father or grandfather of the namesake we have already briefly encountered as Anna Komnene's harried husband) and Tarchaniotes had favoured a defensive strategy and opposed the emperor's rash move into the enemy's territory. Attaleiates' position was that of *krites* of the army, which translates into 'judge', and therefore could denote a kind of provost-marshal who also served as the campaign record-keeper.

The Greeks' faulty intelligence rebounded on them when on 16 August the sultan's forces staged a surprise attack on Tarchaniotes' division of at least 30,000 men at Khelat, sending it reeling. This action has been the cause of much historical debate. Muslim sources insist that it was a clear-cut, simple military defeat. But the picture becomes less clear on the Byzantine side, where one detects a certain sweeping under the carpet; the implication is that Tarchaniotes, a very capable general, was disloyal and deliberately lost the battle at Khelat to hamstring the emperor's campaign. Knowing what we do of the poisoned atmosphere among Romanos' staff, there may well be some truth to this. Indeed, the theory is strengthened by the apparent fact that Romanos knew nothing of Tarchaniotes' defeat that had effectively knocked half of the Roman army out of action.

How far was the Doukas family responsible for this? There can be no clear answer to that question; all that can be said for sure is that Romanos Diogenes was never as popular as he thought he was, and the Doukai could be expected to make plenty of political hay out of that fact. The emperor's haughty and imperious conduct at home would have been common knowledge among the people of Constantinople at least, and not likely to endear him to public opinion. True, there were those—including his inveterate foe Psellos—who admired and acknowledged Romanos' personal valour and fighting spirit. Yet old established powerful families like the Doukai, and the Komnenes waiting in the wings, could not help but regard Romanos as a usurper of sorts, who had shown his true character by his shabby treatment of the imperial lady who had raised him to the throne. And it is not too much to suppose that a good many in those families would have hoped for a good and solid trouncing at Saracen hands that would render Romanos demonstrably unfit for office and a candidate for overthrow. In this light, the lack of initiative and spirit displayed by most of Romanos' generals at Manzikert has a plausible explanation.

Romanos arrived at the fortress of Manzikert to be greeted by volleys of arrows and stones from the Saracen defenders, but on 23 August a detachment of Armenians breached the wall and the garrison surrendered. Romanos set up his headquarters outside the fort, on the slope of an extinct volcano now called Suphan Dag that had a convenient supply of fresh water. Heartened by the Seljuks' precipitate surrender of the fort at Manzikert and believing Alp Arslan to be far away, Romanos authorized a foraging party to scour the countryside on 24 August. This party was unexpectedly ambushed by Seljuk patrols and forced to fall back. The emperor, believing the enemy patrols to be insignificant, ordered Bryennios forward again with instructions to mop them up.

Bryennios aimed to outflank what he thought were small enemy forces but was halted by repeated ambushes. The emperor sent another officer, Nikephoros

Basilakios, with a stronger detachment, but Basilakios, too, found himself cut off from the main camp; apparently knowing little of nomadic warfare, he allowed his formation to loosen during his advance. Worse, he fell into a trap that any soldier worth his spurs would have seen through; the Seljuks, by pretending to retreat, lured him and his men into a gully where they were slaughtered, and Basilakios taken prisoner. Basilakios had commanded the Armenian cataphract heavy cavalry, and his losses and capture were a severe blow to Romanos. But was Basilakios that incompetent? Like any senior Roman entrusted with command in the field, he would have been conversant with the writings of military theorists on the nomads' methods of fighting. Most probably, like the emperor, he simply didn't realize how numerous the enemy actually was. He and Bryennios may also have planned to press the Seljuks back to a point where they would be encircled by the imperial forces. But if that was indeed the tactical plan, Basilakios blew it through his lack of caution.

It must have been clear to Romanos by now that the Turkish force in the vicinity was larger than he thought. But neither he nor any of his staff were in a position to tell how far away the main body of the enemy might be. As we have seen, intelligence was poor to non-existent. To learn more, the emperor sent Bryennios on a reconnaissance-in-force in a wide radius around the camp. When he arrived at the place of the morning's encounters a squad of Turkish mounted archers appeared and attempted to surround Bryennios' force which saved itself by galloping back to camp; Bryennios himself was wounded in the neck and two arrows stuck in his armour. The following morning, perhaps motivated by the Byzantine discomfiture, a detachment of Oghuz Turks in the imperial service deserted to their Seljuk brethren. The Oghuz had been useful as scouts and knew the local terrain well; their loss was another blow to Romanos at a time when he still had no idea of the whereabouts of Alp Arslan.

And he probably still didn't know when a mission from the Turkish sultan arrived in his camp extending feelers for a truce. Romanos interpreted the gesture, wrongly, as a sign of enemy weakness or an attempt to play for time. Actually, Alp Arslan was eager to dispose of Romanos as soon as possible and return to his conquest of Egypt. Romanos, for his part, was careful not to reveal any sign of weakness with the Doukas generals looking over his shoulder. The emperor's reply was rude and brusque, demanding Alp Arslan's full withdrawal from the area and full Byzantine control. Of course, this was unacceptable to the Turks, whose envoys left empty-handed. And so in the morning of 26 August the Roman army, with Romanos at its head, set out in battle array across the treeless wastes in search of Alp Arslan. They marched and rode in the scorching sun, harassed by Turkish cavalry hit-and-run raids. A deserted Seljuk camp was found and looted. It was sometime in the afternoon, with the enemy main force still nowhere to be seen, when Romanos realized that he may have gone too far from his camp—about ten miles. Fearing ambush, he ordered the imperial standards reversed, the signal for a tactical withdrawal.

Unbeknownst to the emperor, the sultan had been watching him all the time, effectively concealed in the surrounding hills. When he saw the imperial standards being turned round he gave the order for a general attack. The moment could not have been better chosen. During the march Bryennios and another commander, Theodore Alyattes, had allowed their men to pursue the Seljuk raiders, scattering the army's formations and unnecessarily fatiguing their men. In fact, such was the indiscipline that the Byzantine army had no right wing to speak of. The left, under Andronikos Doukas, maintained its order but refused to come to the aid of the harassed right. The disorganization was made worse by some mercenary units that didn't understand the signal of the reversed standards and concluded somehow that the emperor had been slain, and promptly broke in flight.

Disaster was quick and overwhelming. Romanos tried to restore some order to his chaotic formations by switching from line to column, but it was now far too late for that, as the Seljuks charged the seething Byzantine mass from all directions. 'It was like an earthquake,' Attaleiates wrote. 'The shouting, the sweat, the swift rushes of fear, the clouds of dust, and not least the hordes of Turks riding all around us.' A Seljuk formation cut in front of Romanos as he was proceeding westwards, forcing him to fight. And fight he did, cutting by far the noblest figure, even when an enemy spear smacked into his left arm at the shoulder. Then his horse, pierced by many arrows, fell dead from under him. He staggered to his feet, intent on keeping up the fight, but fainted from loss of blood; his body was indistinguishable from that of a host of fallen soldiers around him.

Andronikos Doukas, meanwhile, was nowhere to be found, even though his men had so far suffered relatively little. He was, in fact, well to the rear of the action in command of what had become a tactical reserve. Yet this reserve, if that is what it was, remained unused. The main force, it was now clear, had been routed and if Doukas had followed basic procedures he would have used his reserve to try and stem the Seljuk advance and plug gaping holes in the front line. He did nothing of the kind, either out of practical defeatism, believing the battle to be irretrievably lost, or—and there is evidence to argue for this—outright treachery, or a combination of both. In fact, Doukas and his division marched as quickly as they could back to Constantinople with the intention of staging a palace coup. If Romanos was dead, all was well; if not, on his return to the capital he would find the Doukai had already taken his place.

Romanos Diogenes was not dead. All night he lay among the bodies littering the battlefield. The next morning he was discovered by a Turk searching for booty who thought he had found a high-ranking Roman officer alive. He was taken before Alp

Arslan, who at first didn't recognize him until Basilakios told him. Romanos was treated with conspicuous honour as befitting an enemy ruler who had displayed incontestable personal valour. The two became firm friends, taking strolls together and discussing the recent battle. Part of the sultan's conduct can be put down to traditional Islamic courtesy, but there was also an element of calculation: back on the throne of Byzantium where he belonged, Romanos would surely, out of gratitude for the help given him, stop being a thorn in the side of the Seljuk domain and perhaps even become an ally.

This was perhaps asking too much of the people of Constantinople, who received the news of Manzikert with profound shock. In the view of Attaleiates, in one instant 'the whole Roman state [was] overturned'. If Romanos himself entertained any hope of returning to his throne—which he almost certainly did—then he was tragically disillusioned. From Eudokia on down, the prevalent opinion was that Romanos was finished, and could never be rehabilitated after a disaster like Manzikert. Kaisar John Doukas, the brother of the late Constantine X, was the first to rush to fill the power vacuum. Hardly had the dust at Manzikert settled than John Doukas mobilized the Varangian Guard, a body of foreign mercenaries duty-bound to protect the emperor and the palace, sending half of it to the palace to proclaim Constantine's son Michael as emperor, and the other half to arrest Eudokia who was tried and found guilty—on questionable evidence—of aiming to restore Romanos. She was subsequently packed off to a nunnery, and Michael was set up as Michael VII.

Thus, after a hiatus of three years, during which Byzantium suffered one of the greatest military humiliations of its history, the Doukas family was back in power. And what of the Komnene? They appear to have stayed aloof from the tumults and intrigues of the Romanos era, possibly because they didn't trust the Doukai. In fact, one of John Doukas' first acts was to send Anna Dalessene, a sister-in-law of the late Isaac I Komnenos, to a nunnery, which had long been the fate de rigueur for imperial ladies who happened to find themselves on the wrong side of the power balance of the moment. As an administrative punishment, it may have symbolized the essentially religious underpinning of imperial authority. There was nothing sexist in this, as failed male emperors as well tended to be relegated to the monks' cells, the latest being Isaac I. It also ensured that, behind the cloister walls, they would be under observation at all times to prevent any attempt to return to secular power.

Romanos' subsequent actions are hard to explain. Thanks to kind treatment by his captors, he recovered enough from his wounds to be able to scrape together a loyal force with which to march on the capital. He must have known that the Doukas family would already have taken full advantage of his absence; nonetheless, possibly out of sheer bloody-mindedness, he resolutely set out to reclaim his throne from nearly 600 miles away. But his domestic foes seem to have been well warned. Encountering Kaisar John Doukas at Dokeia (modern Tokat), he was stymied, and then roundly beaten by his ex-reserve commander Andronikos Doukas at Adana. Romanos, after agreeing to retire to a monastery, was put on a donkey and paraded hundreds of miles north-west to Kotyaion (modern Kütahya). First, according to the chronicler Skylitzes, on the orders of John Doukas his eyes were gouged out in the crudest way. Then:

> Carried forth on a cheap beast of burden like a decaying corpse... his head alive with worms, he lived on in pain with a foul stench all about him until he gave up the ghost... But in all his misfortunes he uttered no curse or blasphemy, continuing always to give thanks to God and bearing courageously whatever befell him.

That was the summer of 1072. Psellos could hardly hide his delight at Romanos' fate, going so far as to send him a sarcastic letter to the effect that he should be grateful at being blinded, as that way 'the Almighty had found him worthy of a higher light'. Such words could only be motivated by blind hatred, which shows the extent to which personal partisanship had poisoned the political atmosphere in Constantinople. Even when it was apparent that the hapless Romanos was in no position to rule anything any more, the Doukai still feared that he might, and carried Psellos with them. Was anything more personal involved? We have no way of knowing. According to Psellos, Eudokia had been grievously mistreated by Romanos. But in the end she gave her late husband a lavish and honourable funeral. Perhaps an incipient jealousy clouded Psellos' judgement. Whatever the truth, on a broader plane the disaster at Manzikert was the first toll of doom for the Byzantine Empire. The Seljuks, and the Turks in general, were in Asia Minor to stay. A vigorous and capable emperor such as a Basil II or John I Tzimiskes could have turned the situation around and secured the Empire's eastern frontiers. But Michael VII Doukas would prove to be nowhere near up to the job, at a time when not only the Seljuk Turks were consolidating their position in Asia Minor, but the Serbs were threatening from the north-west and Normans from the west. While Psellos and his party ruled in their rarefied adminisphere, other, healthier internal forces were slowly pushing their way to the surface. The Komnenes were among those determined to save the situation from terminal decay and put some spirit back into the shattered morale of Byzantium.

The young man who was so rudely awakened by his mother with the none-too-welcome news that she would marry Romanos Diogenes was now at the helm. Just what kind of ruler he was is hard to tell. We have two main sources of information; one, by Psellos, reveres him as practically one rung lower than a god, while the other, by the historian Skylitzes and almost every other writer, paints him as weak and despicable. If we deem the truth to be between these two extremes, we're not much wiser. About all that can be said with certainty is that Michael VII did little, if anything, to even begin to repair the damage to the Empire occasioned by Manzikert. He conspicuously lacked the qualities to do so, even if he wanted to. Totally under the sway of Psellos, he spent his time in bookish pursuits and dabbled in economics; the unsettled period after Manzikert fuelled an inflation surge, which Michael tried to remedy by debasing the basic currency unit, the *nomisma*, by one-quarter, thus raising the price of wheat by the same proportion. This unpopular move earned him the nickname *Parapinakes*, roughly translated as 'one-quarter-less'.

But if that policy had been Psellos' suggestion, it may have been one of his last, as he very quickly found himself cast aside in favour of a new court favourite named Nikephoritzes, who was a eunuch and therefore in the favourable position of having no offspring's interests to promote. In Skylitzes' damning words, Nikephoritzes assumed total de facto power, leaving the feckless emperor to his 'trifles and childish games'. What Psellos praised as charming modesty, others lambasted as sheer incompetence. In a university or a cloister Michael might have accomplished much as a scholar—but the times called for a soldier, and a tough one at that. An ill-considered move by Nikephoritzes to centralize the grain trade as a state monopoly only raised the price of bread still further, dealing a serious economic blow to the main wheat growers in the Asia Minor hinterland. As inflation ate away at the people's purchasing power and morale, foes beyond the borders were making aggressive noises. The restive Bulgars had elected an aggressive new tsar; farther north, the Hungarians and Croats were turning against Byzantium, while in the east a Norman adventurer named Roussel of Balliol, a Roman army veteran, carved for himself a feudal statelet aiming to stem any Turkish advances in the region.

Throughout this period the Komnenes cultivated an image of patriotic propriety. Though they, along with the Doukai, were the most powerful aristocratic families in Constantinople, their relationship must have been a complicated one. As we have seen, they could often act in concert, sometimes through intermarriage, but there was always an element of rivalry running beneath the surface. The appointment of the promising young Alexios Komnenos to a generalship sometime in the 1070s can be attributed to the families' general rapprochement, probably after his marriage to Irene Doukas, the daughter of the Andronikos Doukas whose absence from the battlefield of Manzikert was credited with ensuring Romanos Diogenes' defeat.

The indefatigable Psellos' devious career had finally caught up with him. Michael VII, whom he had built up as a paragon of a ruler, unceremoniously ditched him as first minister. Some enmity against him seems to have built up in the Doukas family, the causes of which remain vague. Perhaps a snobbish intellectual rivalry was involved, as Anna Komnene informs us that they made strenuous efforts to raise their own cultural level since one of their own was now the emperor. And the eunuch-ridden civil service, as always, must have been crawling with intrigue. In such conditions it is perhaps surprising that Psellos lasted as long as he did. Among all his other activities, he had been working on his *Chronographia* at least since 1063, seven years after he had helped Isaac I Komnenos mount the throne of Byzantium. As we have seen, with the accession of Michael VII he had altered the style of his narrative from impartial reporting to an often nauseous paean to Michael One-quarter-less. Very likely this was done to humour the young and irresponsible emperor, as by now Psellos must have felt his own position tottering. But Nikephoritzes and a disputatious and superficial young firebrand named John Italos now were embedded firmly in the Doukas court. At some point in the mid-1070s Psellos was stripped of his offices and his hair and packed off to a monastery.

The foes of Byzantium, meanwhile, knew of Michael's weakness and sharpened their swords. In 1072 Nikephoros Bryennios was sent to put down a Bulgar uprising which further depleted the Roman manpower after Manzikert. The old Rome, too, was casting covetous eyes eastward; in 1075 the vigorous Pope Gregory VII (the German former monk Hildebrand) set up a papal Croatian kingdom and sent agents to crown the Bulgar Prince Michael of Zeta. And if that were not enough, the Hungarians and Pechenegs were rattling their own sabres. In the face of these multiple threats—not to mention the ever-present Turks—Michael chose to attack the wrong target. This was the Norman Roussel of Balliol (or Ballieul), who had formed his own independent buffer against the Turks in Anatolia and could have been a valued imperial ally. But such was the distorted view from Constantinople that Balliol was seen, most foolishly, as a bigger threat than the Turks. Michael even turned to the Seljuks for help against Roussel, confirming their territorial conquests in Asia Minor in one of the Empire's worst foreign policy misjudgements.

Balliol was captured (as will be recounted in the next chapter), but soon found himself back in imperial service, as the army needed every experienced officer it could get. His commanding general, Alexios Komnenos, needed him to help scotch a plot by Bryennios, who claimed that he was on a palace hit list. In November 1077 Bryennios raised the standard of revolt at Adrianople (now Edirne) and marched on the capital. But he had a rival in the east in the person of Nikephoros Botaneiates, a senior general who had been left out of the Manzikert campaign and since then had governed the Anatolikon theme in what now is west-central Turkey. Botaneiates, who once had been an unsuccessful claimant for the hand of Eudokia and was now getting on in years, decided that the Empire had had enough of the clueless Michael One-quarter-less and set out from the south-east. Intelligence must have reached both pretenders that the people of Constantinople were seeth-ing with economic discontent, and both were happy to wait for the discontent to erupt in mass violence, which it did in the Bread Riots of March 1078. They were an ugly affair. Government buildings by the dozen were torched. The mob seized the eunuch Nikephoritzes, widely held to be responsible for ruinous inflation and grain shortages, and tortured him to death. The terrified Michael lost no time in abdicating—thus probably saving his own skin—and burrowed himself into the monastery at Stoudion. General Botaneiates, bearing the prestige of membership in the old military aristocracy, was crowned Nikephoros III before the month was out. His rival Bryennios was blinded for his pains. And some time during that tur-bulent year of 1078 Michael Psellos passed away, broken in spirit and unmourned.

Little good can be said of the three-year reign of Nikephoros III. Already over 70 when he became emperor, he may have had a respectable record as a military man, but when it came to politics and administration he proved to be completely out of his depth. On his watch the condition of the Empire could get nothing but worse. Alp Arslan's son Malikshah continued his father's aggressive expansion-ist policies until the Seljuk domain swallowed almost all of what is now Turkey. The Seljuks got a vital toehold on the Dardanelles, where they were in a position to harass all the Mediterranean Sea trade out of Constantinople if they wished. Nikephoros himself did not display the best of traits; when his wife died he mar-ried his predecessor's consort, a remarkably attractive Georgian princess. He did this while the ex-Michael VII was still alive, an act not calculated to endear him to the Byzantine people, especially as he ignored the succession claims of Michael VII's young son. To try and placate the muttering masses he spent lavishly on favours for the populace, but all it accomplished was to drive inflation still further and worsen the economic crisis. The day of reckoning was sure to come, and when it did, its driving force was the young general who had tried to stay loyal to both Michael VII and Nikephoros III despite their unpopularity and incompetence, but in the end decided to act to save the Byzantine Empire and its people.

Chapter 6

Enter Alexios

All civil service establishments, in all ages, have an inbred tendency to perpetuate themselves and regard their own interests above those of the nation or sovereign. This was especially true in the Late Roman Empire of the eleventh century, which was called upon to perform a continuous tightrope act, balancing various domestic factional interests against one another while fending off a variety of external foes. Unlike a nation-state of our own time, Byzantium never had any specific geographic boundaries fixed by international convention. One can visualize the Byzantine realm in the shape of a colossal amoeba, now expanding, now shrinking, now extending a finger outwards, now dipping inwards, according to the see-sawing military fortunes at the frontiers. Its nucleus would be Constantinople, a metropolis at the tail-end of Europe but as such, quite off-centre, as by the eleventh century the bulk of the Empire's economy and society was based in Asia Minor. But by the end of that century the Seljuk Turkish steamroller had reduced the Byzantine amoeba to almost half its former size.

This observation raises the question of whether the Byzantine leadership and upper classes thought in what we today would call nationalist terms. If Byzantium had anything resembling a flag, it was the double-headed eagle standard of the emperors. The standard was constant, regardless of house or dynasty, irrespective of whether the monarch inherited the throne from his father or seized it by force. It was the one symbol that any Byzantine army, of whatever ethnic make-up, could recognize and follow. Yet, as we have seen, it was not so much the idea of a Byzantine, or Greco-Roman 'nation' that held the Empire together as the knowledge that state and emperor above all stood for a wider 'Christian nation' (and after 1054 an Eastern Orthodox nation) built on Roman law and Greek in language and culture. The Byzantines proudly regarded themselves as the 'New Chosen People' and their foreign policy reflected this exceptionalism at every turn.

The military strength of the Empire, however, depended to a high degree on the abilities and character of whoever occupied the throne at a particular time. Weak monarchs such as Michael VI and Michael VII, Constantine X and Nikephoros III (plus Romanos IV Diogenes who never got the chance to really prove his worth as an emperor) tended to neglect the army. A powerful and self-seeking civil service also played its part in trying to shunt the military aside, and through most of the eleventh century it succeeded, to the serious detriment of the Empire's fortunes.

Moreover, the devastating reverse of Manzikert dealt a serious blow to the soldiers' morale; mutinies were common during the 1070s, and Alexios Komnenos had his work cut out for him nipping them in the bud. The Turkish advances in Asia Minor had triggered a mass exodus of Christian refugees who crowded penniless into Constantinople, exacerbating the economic crisis and driving up the crime rate. It was becoming too bad to last.

Safe and comfortable in his palace, old Nikephoros Botaneiates settled down with his new wife Maria, the ex-consort of Michael VII. But Maria was young enough to be his granddaughter, and so it comes as no surprise that her time at court was taken up with securing the interests of the Doukas family she had married into. She also had the prospects of her young son, the Kaisar Constantine, to consider. Allied to the Doukai were the Komnenes, of whom the latest able scion, Alexios, was making a considerable name for himself in the field—and sharp-eared courtiers for whom Nikephoros III was their latest meal ticket had taken worried notice of that fact. In 1080 Alexios Komnenos was just past 30, and our sources suggest strongly that he exerted a powerful emotional pull on Maria to complement the political possibilities opening up for him. Nikephoros was in poor health and she must have hoped he was not long for this world. It would not be the first time the wife of an emperor was bowled over by a dashing young military newcomer; the comparison with the torrid business involving Nikephoros II, Theophano and John I Tzimiskes just over a century earlier suggested itself to at least one contemporary writer. Maria set the seal on her favours by making Alexios her official adopted son.

If Constantinople had a mass media, the name of Alexios Komnenos would have been in the headlines almost daily. As it was, it was on everyone's lips. Intellectual and humble labourer alike shared a growing frustration at the incompetence of two emperors in a row and the corruption and arrogance of the eunuchs of the court camarilla. Against this sordid background the reputation of Alexios shone out like a beacon. The public admired the fact that while still very young he had built up a military record that would have done credit to a man twice his age. His noble pedigree was perfect: he was the third son of Kaisar John, the brother of the late Isaac I, and Anna Dalassene, a resourceful lady of high birth who from the first had judged Alexios to be better fitted for the eventual throne than either of his two elder brothers or his younger two brothers and three sisters. In 1071 Anna had flatly—and as it turned out, wisely—forbidden the teenaged Alexios to ride with Romanos IV Diogenes to Manzikert, as he was apparently eager to do. She had ample reason for her decision, as she had just lost her firstborn son Manuel in a skirmish with the Turks and wanted to preserve Alexios, no doubt for bigger things. At about that time, or somewhat later, Alexios married Irene Doukas— better known as Irene Doukaina, according to the practice of adding the suffix *ina*—as the feminine form of a noble surname. This supremely important marriage brought the two strongest military families of Byzantium, the Komnenes and the Doukai, into formal alliance and enlisted the Doukai in the Komnenes' drive for imperial rule. Such a powerful alliance suggested to many that political stability might at last be around the corner—not such a bad prospect in the dismal year of 1080. Anna Komnene, with the benefit of a few decades' hindsight, would write: 'The ground was giving way beneath [our] feet... the barbarian was everywhere on the move, attacking with lightning speed.'

Alexios Komnenos was on the short side, but well-built, with penetrating deep-set eyes beneath bushy eyebrows and a full and ample beard. He spoke with a slight lisp, probably pronouncing the letter 'r' in the guttural French way, as occurs among some people in north Greece today. But what he lacked in stature he more than made up for in character and ability. He was, in the words of the historian Niketas Choniates, 'a dissembler, never saying much about what he intended to do'—the mark of a wise soldier and statesman. He honoured his mother Anna Dalassene and listened to her often-sage advice. After all, she may well have saved him from an untimely demise at Manzikert. And almost certainly she would have had a hand in selecting for his wife Irene Doukaina, who would turn out to be a priceless asset later on. As evidenced by his youthful desire for soldiering while his first beard had yet to appear (as the Byzantines would say), he took to military life with zeal and energy. He appears to have been given the duties of a full general while in his early twenties, rising to second-in-command of the Roman armies, and the first test of his mettle came when he was called upon to deal with the troublesome Roussel of Balliol.

The Byzantine military of the time differed from a modern national army in that it was not too particular about the ethnic origin or allegiance of its members. A Roman soldier took an oath not to Byzantium as a national concept but to the emperor personally; as we have seen, the defence and expansion of Christianity was the overall defining tenet of Byzantine foreign policy over many centuries, and the military was a mere instrument to that end. Therefore it made little difference to the emperor and his senior generals whether Kelts, Franks, Russians, Armenians and even Turks joined the imperial ranks; the last-named, to be sure, were carefully monitored for possible treachery. Good pay and the prospect of plunder usually kept the various contingents in line, but few at the time could guess that the growing proportion of 'foreigners' in the imperial forces would not bode well for the Empire.

The example of Roussel of Balliol should have been instructive. A vain, adventure-loving Frenchman of Norman origin, Balliol appears as a precursor of the crusaders who were to burst into the region twenty or so years later. But he differed from them in that he had no known religious motivation when he arrived in

Byzantium and quickly gathered together a corps made up mostly of Frenchmen like himself. His aim was adventure and feudal lordship, pure and simple. The weakness of Michael VII gave him the chance he needed to set himself up as an independent warlord in central Anatolia. From that base he attacked Roman garrisons in the east, not hesitating to ask for help from the Seljuks, who gave it willingly. More often than not Balliol won his battles by sheer audacity, upon which Michael had the presence of mind to promote young Alexios Komnenos to Grand Domestikos, or commander-in-chief of all the armies. For the soldiery to have followed such a youngster without a murmur, his innate leadership qualities must have been considerable.

Alexios tackled Balliol with skill and determination, gradually forcing him back from his advanced positions. For help Balliol turned to a Seljuk chieftain named Artuk, who owed allegiance to a half-brother of Sultan Malikshah. Here, however, he was thwarted by a Roman technique at which the Byzantines were masters and for which the naive Normans lacked the wit and resources—the simple art of bribery. First, Alexios sent Artuk a message which according to Anna Kommene read something like this:

> Your sultan [Malikshah] and my emperor [Michael VII] are friends. This barbarian [Balliol] is an enemy of both... His whole plan of campaign is carefully thought out: for the moment he is pursuing me with your help; later, when the time is propitious, he will leave me and make war on you.

After sobering Artuk with this no doubt astute observation, Alexios laid out the bait. He advised the Seljuk to capture Balliol, 'for which we will pay you well,' and send him to Alexios in chains. The payment, he added temptingly, would be 'more money than anyone else has received before'. Concluding the mouth-watering offer was an assurance that Artuk would earn the undying gratitude not only of the Christian emperor but also of Malikshah himself (and his powerful vizier Nizam al-Mulk, who was the real power in the sultanate), who would be no doubt glad 'to see so formidable an enemy out of the way, an enemy who trained his men to fight both of us, Romans and Turks'. As a piece of diplomacy it was peerless, appealing to both the Turks' acquisitive instincts and the Muslim sense of honour. Artuk agreed at once, and Balliol found himself delivered in chains to Alexios who was headquartered at Amaseia.

The Norman duly handed over, the money was expected. But Alexios' military talents came up short against financial realities, as the sum promised to Artuk could not, it turned out, be raised. Alexios had some of the money ready, but not all of it; Artuk protested but the emperor merely shrugged, intimating that the whole bribery idea was probably not his anyway. It took a sleepless night for Alexios to hit upon the expedient of raising the rest of the money from the wealthier citizens of Amaseia. When he assembled the citizens and asked for voluntary contributions, they acted as upright citizens normally would in such circumstances, with a cacophony of boos and hisses and insults. Some of the more influential men of Amaseia were in league with Balliol and called for him to be freed. Alexios waited for the storm of invective to subside to remind them that Balliol was an untrustworthy character and would cause trouble for the city if he was not restrained. 'Tell the troublemakers to go to blazes,' he concluded, 'and go home and consider what I have said.'

The muttering citizens dispersed, but Alexios knew that the lull he had achieved was a stopgap measure at best, and at any time during the night the local confederates of Balliol could free him. Balliol himself, however, appears to have been willing to remain a Roman captive rather than take his chances with the Turks, and agreed to an elaborate scheme devised by Alexios. Probably that same day, the word went out to the Amaseians: Balliol would be publicly blinded for the crime of rebellion against the emperor. It was a spectacle few would wish to miss, and Alexios made sure it was a convincing one—as he intended to fake the event from start to finish. The Frenchman was coached to writhe and roar in pretended terror and pain as he lay on the ground facing the official blinder, who in turn was told to grimace horribly at his supposed victim as he waved the eye-gouging irons in his face. It was a great show for the watching Amaseians, who clapped and cheered as it unfolded. Afterwards Balliol was careful to keep a bandage over his eyes and be led around by the hand as 'proof' of his punishment. One of those taken in by this expert show was an officer named Dokeianos, a cousin of Alexios, who bitterly reproached him for treating a brave warrior in so cruel a manner. Alexios must have smiled wryly, taking Dokeianos into Balliol's presence and removing the bandage, to reveal the Norman's eyes as healthy and defiant as ever. Dokeianos at first attributed it to a miracle, but was later told the truth. News of the episode reached Constantinople, where Alexios' reputation rose another notch. The Amaseians, faced with apparent evidence of Alexios' ruthless determination, forgot their previous reluctance and raised the required money for Artuk.

Barely had Roussel of Balliol been dealt with than another, more serious, threat claimed Alexios' attention. This was no mere western 'barbarian' upstart but a respected general of the Empire who had commanded Romanos Diogenes' left wing at Manzikert. Nikephoros Bryennios, with some reason, believed he had a better claim to the throne than his namesake Nikephoros Botaneiates, who despite his rank had taken no part at all in the battle. Botaneiates, now Nikephoros III, was happy to use Alexios against his rival, who had amassed a considerable rebel force in Thrace. As Duke of Dyrrachion (now the port of Dürres in Albania), Bryennios was the most powerful man in the western part of the Empire and in anticipation of his planned march on Constantinople had styled himself Emperor of the Romans. He claimed, probably spuriously, that he was on a palace hit list. He appears to have been one of nature's leaders, tall, good-looking and physically strong. Old Nikephoros III was quite right to be worried, but decided that if a younger man were to replace him, better Alexios Komnenos than Bryennios.

In terms of manpower, Alexios was at a disadvantage. Seljuk Turkish conquests in Asia Minor had deprived the Roman army of potential manpower to the extent that he had to scrape the bottom of the barrel for recruits to the imperial standard. There was a crack battalion called the *Athanatoi*, or Immortals, originally made up of battle-hardened veterans but now consisting almost wholly of green troops. There was also a Keltic unit, competent enough but under strength. Bryennios, on the other hand, could count on his well-armed western army that had remained unscathed by the reverses in Anatolia. The emperor had little choice but to enlist as many Turks as were willing to fight for pay and send them along with the rest under Alexios to settle accounts with Bryennios, and hope for the best.

Alexios probably did not have enormous confidence in the mixed bag of troops under his command, which could explain why he decided to take the offensive before his force had fully assembled. He encamped at the Halmyros River, not far from Bryennios' headquarters, and considered his next moves. His force was outnumbered by the rebels, and moreover, he knew Bryennios to be a capable and valiant commander. A frontal attack with green troops against a superior foe was out of the question. The only feasible tactic was to block Bryennios' line of march to the capital and trust to the imponderables of battle to do the rest. Bryennios saw this and decided to open the action, moving his approximately 10,000-strong force into line formation; he placed himself in the centre, where he was visible to both sides, with his elite Macedonians and Thracians, while his brother John Bryennios commanded the right with 5,000 mostly Italian and Greek veterans, plus a redoubtable cavalry contingent from Thessaly, whose horses and horsemen were renowned since classical times. About 3,000 other Balkan troops formed the left wing. A contingent of Pechenegs stood in reserve in the rear. The gleaming armour and clashing shields of the Thessalian cavalrymen struck fear into a good number of Alexios' inexperienced soldiers.

To meet the attack Alexios hid a detachment in a gully on his left with orders to jump out and ambush John Bryennios' line as it rushed past. The shock was momentarily too much for the Italians and Greeks, but John Bryennios himself turned his horse and cut down one of Alexios' *Athanatoi*. At this the rest of the Immortals broke in turn and Bryennios' right wing surged onwards. Alexios threw himself into the fray, but such was the pressure of the rebels that he soon found himself with no more than half a dozen men by his side. In the heat of the meleé he decided he would get at Bryennios or die trying. But one of his six companions, an experienced soldier who had known him for years, told him it would be suicide and it would be far wiser to make a tactical withdrawal and regroup what forces he could muster. Alexios agreed, but before he could act Bryennios' Pechenegs stormed in, putting Alexios' front ranks to flight. But, as was the Pechenegs' habit, they began looting while the fighting was still going on, throwing Bryennios' offensive into disorganization. The battlefield became a confused mess, which Alexios took advantage of by staging daring individual counter-attacks. He saw a rebel soldier taking one of Bryennios' richly-caparisoned horses from the stable; the horse was wearing the imperial purple saddlecloth, adorned with gold-plated bosses, and carrying ceremonial iron swords—symbols of Bryennios' usurpation of the title of emperor. Alexios could not let this *lèse-majesté* go unchallenged. Drawing down the visor of his helmet, he gathered his six intrepid men and rushed the soldier, knocking him to the ground, and seized the horse.

Already Bryennios' assault had run out of steam, probably because of the Pechenegs' switch at the wrong moment from fighting to looting. Alexios, after leading the captured horse to safety, thought up a stratagem not unlike the deception he had pulled at Amaseia. He detailed a loud-voiced herald to run through the scattered ranks and tell all within earshot that Bryennios had been killed. It wasn't true, but of course the demoralized troops had no way of verifying that, so they took heart and turned back to the battle. The tale gained credence with the sight of the great ceremonial swords Bryennios' horse had been carrying. At about that point a Turkish unit in Alexios' service approached their commander to ask how the fight was going. From a small eminence they saw a field full of milling men but not much actual fighting. The Pechenegs, laden with booty, had already gone. A detachment of Alexios' Franks had deserted to the enemy at the first encounter, encouraging Bryennios to believe that he had won the battle, and his formations were in disorder. This was the moment for Alexios to counter-attack.

When it came, it was savage. Three formations of Seljuk cavalry charged Bryennios' line firing volleys of arrows; behind them rode Alexios with as many men as he could gather up. One of his Athanatoi got a little too enthusiastic and galloped ahead of the rest, hurling his spear at Bryennios' chest; the rebel general drew his sword just in time, slashing his attacker's right arm off at the shoulder and splitting his breastplate. The rebel army withstood the onslaught well, so Alexios ordered a slow withdrawal to draw the rebels after them. The trick worked, and Bryennios' men found themselves ambushed by hordes of Turks who sprang out yelling savagely from their hiding places 'like swarms of wasps'. With arrows raining continuously down on them, the rebel ranks broke and ran to the rear. Bryennios himself, very much alive as everyone must have seen by now, put up a spirited rearguard fight, but as his horse was showing serious signs of exhaustion from the constant charging back and forth, he had to let it rest.

Motionless in the saddle, Bryennios challenged two Turks to come at him. The first charged him with his spear levelled, but Bryennios' sword severed his right hand with the spear in it. The second jumped off his horse and leaped onto Bryennios', clinging to the horse's flank while dodging Bryennios' desperate attempts to shake him off or stab him. This went on for some time until the general's sword arm got tired and he had to give up the fight. Still cutting a majestic figure in captivity, Bryennios was led to Alexios who sent him on to Constantinople. Both rode together for a short distance, Bryennios at any moment expecting to have his eyes gouged out or worse. As Anna Komnene recounts the scene, both men stopped to rest at a grassy knoll, where Alexios dozed off under an oak tree. Bryennios, awake with anxiety, saw Alexios' sword hanging from a branch and had the wild idea of killing his captor and making his escape. But, perhaps reflecting on Alexios' humane treatment of him, thought better of it and stayed a prisoner. A certain code of honour did prevail among members of the military aristocracy, even when they were rivals in civil war.

The revolt did not end with Bryennios' capture. Into his shoes stepped Basilakios, who may have been the Basilakios whose blunders at Manzikert led to the Romans' disaster. When Alexios handed over Bryennios to envoys from the emperor, he received orders to destroy Basilakios who was marching through Greece aiming for the throne. Basilakios is described as a large and powerful man, a valiant warrior and persuasive leader of men. Anna Komnene likens him to 'a long-tusked boar'. If we have seen such glowing descriptions before, it's no accident. The problem with them as they come down to us is that they are stiflingly stereotypical. In the writings of Anna Komnene and others, Nikephoros Bryennios, Basilakios and even Alexios Komnenos himself are very hard to tell apart. Warlords in the late Roman narrative are portrayed in larger-than-life colours as unvarying and formulaic as a Byzantine icon. So how far can we take them at face value? There is no easy answer to this question, except to note lamely that Bryennios and Basilakios were men of more than ordinary ability, and attribute the rest to writers' exaggerations. It would make for more accurate but less interesting history.

Basilakios' reputation was enough to convince Alexios that he would be no easy proposition. Alexios led the imperial forces to meet the rebel at the mouth of the Vardarios River (the modern Axios), where the river empties into the Aegean Sea just west of Thessalonike. Alexios noted that the river at some time in the past had altered its course. A stretch of land about a mile wide lay between the new flow and a dry gully that marked the old course. Seeing the defensive advantages of the location he pitched camp there, ordering his troops to rest in anticipation of an enemy night attack which he thought was highly likely. When night fell, and his men and horses were fed and rested, he put in motion another ruse: leaving all the camp fires burning, he quietly moved the whole army some distance away, leaving only a monk of his entourage named Ioannikios in the general's tent.

As expected, Basilakios fell on the camp with 10,000 infantry and cavalry and was livid when he found no one there. Seeing Alexios' tent lit up, he rushed into it 'with blood-curdling cries' but all he found were Ioannikios and 'a few disreputable servants'.

'Where the hell is the lisper?' Basilakios roared, mocking Alexios' mild speech defect. Turning on Ioannikios (whose name can be translated as Little John), he demanded to know where Alexios was. The cool-headed monk replied only that he and his army had left some time before. As Anna Komnene describes the scene:

> So Basilakios roared his abuse and began a meticulous search turning everything upside down, chests, camp beds, furniture and even [Alexios'] own couch, lest perchance the general might be hiding in any of them.

'Comrades, we've been had!' Basilakios spat as he came out of the tent. But few soldiers are likely to have heard him, because most were busy looting the camp. Which was exactly the moment Alexios had been waiting for; in the moonlight, he and a picked squad galloped up and without waiting for the advancing army to arrive ploughed into the rebels. Alexios noticed a man of prominent rank putting some units into battle order, and thinking it was Basilakios, charged him and sliced off his sword hand. This attack threw the rebel force into confusion, which Alexios and his men took full advantage of, with spear, arrow and wild riding. By now the rest of army seems to have come up, and in the darkness it was hard to distinguish friend from foe. A Kappadokian soldier in Alexios' service named Goules hacked at Basilakios' helmet, only to shatter his own sword. Another soldier, a Macedonian named Petros Tornikios, performed acts of great bravery, cutting down many rebels who were floundering around in the blackness.

Alexios sent a message to the rear of his army to hurry up its march, as parts of the rebel force were putting up a stiff resistance and Basilakios was still in the forefront. There was a very tricky moment for Alexios when a soldier holding a sword 'still reeking with hot blood' emerged from the fray and made for Alexios, aiming his spear at his breastplate. The man in fact was a Kelt, one of Alexios' men who, apparently dazed, had mistaken his commander for one of the enemy. The force of the blow almost toppled Alexios from his horse, and it was only after the general called on the Kelt by name, threatening to behead him, that the soldier realized his mistake and clumsily apologized. When day broke, the situation was still confused. Basilakios' men were still looting Alexios' tents whenever they could, creating an order problem for their general. But the fight had not gone out of Basilakios., whose brother Manuel climbed a small hill and called out to the rebel army that victory was at hand.

It was a vain boast. One of Alexios' soldiers named Basil Kourtikios broke ranks and sprinted towards Manuel, who spurred his horse forward to meet his attacker. Kourtikios dodged the horse and snatched a club hanging from its saddle; with that weapon he struck Manuel, unhorsing him and taking him prisoner. Meanwhile, Alexios was moving his men forward, whereupon Basilakios' army broke and ran the fifteen or so miles east to Thessalonike, where it barred itself inside the city. The people of Thessalonike were at first inclined to support Basilakios, but when Alexios' army appeared outside the walls they had second thoughts. Ignoring Alexios' pledge of a safe conduct if he should give himself up, Basilakios prepared for a desperate defence from the citadel of Thessalonike (probably the present ruined fortress of Yedi Kulle, a former prison). But by now the gates had been opened to Alexios, and the citadel guards handed over Basilakios. Alexios carried him captive on the triumphant way back to the capital. They had not gone very far when messengers from the emperor brought instructions for Basilakios to undergo the standard blinding. It was duly carried out by a spring that for some time thereafter was known as 'Basilakios' Spring'.

The meeting between Alexios and the emperor's envoys must not have been a very cordial one. His victory over Bryennios and enhanced reputation had sent shivers through Nikephoros III Botaneiates and his entourage, and many must have secretly hoped that Basilakios would bring the capable young general to heel. Indeed, it would not be too much to suppose that Basilakios had secret encouragement from Constantinople. The bulk of popular opinion, however, looked to Alexios as the saviour of the battered Empire, and had a powerful champion in the empress, Maria, who as we have seen was impatient to see her doddering husband out of the way. Two palace confidants named Borilos and Germanos, former slaves and described as 'Slavonic barbarians', could not abide the sight of Alexios having the run of the palace with Maria's consent, and plotted to do away with him. In the menace-filled precincts of the palace Alexios Komnenos and his faithful brother Isaac had to move very gingerly indeed. They debated confiding in the empress of their plan to seize power, but decided against it as it could easily leak to the emperor. 'Like fishermen,' writes Anna Komnene, 'they were careful not to frighten away the catch before they were ready.'

Botaneiates, in his declining state, made the mistake that cost him his throne earlier than he would have liked. Out of either forgetfulness or cunning he let it be known that he was considering anointing a young noble named Synadenos as his successor, overriding the far more legitimate claim of Maria's son Constantine Doukas. Maria did a slow burn over this portentous slight and was thus judged to be receptive to the Komnenos brothers' scheme. Approaching her as she was downcast, they assured her of their support for Constantine's claim. Despite the pact of secrecy among the three, Alexios and Isaac felt the cold steel of enmity at the back of their necks; they would visit the palace on alternate days, so that if an assassin struck, one brother would be alive to carry on. One day at the height of the tension Botaneiates invited both brothers to dine with him. The hall seemed filled with their enemies; diners and servants alike were seen whispering in undertones. To counter this menacing atmosphere they made lavish compliments to the chef, among others. The compliments worked, as it was the chef who was coached into bringing the news that the town of Kyzikos, on the south shore of the Sea of Marmara barely 100 miles from the capital, had just fallen to the Turks. When the emperor's face fell at the news, the brothers were quick to reassure him that the Turks would soon 'pay sevenfold for what they have done'. The smile returned to old Botaneiates' face, and the Komnenes were allowed to leave unscathed.

Every day that Botaneiates reigned, however, was a day of deadly danger for Alexios and Isaac Komnenos. Though they could, and did, do everything in their power to cultivate relations with the emperor, they knew that Borilos and Germanos had it in for them and awaited only the suitable opportunity to strike. The two ex-slaves hatched a plan to trump up a charge of some sort against the brothers and have them blinded. But in the swirling eddies of palace intrigue the plot leaked. Consternation seized the brothers. In Anna's evocative prose, they were not prepared to 'wait for the iron rod to take out their eyes and extinguish the light in them'. Fortunately, the affair of Kyzikos gave Alexios the chance to get some army support, as he was ordered to raise a force to counter the Turkish advance. The force, of course, had to be assembled in the capital, which struck fear into Borilos and Germanos who arranged to assassinate the brothers in an ambush. That plan, too, leaked; a senior official who heard it ran to the Komnenes in the middle of the night to warn them.

Time was running out fast. For two days the brothers and their strong-willed mother, Anna Dalessene, waited for the auspicious moment to act. It came when news reached Alexios that the army assembled to stem the Turkish advance was at a village called Tzouroulos (possibly modern Çorlu in European Turkey, about 100 miles west of Istanbul). That same evening he went to see a senior Armenian officer named Pakourianos who had held several important army posts, and explained his predicament. Pakourianos had to balance his loyalty to the emperor with his approval of Alexios' intentions. 'If you leave at dawn, I'll follow you,' Pakourianos replied. 'But if you delay even one day I'll have to inform the emperor.' Alexios in return promised him command of the armies as Grand Domestikos if the plot should succeed. That same night another senior officer named Constantine Humbertopoulos pledged his support.

Before dawn on Monday, 14 February 1081 (at the start of what the Byzantines called, and the Greeks still call, 'Cheese Week' when conspicuous amounts of dairy produce are consumed before the Lenten fast), Anna Dalessene locked the palace doors and slipped out of the precinct with Alexios and Isaac and their sisters, wives and children. They hurried on foot through the darkened streets to the Forum of Constantine, a distance of rather less than a mile. Stopping briefly to make sure they had not been followed, Alexios and Isaac continued on for about three more miles to the Blachernai Palace at the northern city limit, while the women turned back to seek sanctuary in an annexe of the great Sancta Sophia cathedral where the arm of the law could not penetrate. They had to pretend to be provincial ladies on their way home from a shopping trip to Constantinople, and in need of a bit of rest, before the verger would open the doors.

But the palace had been aroused. Before entering the sanctuary Anna Dalassene looked round to see a torch flickering in the dark streets. She recognized its bearer as the tutor of Botaneiates' grandson. She concluded that the emperor had got wind of what was afoot; all she and the other women could hope for was for the emperor and his staff to respect the sanctuary. She in any case intended to return to the palace in the morning and face the music. Nikephoros III was naturally incensed when he learned what had occurred during the night and ordered Anna Dalassene brought into his presence. Before going, she somewhat disingenuously told his messengers to tell him that her sons had no intention of toppling the rightful authority, but they were acting in response to a plot against them by jealous men. 'Just allow me to enter the church of God to worship,' she said with a weary air, and walked slowly inside 'as if she were weighed down with old age and worn out by grief'. With the messengers watching, she bowed deeply twice to the sacred images. The third time she fell to her knees, grabbed the sanctuary doors and cried: 'Unless my hands are cut off, I will not leave this holy place unless I receive the emperor's cross as a guarantee of safety!' The weariness had been an act; the mother of the Komnenes was rising admirably to the critical occasion.

One of the messengers removed a small cross he was wearing and offered it to Dalassene who waved it away with contempt. 'I'm not asking you for a guarantee, but the emperor,' she said, 'and it has to be a bigger cross!' She was not just being petulant. Any pledge of safe conduct made before witnesses, to be valid, had to be made in the presence of a cross of reasonable size in the sight of everyone involved. As the messengers returned to the palace to brief the emperor, Isaac's wife was all for remaining in the church 'even if we have to die'; she would never trust the palace. But Botaneiates was quite taken aback by what his messengers told him and willingly had a large cross of his sent to Anna for the required guarantee. She then consented to return to the palace. Shortly afterwards she and the other women were confined in the Petrion convent in the north of the city, a traditional disposal place for imperial women out of favour. Their possessions and assets remained untouched.

While all this was happening, Alexios and Isaac had broken into the imperial stables at the Blachernai Palace. They seized a number of good horses and hamstrung the others so as not to be pursued. They then rode outside the walls to the Kosmidion monastery where Alexios recruited his brother-in-law George Paleologos, who was persuaded to go along only after 'the most awful threats' by his mother, who would never forgive him if he hung back. According to our sources, Alexios seems at some point to have freed his mother and sisters-in-law from the Petrion monastery and transferred them to safety in the Blachernai Palace. By now the people of Constantinople were fully aware of what was going on and cheered on Alexios. A little ditty, as translated roughly by E.R.A Sewter, made the rounds of the taverns, using the colloquial form of Alexios as the Greeks use it still:

'On Saturday in Cheese Week their [Borilos' and Germanos'] plans went phut!
Alexis, hurrah, had used his nut.
Alexis, he's your boy.'

Presently the brothers joined the waiting army at Tzouroulos. The Komnenes were poised to strike their decisive blow.

The next step was to enlist the aid of Alexios' wife's great-uncle, the Kaisar John Doukas, to keep the Doukai involved. Doukas was living in comfortable retirement on his estate and was none too happy to be rudely awakened by his grandson early in the morning with a message from Alexios. His first reaction was to give the boy a clip on the ear, but soon realized the message was serious. It contained the cryptic phrase that Alexios had 'prepared a very fine dish' and that John should join him as soon as possible 'to sit with us at the perfect banquet'.

'Oh, dear me,' the old man said, covering his eyes and stroking his beard. He may well have thought he was too old for adventures now, but after some consideration he eased himself out of bed, ordered his horse to be made ready, mounted it, and set off to join the campaign. This was family business, and as a good and respected Doukas, he felt duty-bound to come to the aid of the Komnenes. On the way he met a tax-collector bound for Constantinople carrying a cargo of gold and talked him into delaying his journey for a night while they ate and drank merrily at an inn. The next morning the tax-collector wanted to continue on his way; Kaisar John tried to get him to stay, suspicion flared, and in the end the Kaisar had to use force to seize the gold. The hapless taxman had no choice but to go along, as the consequences of returning empty-handed to the imperial treasury were unthinkable. Soon afterwards John Doukas met a company of Turkish free-booting mercenaries who readily agreed—most likely after being promised some of the requisitioned gold—to join the cause.

Alexios, delighted with the unexpected revenue and band of allies, embraced his great-uncle warmly. Without delay the army set out for the capital. Most of the towns along the way cheered his progress. But all was not entirely well in the cause, as a number of soldiers and adherents considered that Isaac, as an elder Komnenos brother, was more entitled to the throne than Alexios. The difference of opinion, fortunately, was kept within manageable bounds; there is no evidence that Isaac himself had anything but the greatest respect for his little brother. And Alexios, for his part, was careful to observe family protocol and defer to Isaac on ceremonial and domestic occasions. Old John Doukas, with his powers of persuasion, argued eloquently in favour of Alexios. The issue came to a head when, in the sight of all the troops, Isaac tried to put the imperial purple sandal on his brother's foot, as a sign that he, Isaac, was not a candidate for the throne. Alexios, crafty even with his nearest kin, pretended to object loudly, but Isaac was adamant. 'It is through you,' he said, 'that God wishes to recall our family to power.' He also repeated an old prophecy, given in the past by a poor priest, that Alexios would one day 'govern with an eye to truth and mercy and justice'. The soldiers cheered till they were hoarse, Isaac rammed his brother's foot into the symbolic sandal footwear, and the issue was at an end. Writes Anna Komnene: 'One would have thought there never had been a difference of opinion.'

Isaac's words to his brother, as recorded by Anna Komnene, are revealing. 'God wishes our family to return to power' reflects precisely the prevailing Byzantine view of political power, its origins and responsibilities. It was not the will of the people, or of the rich, or of the elites, that a certain house should reign, but the will of God. The Empire was too important to be left to humanist theories of governance such as that which originated in classical Athens. Byzantium was the great power of its day. Enemies pressed on it from all sides, all the time. True, there was a Senate, but there is nothing to suggest that this body was anything more than a rubber-stamp organ to which an emperor would have recourse only whenever he sought fit. There was no such thing as a mass media that could give the citizenry a daily snapshot of public affairs and entitle it to judge. The noble houses of the Komnenes and Doukai—the *theia gene*, or 'divine' clans—took the divine bit seriously. To their credit, at no point in their history did they ever dare to presume like the early Roman emperors that they *themselves* were divine; they considered themselves instruments of the Divine Will, but were also capable enough of taking momentous decisions when they were convinced it was the moral thing to do.

One more vulture circling the feeble emperor had to be shot down before Alexios could see his way clear to power. This was a brother-in-law of his named

Melissenos, who had got a force of followers together and was already, according to reports, trying on a purple wardrobe. Melissenos sent messengers to sound out Alexios on the possibility of an alliance and co-emperorship, with Melissenos in charge of the eastern part of the Empire. It would be a return to the mafia-like arrangements that Constantine the Great had fought so hard to overcome seven centuries before. Alexios and Isaac saw through the offer, but couldn't afford to dismiss Melissenos entirely, so they agreed to appoint him as Kaisar and give him the revenues of the major port of Thessalonike in Greece. Melissenos' envoys demanded a chrysobull, or sealed imperial rescript, to confirm the appointment. We are told that Alexios' private secretary kept putting off drafting the chrysobull on various pretexts, apparently fearing that Melissenos might demand even more privileges. Very likely Alexios himself had second thoughts about the pledge and to be on the safe side had no wish to see it set down in imperial red ink.

Soon after this Alexios and the army reached Aretai, a village on a hill, and were able to gaze down at the urban mass of Constantinople before them. The Komnene set up their siege headquarters in a former summer villa of Romanos IV Diogenes. A few miles away in the palace, Nikephoros III Botaneiates wallowed in fear, convinced the end was near. But Alexios, viewing the long walls of the city, was under no illusions that his task would be an easy one. The palace itself might be ripe for the taking, but he fretted about the uneven quality of his own troops. As a melange of Greeks, Normans and Turks, to name just three ethnic groups that needed just a spark to start brawling, it had to be watched all the time; at any moment, on any pretext, any unit might desert or refuse to fight, and there was always the joker in the pack, Melissenos, to keep an eye on. Alexios spent a sleepless night worrying about it all, and in the morning asked Kaisar John Doukas to go with him to inspect the defences of Constantinople. But John Doukas had rather been hoping that his role in Alexios' rebellion was over, for in the meantime he had donned a monk's habit to signify that though he was glad to help his kinsman, he was too old to play soldier any more. John grumbled, and some of the soldiers snickered at his monkish garb, but he reluctantly accompanied Alexios right up to the city walls.

With a casualness that seems barely credible in our age, Kaisar John engaged some of the defending troops in conversation, asking them who they were. They were mostly foreign mercenaries—Germans and Anglo-Saxons (already renowned for their prowess with the battleaxe) plus the crack Immortals. Of these, the Germans were believed to be the least reliable and Alexios decided quite simply to buy them off—never difficult with mercenaries. After some negotiation (and almost certainly the promise of a good reward) the Germans' commander agreed, when the time came, to allow the rebels to scale the wall in his sector. At this juncture Melissenos stormed up and demanded his chrysobull. Alexios' secretary insisted disingenuously that it had been mislaid, but Alexios himself, his patience now exhausted, fobbed off Melissenos with a promise of future consideration; now, he insisted, taking Constantinople was the immediate priority. George Paleologos, known as 'the smiter of walls', was sent to the German commander to confirm the arrangements made earlier: on a signal from Paleologos, the gates would be opened and Alexios' men would pour in.

It was an early morning in Holy Week, sometime in April 1081, when the Charisian Gate in the northern section of the wall was opened and Alexios' army surged in with great *élan*, straight down the great commercial avenue, the Mese. All discipline was lost as the rebels fanned out through Constantinople on a rampage, robbing and looting and raping (though Anna Komnene claims no one was murdered). Botaneiates, thoroughly unnerved by the events, had decided to abdicate, but preferred Melissenos rather than Alexios to take his place. He detailed an envoy to cross the Bosporus and collect Melissenos, who was waiting at Damalis on the Asian side. But the rebels were too quick for him; Paleologos, armed for combat, had reached the sea, probably at the Golden Horn, where the Byzantine fleet was stationed. He noticed the fleet guardsman to be an old friend of his, and thus managed to get on board the ship being prepared to fetch Melissenos. He then addressed himself to the seamen to the effect that Botaneiates' cause was hopeless and that Alexios Komnenos was already master of the situation.

> Come and look round the city [Paleologos urged]. See for yourselves that the whole army is within the walls. See the standards. Hear the loud cries of acclamation. See Alexios on his way to the palace, already invested with the authority of an emperor. Turn the prow.

The crew obeyed, all except the fleet guardsman who remained stubbornly loyal to Botaneiates and to break his resistance had to be threatened with being chained to the deck or cast overboard. Back at the fleet anchorage Paleologos, his sword and buckler prominently displayed, took over the fleet in the name of the Komnene, arresting the envoy whom Botaneiates had sent. Cheers echoed off the shore as Paleologos led the fleet off the Acropolis point beneath the palace at the mouth of the Golden Horn. But at this point Paleologos found himself up against an unexpected adversary, none other than his own father, Nikephoros.

Paleologos senior had chosen that moment to turn up in a ship in support of the emperor. His son only realized his father was on board when he moved to cut off the approaching vessel. 'What are you doing here?' Nikephoros Paleologos called to his son, adding that he was a fool for supporting the rebels. Disembarking, the father made his way to the palace where he suggested mobilizing the English portion of the imperial guard to repulse the rebel advance. But Botaneiates, now thoroughly dispirited, replied that it would be no use, and sent away the elder Paleologos with a message for the man who was about to displace him:

> I am a lonely old man, with neither son nor brother nor relative. If it is agreeable to you, you can become my adopted son... I will [not] share in any way your authority as emperor, but will merely enjoy with you the title, the acclamation, the right to wear the purple sandals and to live quietly in the palace.

By now Alexios and Isaac were in the palace grounds and were inclined to agree to the terms, but Kaisar John Doukas intervened forcefully. Glaring at Nikephoros Paleologos, he snapped at him that 'there is no place whatever for further negotiations. Let him vacate the throne and look to his own safety'. John may well have had the impression, probably rightly, that old Botaneiates selfishly wanted to keep the pomp and comfort of the throne while abandoning all real responsibility.

One faint hope remained to the emperor in the person of the intriguer Borilos, who had a guards unit under his command and urged a counter-attack as the rebel army was occupied with looting around the city. But the head of the church, Patriarch Kosmas, a wise and saintly man, advised Botaneiates to step down rather than shed more Christian blood. The old emperor then wrapped his imperial robes around him and set out for Sancta Sophia to find a few moments of solace and peace. On the way he suffered one last indignity: Borilos, the unhesitating turncoat, roughly pulled off Botaneiates' richly embroidered cloak and its pearl clasps with the mocking remark that 'it really suits us now'.

Alexios could not be certain that the deposed emperor would not become a magnet for a counter-revolution, so he sent a relative to accompany Botaneiates from the cathedral to the shore, where he was put into a boat and rowed to the bleak and sprawling Peribleptos monastery (roughly where a large Istanbul hospital stands today). Apparently still hoping for some miracle, he dithered for a while, but was eventually browbeaten into having his head shaved and donning the monk's habit. In the end the only thing that bothered him about his new surroundings, as he confessed, was its meatless diet. The month was February 1081.

Chapter 7

Holding the Empire together

Once crowned and seated on the Roman throne, Alexios I Komnenos lost no time in disbanding his rebel army and sending the troops back to the barracks. Enough mayhem had been committed while Constantinople was in the process of being taken; now the return of civil peace and order was the first priority. And while the streets and squares quietened down and returned to normal, the domestic situation in the palace itself required urgent attention. The Empress Maria, widow of Michael VII and now ex-wife of Nikephoros III, and her 7-year-old son Constantine had witnessed the tumultuous transfer of power at close quarters. Maria, a Georgian princess, had every reason to stay on; she had made Alexios her adopted son—if she was not actually smitten with him—and was fiercely protective of the fair young Constantine, who in Anna Komnene's words was 'a gorgeous child... seemingly endowed with a beauty not of this world'. Moreover, as a Georgian and hence a foreigner, Maria had no one outside the palace whom she could trust for protection.

Probably so that he could work undisturbed, Alexios moved his quarters to the so-called Upper, or Boukoleon Palace, which abutted the Lower Palace on the south and overlooked the Sea of Marmara (in what is now the Cankurtaran district of Istanbul); he took with him his mother Anna Dalassene, his brother Isaac and several other close relatives, leaving his wife Irene, all of 15 years old, in the Lower Palace with her mother and sisters and the venerable Kaisar John, Irene's grandfather. Tongues wagged when it was noted that Maria was also housed in Boukoleon. Maria seems to have been a very attractive lady, classically statuesque, tall and willowy with a rosy complexion and magnetic blue eyes, and Kaisar John, for one, feared that she might steal Alexios' heart and trigger dynastic troubles. John strongly suggested removing her from the palace, but Alexios and Isaac just as strongly objected. The issue became public and acrimonious, with arguments flying back and forth on all sides.

Indeed, the precise relationship between the Komnenes and the Doukai at this point becomes murky. Anna Dalassene had never quite liked the Doukai, which could have been why Alexios kept his young Doukas wife and his mother apart. George Paleologos, an ardent partisan of the Doukai, did not hide his suspicion that Alexios might want to shunt them aside. The suspicion deepened when Alexios was crowned alone, without the customary simultaneous crowning of the wife as empress.

The Doukai naturally raised an outcry; was Alexios proving to be too pliable by his mother? On the face of it, it would seem so. Anna Dalassene tried to manipulate the selection of a new patriarch, but incumbent Patriarch Kosmas was of sterner stuff, and insisted not only on staying put but on crowning young Irene as well, which was accomplished within the week. A possible break with the Doukai had been averted.

A job, meanwhile, had to be found for Alexios' faithful brother Isaac. The new emperor accordingly created the office of sebastokrator, a kind of vice-emperor situated between the throne proper and the office of kaisar, and hence the second highest position in the state. It entitled Isaac as well as John Doukas to wear diadems decorated with pearls and precious stones, though on a scale smaller than Alexios' own lavish skullcap-shaped crown that featured strings of gems hanging down on each side of the face. Several other grandiloquent-sounding titles were created for other worthies who needed to be kept happy. As for Maria, Alexios agreed to her demand that her son Constantine be proclaimed titular co-emperor with the right to wear purple sandals and a crown; the emperor certainly saw no threat from that quarter and could afford to be generous. Thus satisfied, Maria retired to private life.

Alexios had weightier matters on his mind than fixing up domestic arrangements, and one of the weightiest was his own conscience. He could never quite get over the fact that the army that he had commanded, and which he had led to Constantinople to clear the slate and set up a new status quo, had celebrated its victory with orgies of looting and destruction. This was definitely not the image he wished for himself and his cause. As his daughter was to write later, he feared that 'somehow he might be the scapegoat, the object of God's vengeance'. There can be no doubt that he was a devout man and viewed his mission as a call from God, an ideology unchanged since the days of Constantine I who in 312 reported seeing a radiant cross in the sky before the decisive Battle of the Milvian Bridge near Rome that set him on his triumphant career as the founder of Constantinople and the classic divinely-ordained model of the Roman imperial office. But unlike Constantine, whenever Alexios found himself unable to stick to Christian ideals, it bothered him a great deal. After all, whoever may have been responsible for the damage to the city, the buck inevitably stopped at his feet.

After unburdening himself to his mother and Patriarch Kosmas the emperor agreed to do penance for his sins, real and attributed. This involved fasting and wearing a prickly sackcloth next to his skin for forty days—the time Christ spent in the desert—and sleeping on a bare floor with nothing but a stone for a pillow. All the Komnene men and their wives willingly submitted to the ordeal from which Alexios emerged hugely relieved in conscience. It also did his public image a lot of good. Anna Dalassene made sure her guiding (some might say controlling) hand shared the helm. In August, when the emperor was distracted by strategic issues, he formally handed his mother full domestic authority in his absence.

I, your emperor [read the imperial chrysobull] decree explicitly [that] because of her vast experience of secular affairs... [w]hatever decisions or orders are made by her, written or unwritten, reasonable or unreasonable, provided that they bear her seal... shall be regarded as coming from myself.

The 'reasonable or unreasonable' clause must have struck many as proving Alexios' total submission to his adored mother. And they were not wrong. But as he was yet young and inexperienced in rule, her rock-like presence may well have been more help than hindrance. Anna Dalassene was indeed the power behind the throne in this early stage. 'It was as though,' wrote Anna Komnene, 'she drove the imperial chariot while he ran alongside.' Dalassene's granddaughter also credits her with cleaning up the morals of the palace women's quarters, plagued until then by 'utter depravity', and attending church services daily.

Alexios' mother's strength enabled him to concentrate on foreign and military policy. Two main threats were pressing on the Empire from opposite directions, trying to squeeze the life out of it. These were the Turks in the east and the Normans in the west. The Seljuk sultan, Alp Arslan, the magnanimous victor of Manzikert, had in the year after that battle extended his sway to Damascus, which he seized from the Egypt-based Fatimids. In December 1072 he was campaigning in Persia when an assassin struck him down. Into his shoes stepped his vizier, Nizam al-Mulk, who was supposed to be guardian of Alp Arslan's young son Malikshah but arrogated complete power to himself as *atabeg*, or 'sultan's guardian'. Nizam al-Mulk inaugurated a period of prosperity in the Muslim domains, beefed up by an internal security system. While he consolidated control over Syria and Palestine, his cousin Süleyman concentrated on keeping Asia Minor under Turkish control. The Seljuk attempt on Kyzikos, the event that triggered Alexios' march to power, was a part of this unceasing pressure on the shrinking boundaries of the Empire.

But the Turkish threat was relatively minor compared to that unfolding on the western frontiers, where a Norman adventurer and warlord named Robert Guiscard had solidified control over south Italy and Sicily, had his eye on the warm southern seaboard of Greece and nursed dreams of one day seizing rich Constantinople itself. A mere fifteen years before, Norman arms had scored a notable success when William of Normandy invaded England, routing the Anglo-Saxons at Hastings and establishing himself as William I (known subsequently as the Conqueror). At about the same time, in the inimitable words of Will Durant, 'with no taste for peaceful poverty, and with a zest for adventure and rapine still warm in their Viking memories,' some Normans hired themselves out for service in Italy, fighting on behalf of rival local dukes. A dozen years before Hastings, Robert Guiscard (meaning the Wily) was already the master of Calabria in the toe of Italy and had struck a deal with Pope Nicholas II to let him keep his gains. He was already 66 when Alexios I became Roman emperor, and could have spent the rest of his days on his sunny Italian estates. Instead, driven by an insatiable lust for yet more power, he schemed to become emperor himself.

Judging from the descriptions that have come down to us, Robert the Wily's appearance matched his manner and character. Very tall and powerfully yet athletically built, he had a ruddy complexion and fair hair, and eyes that glared penetratingly. He had started out from Normandy with a mere three dozen men and established himself as a ruthless brigand in Lombardy, where Anna Komnene credits him with frightful atrocities. While Guiscard was ruling his Italian domains, his eye was never off Constantinople; indeed, as much of the native population of south Italy and Sicily still spoke Greek, it probably struck him that he was already a Byzantine ruler of sorts, so why not go for the real thing? His chance came in 1073 when Michael VII, for reasons that remain vague but maybe had to do with neutralizing the Norman threat, wrote to Guiscard proposing that the emperor's brother marry Guiscard's daughter Helena. The Norman warlord didn't bother replying, but sat up when another royal missive arrived altering the terms somewhat: Michael's baby son Constantine would now be Helena's prize when he grew up; in addition, Guiscard and his nobles would be given nearly four dozen imperial titles, and 200 pounds of gold as a sweetener.

That did it. Guiscard showed the letter to his warrior-wife Sichelgaita, who at least had the decency to advise him against making war on fellow Christians. Here, he said, was proof that the way to Constantinople was open. He then, according to Anna Komnene's account, produced his *coup de grâce*: he brought in a monk who claimed to be the ex-Michael VII and fabricated a tear-stained tale of being hounded out of his Empire by the usurper Nikephoros Botaneiates. In 1078, as we have seen, Botaneiates actually did topple Michael and become Nikephoros III, dashing the chances of Guiscard and young Helena, who had already travelled to Constantinople and converted to the Greek Orthodox Church in preparation for her betrothal. Guiscard in fury sent his son Bohemond, by all accounts a younger replica of himself, to ravage Byzantine territories on the eastern shore of the Adriatic, around Avlona (what is now the Albanian port of Vlorë).

Guiscard meanwhile gathered a fleet at Brindisi for the planned big push on Byzantium. He sent an envoy, Count Radulf of Pontoise, to Botaneiates to protest at the apparent ditching of the plans for Constantine and Helena. Radulf returned with sobering news: that he had seen the real Michael VII living in monastic retirement (exposing the charade by the monk), that Botaneiates had been sent packing and that Alexios Komnenos was on the throne. Radulf argued strongly against war. Since Botaneiates was no longer in power, he said, the Normans' *casus belli* had evaporated. They had nothing against Alexios. Radulf went so far as to disparage all the war preparations that Guiscard was making. But of course, that was the last thing the warlord wanted to hear. He would allow nothing to hold him back from his planned conquest of the Byzantine lands. Such was his rage (and that of the Michael-impersonator) that Count Radulf was lucky to escape with his life. He fled for refuge with Bohemond at Brindisi.

Some 1,500 Norman knights and thousands more auxiliaries and 150 ships are reported to have assembled at Brindisi, but many, if not most, of the men were inexperienced and ill-trained. The plan was to sail across the Strait of Otranto—as quickly as possible because of the onset of winter and rough seas—to Avlona, and once a foothold was established on the west shore of the Adriatic Sea, move north to Dyrrachion from where the old Roman Via Egnatia ran right across north Greece and Thrace to Constantinople. The expedition sailed in May 1081. At first it went well; Corfu fell, along with its fortifications. Then a storm hit the fleet as it was sailing north to Dyrrachion and sank many ships at a great cost in lives. The Byzantine governor of Illyrikon, of which Dyrrachion was the chief town, George Monomachatos, was a Botaneiates appointee and felt his position to be vulnerable. The result was that Alexios, unable to rely on the governor, was forced to act at speed.

But with what? He had no more than 300 available soldiers in the capital, all green troops. There were many more experienced men guarding the eastern forts and frontiers, but they would take many days to switch to the western front, even if summoned by the swiftest messenger. Letters were despatched to the fort commanders ordering them to report to the capital at once with as many experienced soldiers as they could muster without denuding their own defences. Alexios also mobilized the diplomatic front, sending his trusted brother-in-law George Paleologos to unseat the uncooperative Monomachatos, who he feared might well join Robert Guiscard, and strengthen the defences of Dyrrachion. He sent messages and money to northern and western European leaders, including Holy Roman Emperor Henry IV. Anna Komnene adds that an appeal was also sent to Pope Gregory VII (the German ex-monk Hildebrand), though that seems unlikely, as the pope actively backed Guiscard's campaign against what the Catholics called the 'schismatic Greeks'.

The appeal to Henry IV was especially treacly, beginning: 'Most noble and truly Christian brother, I pray that your mighty realm may flourish and enjoy even greater prosperity,' and going on to heap compliments on the very monarch whom the Byzantines officially considered a counterfeit. The 700-word letter condemned Robert Guiscard as 'that most iniquitous of men... murderer and criminal', and buttressed the honeyed words with the promise of 250,000 gold pieces and 100 purple cloths of the best silk. Alexios ended the appeal with a suggestion that his young nephew (Isaac's son) could eventually marry into Henry's family to seal an alliance between the two Roman Empires. This left Alexios temporarily free to tackle the Turks who were always threatening from the Asian side of the Bosporus. He organized hit-and-run commando groups from the troops transferred from the east and sent them on night-time boat raids against Turkish camps. These raids were successful to the point at which they grew into proper campaigns that drove the Turks out of large parts of Bithynia (now north-west Turkey) and forced Sultan Süleyman I to ask for a truce.

By the middle of June 1081 Guiscard was firmly entrenched outside Dyrrachion, where George Paleologos was busy strengthening the defences, setting up catapults on the walls and exhorting the soldiery to courage. They would need it, for Guiscard had built up a formidable offensive array with the full complement of siege engines and catapults mounted atop a tower as high as the walls. Paleologos put a spokesman on the wall to ask the attackers why they were there. The reply came in the form of a lavish procession featuring the pseudo-Michael, accompanied by clashing cymbals, beneath the walls. As soon as he appeared, the reply from the defenders was a hail of insults and catcalls on this obvious impostor. Guiscard, his propaganda point made, took it in his stride and prepared for an assault.

His forces greatly outnumbered, Alexios could rely for help on two very different sources: the Catholic Venetians, whose naval power was threatened by the Normans, and the Muslim Seljuk Turks, who it seems were easily bribable. The Venetians, too, had to be bribed, but once that business was out of the way they fitted out a large fleet that sailed down the Adriatic and put in at Pallia, some miles north of Dyrrachion. Guiscard sent his son Bohemond to browbeat the Venetians into joining the Normans, but the Italians merely laughed at his beard. Enraged, Bohemond launched an ill-advised sea attack which went badly; the Norman ships were pushed back in disorder and Bohemond himself narrowly escaped drowning. The Venetians jumped ashore at Dyrrachion and continued the fight, soon to be joined by Paleologos' troops who sortied from the city and pushed the Normans back with some slaughter. Round one to Alexios.

In August the emperor decided to take matters in hand personally and march to meet the Norman nuisance. He left behind Isaac to keep order in Constantinople and 'quash the sort of nonsense which poorly disposed people are prone to indulge in'—meaning probably the outbreaks of sedition that tended to arise when an emperor was absent. As senior general he took along with him a long-time supporter, Gregory Pakourianos, with the experienced soldier Nicholas Branas as second-in-command. The force included the Corps of Excubitors, an elite unit dating back to the fifth century when Emperor Leo I wanted a more reliable palace guard. By Alexios' day the Excubitors—whose name meant 'out-of-bed', as they had to be available for emergencies at all hours—had become a kind of military police, tasked with keeping civil order. Now, commanded by Constantine Opos, they took their place in the emperor's battle line-up. There was also a contingent of Franks commanded by Humbertopoulos, a Frank who by his name seems to have reinvented himself as a Greek, and an old supporter of Alexios.

On the way to Dyrrachion the emperor gained accurate intelligence of Guiscard's strength. Paleologos, in the meantime, had been hard-pressed to keep up with the constant battering by the Normans' siege engines. On one occasion he lost patience and, flinging open the gates, attacked the enemy. In the hard fight that ensued, Paleologos sustained several wounds, including an arrow in the temple; he broke off the shaft but the arrow head remained stuck in his head. By nightfall nothing had been decided and Guiscard was as strong as ever. Paleologos then decided that the Normans' tall tower had to be neutralized. He and his men spent a feverish night building a tower that featured a swinging beam that could be aimed at the Normans' tower when it was at the wall and the men on it were attacking. It worked perfectly, stalling Guiscard's attempt to send men over the wall. Minutes later, the Byzantines set fire to the Norman tower; while its occupants fled, Paleologos' men hacked the remains to bits. Guiscard was on the point of readying a second tower when Alexios and the army came into sight.

On arrival at Dyrrachion Alexios personally scouted the ground. He decided to set up camp on a promontory near the city, and once that was done, summoned Paleologos. At first the general was reluctant to leave his post at a time of extreme danger, and probably suspected a trick. He said he would go only if he saw the emperor's ring. It was duly brought to him, and so he went, taking some warships with him. Alexios' aim was to consult Paleologos and other senior officers—who we are told included the sons of three previous emperors: Constantine X, Michael VII and Romanos IV Diogenes. Paleologos and the older men flatly advised against a pitched battle with Guiscard and favoured a tactic of attrition by constant skirmishing. The younger nobles, however, including the sons of the emperors, were all for dashing into battle. In the middle of the debate envoys arrived from the Norman camp bearing proposals from Guiscard. We are not told what precisely those terms were; they probably included a demand for redress for the humiliation suffered by his daughter Helena. But they seem to have been sufficiently unacceptable for Alexios to reject them at once. Guiscard, told of the rejection, called his counts together. Addressing them, he acknowledged Alexios as 'a brave soldier, who has acquired an experience of the military art beyond his years', and urged them to a supreme effort. He ordered his baggage trains to be burned and his ships sunk, so that there could be no possible way but forward.

Alexios initially settled on a sudden night attack on the Norman camp from two directions at once, with allied forces moving on the Normans' rear. He had to change his plan somewhat after Guiscard moved his whole force out of his camp into the plain between it and the sea. The emperor's Varangian Guard was already

Above: Michael Psellos and Michael VII (Mount Athos)

Right: Joshua of Navi, an emblematic Old Testament figure in twelfth century Byzantine military attire (Hosios Loukas monastery, Greece)

Below: Gold coin with the image of Isaac I Komnenos (Numismatic Museum, Athens)

Above left: Alexios I Komnenos (Hellenic War Museum)

Above right: Image of Irene Doukaina in St Mark's, Venice (*Der Spiegel/Geschichte*)

Left: Anna Komnene in a nun's habit (Greek illustrated youth magazine, c. 1965)

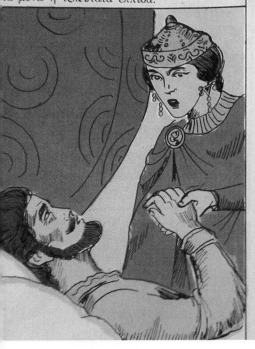

Above: Anna Komnene and John II (Greek illustrated youth magazine, c. 1965)

Right: Small battleaxe used by the Varangian Guard (Hellenic War Museum)

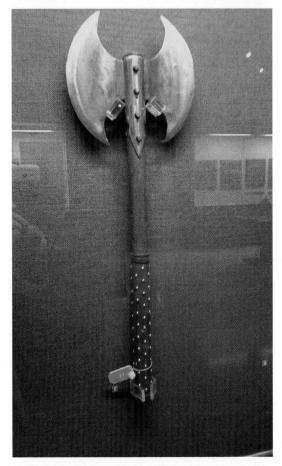

Above left: Model of a Greek fire-throwing engine (Hellenic War Museum)

Above right: Model of a Komnene-era Byzantine siege-tower (Hellenic War Museum)

Below: Twelfth century naval battle (Hellenic War Museum)

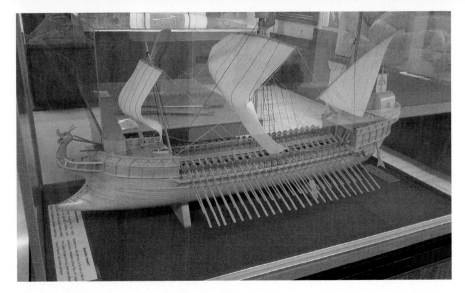

Above: The dromon, a Byzantine warship of the Komnene period (Hellenic War Museum)

Below: Period painting of the simultaneous eye-gouging and castration of a conspirator (*Der Spiegel/Geschichte*)

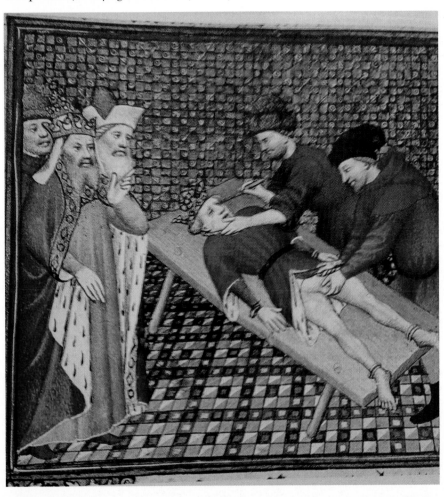

Above: John II and Irene
(Ekdotike Athenon)

Left: Manuel I and his second
wife Maria (Ekdotike Athenon)

Above: Crown of Nikephoros II Phokas (Ekdotike Athenon)

Right: Andronikos I (Hellenic War Museum)

Below: John II, Manuel I and Alexios II (Hellenic War Museum)

Alexios III Grand Komnenos of
Trebizond (Ekdotike Athenon)

The monastery of Hosios Loukas,
Greece, an example of Komnene-era
ecclesiastical architecture
(Author's photograph)

on the move; it was recalled and slotted into the Roman lines opposite the Normans. On 19 October the action opened with both sides carrying out cautious skirmishing. Alexios, as was the imperial custom, rode front and centre. Stationed on the right was the Kaisar Melissenos, with Pakourianos—now Grand Domestikos of the army—in charge of the left. The emperor planned to send a squad of archers forward first and instructed Nampites, the Varangian Guard commander, to open his ranks to let them pass through. The archers were to hit-and-run, withdrawing to the protection of the Varangians when chased back, to re-form and attack again.

The action sped up when a Norman unit impetuously attacked the Varangian Guard. A good portion of the Guard was made up of Norman-hating Anglo-Saxons (of whom more in the following chapter) who used their battleaxes to good effect and drove the enemy back, literally into the sea. A popular story given currency by Anna Komnene relates how Guiscard's wife Sichelgaita put herself in the path of the fleeing Normans and yelled at them to turn round and 'be men'. Some heeded, in time to join a counter-attack against the Varangian Guard, who in their enthusiasm had become dangerously cut off from the main Byzantine force. The newly-energized Normans hit the Anglo-Saxons like a hammer, driving those who survived into a nearby church where they were burned to death when the Normans torched the church.

Guiscard now fell on the Byzantines like a whirlwind. Many of Alexios' distinguished officers perished on the field, such as Prince Constantine, the *porphyrogennetos* son of Constantine X Doukas, Synadenos and George Paleologos' hot-tempered father, Nikephoros. Alexios tried desperately to stand his ground, but three Norman nobles drew a bead on him and charged him, their spears aimed. The first missed; Alexios parried the second with his sword and sliced off its owner's arm; the third was too quick for him to avoid, and acting instinctively, he bent back; still, the spear grazed his cheek and severed his helmet strap. Helmetless, the emperor righted himself on his plunging horse. His admiring daughter paints a vivid picture of the moment:

> He was dusty and bloodstained, bareheaded, with his bright red hair straggling in front of his eyes and annoying him (for his horse, frightened and impatient of the bit, was jumping about wildly and making the curls fall over his face).

What Alexios saw around him was not encouraging. His allied Turks were fleeing en masse. Watching from the wings was one of his chief allies, the Bulgar Tsar Constantine Bodin who, never a very willing ally, decided that the cause was lost and fled in his turn. Alexios had no choice but to retreat with the enemy hot on his heels. At a place sinisterly called Bad Side (Kake Pleura) they caught up with him and would have finished him had not his horse made a tremendous leap forward, leaving some of the Normans' spears stuck in his clothes. Still, the enemy chased him until at one point he wheeled about and transfixed one Norman with his spear.

The danger was far from over. Soon Alexios found his way blocked by a line of Normans standing shield to shield, hoping to capture him. In the line was an imposing armour-clad figure who he figured was Robert Guiscard, so, 'he gathered his wits,' levelled his spear, and charged the man, who charged back in a deadly joust. Again, we must quote Anna Komnene, who employs terms reminiscent of Homer's *Iliad*:

> The emperor was first to strike, taking careful aim with his spear. The weapon pierced the Kelt's breast and passed through his back. Straightaway he fell to the ground mortally wounded, and died on the spot. Thereupon the emperor rode off through the centre of their broken line.

The hapless Norman turned out not to be Guiscard but his number two; as for Guiscard himself, he raged futilely at Alexios' escape. For two days the wounded and exhausted Alexios rode through the mountains across what is now central Albania until he reached Lake Ochrid, where he could rest. He could take a spot of comfort at least, despite the loss of all his army's equipment and supplies, that he had stayed alive to fight another day.

After recuperating at Ochrid Alexios gathered together what remnants of the army that he could and sent messages scheduling a staff meeting in Thessalonike. He had frankly not expected his force, with some notable exceptions, to perform so poorly. He did not have to look far for the answer. Though ten years had passed since the debacle at Manzikert, the Roman army was still far from up to strength. Traditional sources of manpower such as the Asia Minor hinterland had fallen under Turkish control. Most of Alexios' force had consisted of green troops with very little, if any, basic training, and many had simply deserted. Even the redoubtable Varangian Guard had been caught napping through a lack of battlefield discipline. Keeping armies in the field also costs a lot of money, and at this point there was hardly any left in the Constantinople treasury which, we are told, remained unlocked because there was nothing to steal from it.

Besides abdicating in despair, which Alexios' indomitable spirit forbade him to do, there was just one road open to him: scrape together funds from wherever he could to pay for a new army and hope that a revived spirit of patriotism would do the rest. Isaac Komnenos and Anna Dalassene were among the first to respond eagerly to the call, sending all their family heirloom jewellery to the mint to be melted down. They found many imitators, but still the money raised was nowhere near enough to pay the required number of mercenaries what they were demanding. There was only one more possible source of wealth, the Church. Isaac approached the Holy Synod with a proposal to melt down some of the superfluous ecclesiastical gold and silver. There had been a precedent for such a desperate measure: in 618 the Church had placed its riches at the disposal of Emperor Heraclius to counter a serious Persian threat. After a stormy argument, the Synod agreed, though a couple of senior clergymen became bitter foes of the Komnenes as a result, and would pass up no future chance to disparage them.

At Thessalonike Alexios had the satisfaction of seeing recruits flocking to his banner. He sent a bishop as envoy to Henry IV in Germany with a message urging him to invade Lombardy to draw off Guiscard from the Balkans. Leaving Grand Domestikos Pakourianos in charge at Thessalonike, Alexios returned to Constantinople to concentrate on rebuilding the army. Guiscard was surprised and discomfited by the news that Henry IV's army had arrived in Lombardy. He felt he had to return to meet the threat in person and entrusted his son Bohemond with maintaining the front at Dyrrachion. On the way he enlisted Pope Gregory VII in his cause. Then Henry IV got word of the Byzantine disaster at Dyrrachion and his resolve suddenly evaporated; he turned tail and was barely able to escape pursuit by Guiscard who looted the Germans' camp. Bohemond, for his part, moved south and east into Epiros, fortifying himself in the lakeside town of Ioannina and raiding the surrounding countryside.

For the next two years or so Alexios was in the position of a cornered boxer under constant pummelling. Bohemond was proving to be a carbon copy of his hard-as-nails father. In May 1082 the emperor emerged from the capital for another crack at the Normans in northern Greece. Outside Ioannina, after assessing the enemy's strength and finding it considerable, he hit on the idea of using small wagons to break up the expected Norman charge; how exactly this was to be done remains unclear from our extant sources, but somehow Bohemond got wind of it and split his attacking force to hit the Byzantines on the flanks. Alexios as usual fought valiantly, but could not stop the rout of his army. After a rest at Ochrid the emperor marched to take on Bohemond once more near Arta. This time he had spiked iron balls called caltrops strewn on the ground in the path of the Norman cavalry's expected advance, to pierce the horses' hooves. But again the enemy learned of the scheme—Byzantine security must have been calamitous— and it was Ioannina all over again: a simultaneous attack on the wings to outflank the centre, and a wild flight of the Byzantines.

Bohemond moved to secure control over the Greek districts of Epiros, Thessaly and Macedonia, but all was not well in his own camp. His domineering character alienated several of his nobles, who seriously considered defecting to the Byzantines. At least two are reported to have tried, and Bohemond took a page from the Byzantine punishment manual by blinding them for their pains. Back in

Constantinople, Alexios scoured the realm for more manpower, including Turks if necessary. In April 1083, in the midst of these preparations, Alexios received news that Bohemond had reached Larissa in central Greece, an important market town and source of grain and cavalry horses. In command of the imperial garrison in Larissa was Leon Kephalas, who held out against the Norman siege with increasing difficulty; food was scarce, and Kephalas sent a strongly-worded message to Alexios to the effect that if he did not send help soon, he would 'be the first to be charged with treachery'.

Fortunately for Kephalas, Alexios was already close at hand, encamped at Trikala about fifty miles to the west. He had closely questioned one of the senior citizens of Larissa about the lay of the land around the city, planning to ambush the Normans instead of engaging them in pitched battle where they so far had proved invincible. Anna Komnene reports that one night, during an exhausted sleep, he dreamed that an icon of Saint Demetrios (a Roman officer put to death in 308 in Thessalonike for espousing Christianity) spoke to him, saying: 'Cease tormenting yourself and complaining, for tomorrow you shall prevail.' This may sound suspiciously like the vision that occurred to Constantine I before the Battle of the Milvian Bridge seven centuries before, and the temptation may be to dismiss it as propaganda; but we must always remember that in the Roman-Byzantine world such divine revelations were taken very seriously, and in a supposedly secular age we still have no real grounds for dismissing them. And, of course, who is to say that Alexios did not have such a portentous dream? If Anna Komnene recorded it, we may be reasonably sure that her father told her of it.

At Larissa the emperor decided on a plan at least as old as Alexander the Great: to employ a tactical withdrawal that would lure the enemy centre into a headlong frontal attack, when hopefully the enemy would advance too far in their enthusiasm and prove vulnerable to ambush. In an added twist, he intended to leave overall command, including all the imperial standards, in the hands of his generals, while he himself would lead a picked squad and hide in a defile to emerge at the opportune moment. His movement was screened by a diversionary skirmish by the main force. All night Alexios and his squad stayed under cover, kneeling in prayer, the emperor with his 'reins in his hands'.

At daybreak Bohemond looked across to the Roman lines, saw the imperial standards flying, and the horses flaunting the purple saddlecloths, and promptly fell into Alexios' trap. From his hiding place the emperor watched as the Normans swept down like a scythe on the Byzantine centre which, as it had been instructed, fell back. When he judged that the Norman leader had galloped onwards as far as a place called Lykostomion (Wolf's Mouth), he and his squad made straight for the Norman camp, killing many of the enemy and seizing booty. Then Alexios called on George Pyrrhos, a commander of the archers, and ordered them to rain arrows on the Normans from a safe distance in their rear. This unexpected attack threw the Normans into confusion. In the words of Anna Komnene—who was almost certainly relaying a judgement by her military husband Bryennios:

> All [Normans] when on horseback are unbeatable in a charge and make a magnificent show, but whenever they dismount, partly because of their huge shields, partly too because of the spurs on their boots and their ungainly walk, they become very easy prey, and altogether different as their former enthusiasm dies down.

Lykostomion was indeed the 'wolf's mouth' for many Normans, who milled about chaotically, blinded by the great clouds of dust raised by the circling horses and felled by Pyrrhos' hail of arrows. When news of the discomfiture reached Bohemond he was gobbling down grapes and crowing about the victory he imagined he already had in his grasp. Keeping a cool head he sent some Norman cavalry to climb a ridge overlooking Larissa, where they repulsed at least one Roman attack.

On the following morning Bohemond shifted position to a wooded defile between two hills west of Larissa, ideal for defence. The Byzantines followed him there, and were incautious enough to attempt a few costly sallies into the mouth of the defile. One rather clever soldier named Ouzas, probably a member of an Asian nomadic tribe, speared Bohemond's standard-bearer who had been chasing him, seized the standard and turned it upside down, bamboozling the other Normans into thinking that the pursuit had been called off. At this point hostilities seem to have petered out, with Bohemond retiring west and north to Trikala and Kastoria, and Alexios to Thessalonike. The encounter at Larissa had been a stalemate, but it had halted the string of reverses that Byzantium had suffered in Greece for two years, and enabled the long-suffering Alexios to spend the summer back at home, planning his next moves.

Domestic politics in Byzantium were rarely free of turbulence. True to the official Christian ideology of the state, the Orthodox Church always had a considerable say in the running of affairs; individual patriarchs, according to the character of each, had intervened overtly or covertly in imperial policy, and often carried a large part of public opinion with them. When Alexios returned to Constantinople in the late spring of 1083 he found he had to contend with not a stubborn clergy so much as an aggressive public speaker named John Italos who set himself up as a teacher of philosophy and gained enormous popularity debating cleverly in the manner of an ancient Athenian sophist. In the opinion of the palace Italos, a student of the late Michael Psellos, preached outright sedition, not to mention unorthodox doctrines that turned the Church against him. Alexios ordered him to face an ecclesiastical tribunal. As word of Italos' teachings spread beyond the chattering classes to the more conservative and devout populace, the orator felt himself in danger. At one point he fled to the roof of Sancta Sophia to escape an angry mob that would, in Anna Komnene's opinion, have 'hurled [him] from the galleries into the centre of the church'. Italos sought the protection of some sympathetic nobles. Nonetheless, the emperor ordered him to retract his heresies, bareheaded and in public, in Sancta Sophia. This he did, but soon resumed his old ways. There followed an excommunication from the Church, but we are told that the garrulous philosopher later recanted of his own accord.

Of course, the Balkan campaign was far from over, as long as Bohemond held sway in north Greece. The autumn of 1083 found Alexios back in that theatre, trying to eject the Normans from Kastoria, a strongly-fortified lakeside town. He planned a two-pronged attack on the town, himself from the landward side and George Paleologos with a water-borne landing from the lake. As the assault progressed, a good number of defenders deserted to the imperial side. This forced the defence into abject surrender, and Alexios was able to return home with another feather in his cap. On the way back he was called on to settle a troublesome theological-cum-security affair. A heretical sect called the Paulicians, whose beliefs had elements of old Persian Manichaeanism, had recruited a rebel force and were seen as dangerous insurrectionists. Alexios called on the Paulician leaders to meet him at Mosynopolis (roughly where the Greek town of Komotini is today) and arrested all the members of the sect he could find.

But on his return to Constantinople Alexios was in a worried frame of mind. There hung over him the charge of having denuded the Church of its assets to fight his wars, and he was anxious to set the record straight. Calling a high-level meeting at the Blachernai Palace, the emperor subjected himself to cross-examination by senior clergy, the Senate and the senior military commanders. It was found that the Church had not been deprived of as much as was claimed, and that Alexios' exactions were but a drop in the ocean. Thus exonerated, the emperor delivered a justification for what became the chief characteristic of the Komnene dynasty— the militarization of the state:

> It was my misfortune to find the empire surrounded on all sides by barbarians, with no defence worthy of consideration... You know the many dangers I faced, almost myself becoming a victim of the barbarian's sword. Those who shot arrows at us from east and from west vastly outnumbered our forces.

If necessary, he went on to say, the Church must be subordinate to military considerations, and used the Bible to justify the doctrine:

For we hear that even the prophet-king David, when he was reduced to
the same necessity, ate of the sacred bread with his warriors, although it
was forbidden...

Roman canon law, he added, allowed church money to be used to ransom
prisoners-of-war. Now that Constantinople and the rest of the shrunken Empire
were in direct danger of capture, in a manner of speaking, then it was nothing less
than the duty of clergy to contribute to the defence by all economic means available. He won that argument, but left a simmering resentment among some senior
generals and senators that would have erupted into a mutiny had not Alexios' intelligence network informed him in time. The plot ringleaders were treated relatively
leniently, merely being exiled and stripped of their property. Perhaps Alexios felt
he could be generous because at about this time Irene Doukaina gave birth to their
first child, their *porphyrogennete* daughter Anna.

She preserves for us a legend that we have already mentioned—that her mother
was seized with labour pains in December 1083 while Alexios was on his way
back from his latest scrap with the Normans. We may assume that couriers had
informed Irene Doukaina of her husband's progress, as when the time came for the
baby to be delivered she made the sign of the cross over her womb with the words:
'Wait a while, little one, till your father's arrival.' Irene's own mother, helping out,
snapped at her: 'What if he takes a month?' But Irene was adamant, and she turned
out to be right; Alexios was home in time for him to take his firstborn into his arms.
All of Constantinople rejoiced.

Farther afield, Robert Guiscard was gobbling up as much of Italy as he could; on
27 May 1084 his forces burst into Rome, freed Pope Gregory VII from self-imposed
imprisonment and thoroughly sacked the Eternal City in an orgy of flames and
blood. But across the water in Avlona his son Bohemond was not having an easy
time of it. After his failure against Alexios at Larissa, he had retired to the Adriatic
coast to face George Paleologos who in the meantime seems to have brought more
Norman counts into imperial service. Depressed at these defections, Bohemond
sailed to Lombardy to ask his father's advice. The elder Guiscard's response was
typical: put together a new army and fleet and regain the initiative in the Balkans
by sheer persistence. A few months later Guiscard sailed back to Greece with 150
warships; off Corfu they were trounced by a Venetian fleet, but Guiscard managed
to assemble the remnants of his own fleet and take his revenge on the Venetians.
The Normans wintered on Corfu. Then plague struck, in the form of what was
most likely typhoid fever. Hundreds of Norman knights and ordinary soldiers perished; Bohemond sickened, and was sent to Italy to recuperate. Nonetheless, such
was Guiscard's drive that he imagined he could continue his conquests south to
the island of Kephalonia. In the early summer he sailed to join the advance force

which he had sent under his son Roger Borsa. On the voyage the plague struck him. By the time he put in at a fishing village on Kephalonia he was sinking fast. He died on 17 July 1085, aged 70, as Roger Borsa wept at his bedside. The village in which he breathed his last has ever since been called Fiskardo—a corruption of Guiscard.

As Bohemond arrived to accompany his father's body to Italy, and almost saw the coffin washed overboard in a severe storm, Alexios reacted to the news of the terrible Norman's demise 'like a man throwing off a great weight from his shoulders'. He was now free to exercise the highly effective Byzantine art of bribery, which he practised on the Venetians holding Dyrrachion with such success that the city was soon back in imperial hands without a drop of blood being shed. Then he could afford to turn his attention to another enemy pressing on the northern frontiers—the Pechenegs, who for at least 200 years had a fearsome reputation for violence, treachery and rapaciousness. Many considered them worse than the Normans, who were at least Christian. Emperors as far back as Constantine VII had been careful to keep the Pechenegs docile with copious bribery; but from Romanos IV Diogenes onwards that policy had changed, and by the time of Alexios I the Komnenes' proud policy of aggressive defence and aristocratic principle had fired the Pechenegs' enmity anew. War broke out in 1086 when they began a major campaign against the Empire.

Alexios sent his trusted Grand Domestikos Pakourianos, who had helped him defend Dyrrachion, and Nicholas Branas to meet the advance. On the way Pakourianos learned that the Pecheneg force was larger than he had thought and decided that the best tactic would be defensive manoeuvring, avoiding a pitched battle. But as happened so often when command was shared, disagreement arose. At the camp at Beliatoba Branas was all for a brash frontal attack; Pakourianos, fearing he could be called a coward, reluctantly agreed. Unfortunately, Pakourianos was right. The first charge ended in utter and complete rout; Branas was fatally wounded, while Pakourianos during a furious charge somehow collided with an oak tree at great speed and was killed instantly.

The news came as a great shock to the emperor, who had valued the Grand Domestikos' friendship and loyalty, but there was no question of not carrying on the fight. He ordered a general, Tatikios, up to Adrianople post-haste with money to pay the troops (one suspects that part of the reason for the defeat at Beliatoba could have been poor morale on the part of unpaid soldiers) and raise new levies. Humbertopoulos and the Varangian Guard were sent to join him. While Tatikios was setting up camp at Philippopolis (now Plovdiv) he noticed a force of Pechenegs returning from a raid. On the banks of the Evros River he divided the army in two and ordered each section to fall on the enemy flanks, which they did with great *élan*. The Roman victory was complete, but Tatikios knew that the force he had beaten was a mere drop in the ocean of Pechenegs swarming around the Bulgarian countryside. When he received reports of a large Pecheneg force at Beliatoba, he marched cautiously to meet it, by no means confident of the result. He came on the enemy at the Evros River.

> Both armies [writes Anna Komnene] were afraid and put off the moment of conflict, the Romans because they trembled before the overwhelming numbers of the [Pechenegs], the enemy because they feared the sight of all those breastplates, the standards, the glory of the Roman armour and the brightness reflected from it like rays of starlight.

Both armies remained tensely where they were, neither daring to take the initiative. Humbertopoulos' warlike Kelts, 'sharpening teeth and sword alike,' had to be held back. For no fewer than three days in a row, the opposing armies would move into formation, stay put all day, and retire in the evening. The Pechenegs were the first to break and turn tail after the third day of this elaborate game of chicken. Tatikios gave chase, picking off stragglers, until satisfied that the Pechenegs had been chastised, and returned to the capital.

But the Pecheneg menace was not over by a long shot. In the following spring a new leader of the Pechenegs named Tzelgou, aided by a deposed ex-king of Hungary named Solomon, crossed the Danube and began to ravage Bulgaria. The Byzantine general sent to deal with them was Nicholas Maurokatakalon, helped by Alexios' younger brother Adrian. Like Pakourianos before him, Maurokatakalon was sobered by the size of the enemy force he saw before him. Near the village of Koule he divided his force like Tatikios had done at the Evros River, and after a fierce battle trounced the Pechenegs. Tzelgou, after fighting bravely, was killed; many of his fleeing men fell into a river and were drowned, trampled by the mass behind them. Adrian Komnenos, for his part in the battle, was promoted to Grand Domestikos of the West.

But as long as the Pechenegs remained south of the Danube and in imperial territory, the emperor could not rest. Fearing that they could at any moment filter through the mountain passes in the direction of the capital, Alexios personally rode with his army to Adrianople and from there to Lardeas (approximately at modern Veliko Turnovo in Bulgaria). At the same time his general, George Euphorbenos, was sent by sea to enter the Danube and set up a command at Dristra (perhaps today's Silistra). Alexios spent six weeks preparing a campaign which he hoped would see off the Pecheneg menace for good. With the emperor himself confronting them, the Pechenegs sent a peace mission to him; Alexios, with good reason, believed it to be a mere time-gaining stratagem and refused to parley. At this point, Anna Komnene tells us, a secretary who probably had some knowledge of astronomy whispered in the emperor's ear that an eclipse of the sun was expected any minute. The secretary's intention was probably to impress the rude barbarians with evidence of the emperor's prophetic powers. Alexios told the envoys that God would soon give a sign in the sky, and a few hours later the predicted eclipse occurred. The stunned envoys were duly escorted out of the camp. As they were on their way to Constantinople under guard, they overcame their captors, killing some, and escaped.

Near Dristra the Pechenegs launched a surprise attack on Alexios' camp. In the resulting confusion the imperial tent came down, but his men recovered in time to drive the attackers back. Yet the Pechenegs remained in control of Dristra, foiling Alexios' attempts to besiege it. Maurokatakalon and Paleologos suggested that the army move to Preslav, the main Byzantine administrative centre in the region. Preslav, they said, could be a secure base from which to launch raids on the enemy; it would make more tactical sense than wandering about the countryside at the mercy of the barbarians. But that wasn't Alexios' style; he was all for taking the initiative wherever he could, and in this he was seconded by the two sons of the late Romanos Diogenes, Nikephoros and Leon, 'young men [with] no experience of the misery of war'. Thus he hatched another of his crafty schemes: he ordered a complete blackout of the camp for that night—no fires or lamps were to be lit. The troops and horses were kept awake and alert, and dawn found the emperor ready on horseback in the centre of the army drawn up in combat formation.

In charge on the left wing was the emperor's brother-in-law Nikephoros Melissenos; part of the right wing was under Tatikios. Adrian Komnenos and the Latin contingent stayed close to Alexios, who detailed six senior officers to be his bodyguard and look out for him at all times, regardless of what else was happening on the battlefield. These men included Romanos IV's sons Nikephoros and Leon, Maurokatakalon and Nampites, the commander of the Varangian Guard. The Pechenegs soon appeared on the horizon: masses of men in close order, backed up by covered wagons carrying their women and children—indicating that for the Pechenegs retreat was no option. Alexios gave strict orders that no man was to advance alone and break the line, which had to be kept as strong as possible for the impending clash which, when it came, was violent. All day the bloodshed continued; Leon charged impetuously, galloped farther than he should have, and fell mortally wounded. It seemed all but impossible to break the Pecheneg lines; Adrian Komnenos managed to reach the wagons but had to fall back with only seven survivors from his contingent. A shudder of despair ran through the Roman ranks when what appeared to be many thousands more of the enemy materialized on the horizon.

There was no alternative but to sound a general retreat, but Alexios was determined to fight every inch of the way. In his right hand he wielded his sword; in his left he clutched what was believed to be the Virgin Mary's original cape, the *Omophoron*, held up like a standard. As twenty horsemen defended him as best as they could, three Pechenegs jumped at him. Anna Komnene paints the scene in vivid colours:

> Two seized his horse's bit, one on either side; the third grabbed him by the right leg. Alexios immediately cut off the hand of one and raising his sword and roaring loudly put him to flight. The man who was clinging to his leg he struck on the helmet. He only struck him rather lightly, however, rather than with full force since he feared one of two things would happen if he hit him too hard: either he might strike his own foot, or he might hit his horse... He delivered a second blow, but this time took careful aim.

Michael Doukas, Irene's brother, called out to him: 'Why are you trying to hold out here any longer? Why lose your life?'

'Better to die fighting bravely than seek safety in an unworthy manner,' Alexios reportedly replied.

'If you were an ordinary soldier, that would be fine,' Doukas said. 'But when your death would endanger everybody else, why not choose the better course? If you're saved, you can fight another day and win.'

The emperor appreciated the logic of Doukas' words, but still felt bad about abjectly retreating. He gestured to the Pechenegs close at hand. 'If we go back the enemy might meet us,' he said. 'We must charge them hell-for-leather. That way we'll get behind them and withdraw by another route.'

It was much easier said than done. Doukas spurred his horse forward, but the animal slipped and threw him; luckily an aide was present to give him his own horse. Alexios grimly pressed forward, slashing at every Pecheneg who tried to stop him. He was lucky enough to spot an enemy horseman who was about to fall on Nikephoros Diogenes from behind. A quick warning shout from the emperor, and Nikephoros turned just in time to fell his attacker. But Alexios by now was justifiably feeling the strain on both his arms, the one wielding the sword and the other holding up the revered *Omophoron*. A stiff wind was also making it hard for him to keep the standard upright. Then a spear slammed into his buttock; it didn't break the skin but caused an agonizingly painful muscular spasm and most likely a severe bruise. Our sources are vague on what happened next, but it seems Alexios was forced to dismount and hide the *Omophoron* under a bush; at that hour night was falling, and Alexios somehow was able to get away to safety and take some rest at Beroe. He left behind Melissenos, who had been captured. That was almost the fate of Paleologos as well, but the general managed to elude his pursuers and

wandered around the Bulgarian mountains for eleven days before eventually finding the road home.

Recuperating and reorganizing at Beroe (perhaps modern Kazanluk in
Bulgaria), Alexios had a visit from Count Robert of Flanders who was returning
from a pilgrimage to Jerusalem. The count promised to send 500 horsemen as soon
as he got home. Alexios then moved the army to Adrianople, to be closer to home
and sent an ambassador to the Pecheneg camp suggesting a truce. The Pechenegs
were amenable because they themselves were being threatened by another aggressive nomadic tribe called the Cumans—descendants of the Scythians who were
a considerable thorn in the side of the Greeks in the late sixth century BC. Both
sides appeared to be on the verge of cementing a peace deal when the Pechenegs,
angry over Alexios' failure to halt the Cumans, broke off the talks and reverted to
their old raiding and pillaging ways. By the autumn of 1089 they had occupied
Philippopolis and were preparing to march on Constantinople itself.

Playing for time, Alexios sent his General Migdenos, a reliable associate ever
since the battle at Larissa, to gather mercenaries for another expected showdown.
In the spring of 1090 Alexios, having wintered at Bulgarophygon (now probably
Lüleburgaz in European Turkey), felt confident enough to tackle the pernicious
Pechenegs one more time. In view of his travails in two great lost battles, where his
life was repeatedly in the greatest danger, Alexios' energy appears remarkable. But
he was never one to shrink from a fight, no matter how great the odds against him
seemed. He was still young, in his twenties, and at the peak of his physical powers.
He was almost certainly sincere when, in the anxious moments fending off attackers
at Dristra, he said he preferred death in action to retreat. When he saw Pecheneg
formations making aggressive demonstrations at Bulgarophygon he decided to
send in a new detachment that he had raised. These were the sons of soldiers who
had fallen in action, 'all with beards barely grown,' but eager warriors thanks to the
special training they had received. They were called the *Archontopouli*, or 'young
nobles,' and numbered 2,000, which was supposed to be the number of the Sacred
Band, an elite unit of ancient Thebes. But though bursting with fighting spirit,
the *Archontopouli* were inexperienced and possibly ill-led, as their first impetuous
attack fell into a Pecheneg ambush, and soon 300 of the young nobles lay dead on
the field. Alexios was sorely grieved for them, as he considered them almost his
own sons and knew all of them by name. Tatikios, the Latin contingent and the
imperial guard were sent to scout the menacing countryside; coming across some
Pechenegs on a foraging expedition one morning, they swept down on them and
eliminated them. Then the 500 horsemen promised by Count Robert of Flanders
turned up, bringing with them 150 more well-bred mounts as a present for Alexios.

Besides the titanic struggle against the Pechenegs, the emperor had to keep an
ear open for news from the east, where stability could never be taken for granted

as long as the Turks remained a potential menace. Alexios had managed to make peace with many of the mutually-quarrelsome Seljuk Turkish potentates who were in charge of several key cities in Asia Minor; one of these was the emir of Smyrna, Çaka, who had extended his control over the whole Aegean seaboard and was thought to be Alexios' ally. But when the Pechenegs attacked from the north, Çaka showed his true colours and moved, like Robert Guiscard before him, to seize the Byzantine throne.

An army sent to stall Çaka's advance found itself besieged on the island of Chios, while the Turks' ships ran rings around the ill-led Roman flotilla whose commander, Constantine Dalessenos (of Alexios' mother's family) asked for a meeting with Çaka. At the meeting the Turkish leader complained that, as he had been an ally of Byzantium, 'since Alexios Komnenos seized power everything has gone wrong.' The emperor's reputation as an implacable warrior unwilling to put up with the status quo had certainly spread far and wide. Çaka suggested a marriage alliance as well as a truce, but Dalessenos was not taken in; instead he got Alexios to bring in John Doukas, his wife's brother, who had held the command at Dyrrachion and was now given command of the fleet at Chios. After a sharp fight the Byzantines held on to Chios, but Alexios was already concerning himself with yet another incursion by the Pechenegs, who had penetrated almost to the Gallipoli Peninsula. Alexios sped westward, coming on the enemy at Rousion; intending a surprise attack on the enemy, he kept his men awake all night by having the imperial falconer go around the camp beating a drum so that the troops could be ready to attack at first light.

Hardly was the sun up, however, when a sordid event disturbed Alexios' plans. A Pecheneg renegade named Neantzes was sent to scout the enemy position; unknown to the emperor, however, Neantzes was a double agent who crossed to the enemy to reveal the Roman plan. He seems to have been overheard, and his treachery reported to the emperor; when exposed by questioning, Neantzes promptly decapitated the one who had informed on him. Alexios and his staff seem to have been too stunned to react at once. Besides, there was a battle about to be fought, and the emperor had more immediate things on his mind than punishing Neantzes. The delay proved to be an unfortunate lapse of judgement, as Neantzes then had the effrontery to ask Alexios for a better horse; once seated on it he pretended to charge, but instead rode straight to the enemy and gave them as much intelligence as he had, which was quite considerable. The result was predictable: at the first clash the Byzantines were almost routed. Alexios, his teeth chattering with fever, managed to draw up his army again. At the sight of the massed Roman ranks the Pechenegs withdrew.

From his sickbed Alexios incessantly conferred with his officers on what to do if the enemy were to attack again. He was especially concerned about the mounted archers, and carefully coached them on how to fire their arrows and when to dismount. All night he was busy briefing the men, and in the morning, after a minimum of sleep, he felt well enough to get out of bed and take his accustomed place in the centre of the line in time for the expected Pecheneg attack. His archers opened the action by dismounting and moving on foot against the enemy, firing a storm of arrows all the time. Alexios and the army followed close behind. After the initial hard clash the Pechenegs broke and ran; perhaps the volleys of arrows unnerved them, or maybe campaign fatigue had set in. We must handle with caution Anna Komnene's proud assertion that the mere sight of her father caused the flight; often enough in the past the Pechenegs had been unfazed by his presence, and there was no apparent reason why they should be terrified now. Many of the enemy fell while fleeing and for the first time in a long while, Alexios could taste the sweetness of a resounding victory.

But one victory, however smashing, is rarely enough to win a war, and so Alexios maintained a defensive posture, moving north to Tzouroulos, which had been his forces' rendezvous point preparatory to moving on the capital and seizing power some ten years before. Tzouroulos was on a heavily-fortified hill, and thus the Byzantines got a good view of the pursuing Pechenegs as they swarmed over the plain below. After another night spent mulling over the problem—he seems to have had the extraordinary ability to get by on little or no sleep—the emperor thought up one of his stratagems: he requisitioned all the local horse carts and ordered their wheels and axles removed; these were tied to ropes and hung over the walls like Christmas tree decorations. Orders went out to the archers to dismount and advance towards the Pecheneg line in the plain below, firing arrows as they went; this was intended to provoke an enemy charge. Alexios, conspicuous as the only man on horseback, rode with them to keep them steady as the next phase of the movement would require a high degree of coolness and discipline: as soon as the yelling Pechenegs charged, the archers would have to stop and very slowly shuffle back in good order, 'shifting knee past knee,' in a phrase first used by Homer in the *Iliad*. At the right moment they split to open a gap in the Roman line, through which the Pechenegs rushed in a tumult, right up to where the defenders were ready to cut the ropes holding up the wagon wheels. Again, we must resort to Anna Komnene for a high-fidelity description of what happened next:

> The wheels crashed down with a great whirring noise, all of them rebounding more than a cubit from the rampart as the curving wheels were thrust away like bullets from a sling... The normal weight of the wheels, falling in this mass descent, acquired tremendous momentum from the downward incline of the ground. They toppled down on the barbarians with great violence, crushing them in all directions and

cutting off their horses' legs like mowers in a harvest field; with fore- or hind-legs severed... the horses sank down and threw their riders forward or backward.

At that moment Alexios ordered his ranks to close in on the struggling mass. Those Pechenegs not killed by arrows or lances fled in panic from the juggernaut of wheels, and many were drowned trying to cross a watercourse.

Such was the warlike drive of the Pechenegs that even after this debacle they did not give up and made ready to renew the battle the following day. Their man-power was limitless, it must have seemed to Alexios as wearily he once more took up his position in the centre of his army. But this time there was a difference; the past two encounters had been won decisively, and Roman army morale must have soared as a result. This renewed morale may well have been the deciding factor in the Byzantine victory that day. It was now winter—probably January or February 1091—and high time to return home. He left Maurokatakalon in charge of a gar-rison to keep watch in case the enemy should renew hostilities.

The emperor was not able to rest even a week at the palace when news arrived that the Pechenegs were on the march again. He hastened back west with 500 new recruits and occupied the town of Choirovachoi, probably not far from Tzouroulos. He locked the town gates, forbade anyone from leaving and entering, and called for volunteers to man the walls. Soon several thousand of the enemy appeared on a height opposite the walls, and Alexios realized that a pitched battle with such a superior force was out of the question. Just how many soldiers he had under him remains vague; 500 seems to be an especially low number with which to meet the far more numerous Pechenegs, and it may have been that Maurokatakalon was able to pitch in with some more. But the emperor felt he could not even waste a day, and if only a few hundred troops could be mustered, so be it. 'If we are all of one mind,' he told his anxious men, 'I am absolutely confident of victory.'

But for once that vaunted confidence failed to work its magic. The men refused to believe him. He became sterner, reminding them that if they shrank back they would certainly perish. Their only hope was to fight. At this point we can imagine him mounting his horse. 'For my part I am going out now,' he said, adding that anyone with a faint heart was not entitled to come with him. Some—we don't know how many—agreed to follow him. A first encounter ended in Alexios' favour; a number of severed Pecheneg heads were carried back to Choirovachoi in tri-umph. While still in the field the emperor ordered some of his soldiers to dress in Pecheneg garb; these lay in wait for the enemy returning from a plundering expe-dition and massacred them. This Roman detachment was still in its Pecheneg dress when it came on a column under Paleologos that had hurriedly marched up from Constantinople. We are told that Alexios kept them deliberately like that in order to play a practical joke on Paleologos' men. At any rate, a potentially fatal misunderstanding was averted only by Alexios' own appearance at the proper moment.

Those Pecheneg heads which the Byzantines had harvested at Choirovachoi were carried in triumph into Constantinople, followed by columns of chained prisoners of war. Such was the public adulation in the city that Paleologos felt peeved that he hadn't been in time to share much of the glory. People sang and danced in the streets. But some of the nobility felt differently; it seemed to them that Alexios was milking all the popularity on false pretences, as the Pechenegs were still roaming back and forth on the borders of the Empire, raiding and pillaging at will. Four victories did not seem to have made a significant dent in this fearsome barbarian mass that seemed to be everywhere. Meanwhile, Çaka was lording it in the eastern Aegean, coordinating moves with the Pechenegs. As heavy snow fell on Constantinople, blocking the streets and rising above the house doors, Alexios sat in his palace and planned strategy for the coming spring.

Operations resumed as soon as warmer weather returned in April 1091. While Melissenos was sent to Ainos on the north Aegean coast (about where the present Greek-Turkish border lies) to secure it as a naval base, the emperor followed with the 500 Flemish warriors that Count Robert had sent and had since remained in Roman service. Ainos was where the wide Evros River flows into the sea; Alexios took time scouting both banks and decided on taking up a position between the river and a swamp. As was expected, a great mass of Pechenegs appeared on his front, supplemented a few days later by many thousands more Cumans. If the emperor had any hope of prevailing, he had to try and win over the Cumans, whose allegiance was already far from certain. He invited the Cuman leaders to a sumptuous banquet in his tent and promised them that if they turned their weapons on the Pechenegs and prevailed, they could keep all the booty. Having gained their enthusiastic agreement, he evacuated his force to the other side of a river by means of a hastily-built bridge. During the next few days he had to fend off several Pecheneg attacks, some of them costly to both sides, and ended up on a hill called Lebounion.

There wasn't enough room on the hill for the whole Byzantine force, so Alexios ordered a trench dug around the lower slopes to hide the mass of the army from enemy observation. While at Lebounion he had a visit from the Pecheneg turncoat Neantzes, who hoped no doubt to profit from some secret negotiation, but the emperor clapped the man in irons. The time for games was over. The Cumans, for their part, were inclined to join the Byzantines, but were getting impatient at the inaction; one afternoon they confronted Alexios and told him they intended to attack the Pechenegs in the morning, orders or no. The emperor was delaying in the hope that expected reinforcements could arrive from Constantinople, but realized that time had run out. And could he really trust the Cumans? There was only one way to find out. He called the army together.

What followed, as narrated by Anna Komnene, was an extraordinary event. Alexios led the whole army in hymns and prayer as detachments of troops marched in a torch–lit procession (though some of the more loutish men had to be ordered to take part).

> At the moment when the sun set below the horizon, one could see the heaven lit up, not with the light of the sun, but with the gleam of many other stars, for everyone lit torches, or candles, according to what they had available, fixed on their spear points. The prayers... were borne aloft to the Lord God Himself.

At midnight emperor and army retired for a short sleep. Well before dawn he sprang up to see that the light-armed troops were properly equipped for action; those men lacking armour were given silken breastplates and caps whose metallic shine, it was hoped, would deceive the enemy into thinking it was real armour. The sun was up when the army assembled in battle formation: Alexios in the centre, Paleologos on the right and Constantine Dalassenos in charge on the left. The Cumans were probably in the rear, with Humbertopoulos and his Varangians next to them. Squadrons of cavalry protected the wings. Then came the trumpet call sounding the charge, and Alexios spurred his horse forward, the war cries and prayers of his men echoing in his ears. The shock of collision threw the Pechenegs into disarray; the emperor, however, was still preoccupied about whether the Cumans might switch sides and kept close tabs on their contingent. The fight was ferocious—'a slaughter such as no one had ever seen before'.

That spring day was a warm one, and around noon the Romans were becoming tired and thirsty. Alexios sent a foraging party around the farms in the vicinity to collect wineskins full of water; the peasants were glad to comply, having suffered from Pecheneg raids for years. Duly refreshed, the Byzantines fell on the Pechenegs in an orgy of butchery. They burned with insane revenge for years of stinging defeats at the hands of this wily and dangerous foe. Not even the women and children in the enemy camp were spared. The soldiers' sword arms ached with the incessant effort. In a single afternoon an entire ethnic tribe was exterminated, except for a few thousand taken captive. The Pechenegs were essentially erased from history. The few survivors would henceforth be subjects of Byzantium.

As Alexios that evening sat down to a well-earned dinner, a general, Synesios, fretted to him that the sheer number of prisoners taken was a potential threat; at any moment they could overcome their captors, and therefore they should all be put to death at once. The emperor, in the name of Christian charity, refused to authorize such a barbarous act. Yet in the middle of the night Synesios, without orders, had all the prisoners massacred. In the morning the emperor tore a ferocious strip off the general and clapped him in chains. By that time the Cumans had made off with whatever booty they had been promised. A stench was arising from the corpse-strewn battlefield, so the army moved east. On the way Alexios met Melissenos, who was coming up with reinforcements but was too late to take part in the battle at Lebounion. The emperor reached home in May, hopeful now that he could rest from the rigours and dangers of battle and concentrate on being a ruler.

Chapter 8

The road to Micklegarth

If the previous chapter reads like a tiresome list of Alexios' battles against a variety of enemies, we need to be reminded that the Roman struggle against the Normans and Pechenegs each lasted several years, as long as both the world wars of the twentieth century. Our telescoped account does not do justice to the complexity and length of the campaigns, which are described in far more (and sometimes confusing) detail by Anna Komnene in her acclaimed *Alexiad*. For the present we may leave an exhausted Alexios I walking away from the heaps of barbarian bodies at Lebounion, and take a look at one of the units who stood by him in his defeats, helped him in his victories, and at home guarded his palace. This was the conglomeration of Russians, Scandinavians and Anglo-Saxons known as the Varangian Guard.

In the quarter-century since the 1066 Battle of Hastings, as we have seen, a good many Anglo-Saxons could not live under Norman domination in England and fled to a Christian power where their martial skills could be employed and appreciated, and which would offer them a chance to measure swords with their old enemies. The flight had begun almost at once; a year after Hastings, several Anglo-Saxon counties in the north and west of England rose in revolt against the new Norman king. William had hurried back from Normandy to undertake his notorious punitive 'harrying of the north' which set back that region's economy for centuries and established Norman rule in England as a frankly ruthless dictatorship. Sporadic Anglo-Saxon insurrections continued; Ordericus Vitalis, an English monk-historian who lived at that time, lamented that his countrymen 'groaned aloud for their lost liberty and plotted ceaselessly to find some way of shaking off that what was so intolerable and unaccustomed'. One of the rebels could have been the man subsequently immortalized in legend as Robin Hood.

There is evidence that English mercenaries had filtered down to Byzantium before 1066, specifically after the death of King Canute in 1035, when Anglo-Danish *huscarls* (house-guards of the king), fleeing the resulting instability, found their way to the Empire. But the exodus began in earnest after Hastings, triggered by the sheer weight of Norman oppression. Some of the leavers hoped to enrol some foreign ruler to help them topple William I, though it's hard to see how effective a Byzantine emperor could have been to that end. Nonetheless, writes Ordericus Vitalis, 'some still in the flower of youth... bravely offered their arms to Alexios, emperor of Constantinople, a man of great wisdom and nobility.' Alexios' reputation was thus well-known in England. It also seems to have been common knowledge that the Norman adventurer Robert Guiscard was threatening Byzantium, hence 'the English were warmly welcomed by the Greeks and were sent into battle against the Norman forces, which were too powerful for the Greeks alone'.

The English arrivals were incorporated into the Scandinavians and Russians of the Varangian Guard. Among the first actions undertaken by Alexios' Anglo-Saxon contingent, as we have seen, was the disastrous charge at Dyrrachion, in which the troops were trapped in a church and burned to death. A recently discovered source, the *Chronicon Universale Anonymi Laudunensis*, notes that in 1075 more than 250 ships carrying 'a group of English notables', (somewhere in the region of 4,000, including whole families) sailed into Constantinople. According to this document, some stayed to take up service with Michael VII, while most sailed on for six days to found a township they called 'Nova Anglia' (New England). No one knows where this Nova Anglia was, or whether it even existed historically; yet most commentators agree the story contains a germ of truth. More information comes from the Jarvardar Saga, a Scandinavian epic, which appears to confirm the arrival of these English in 'Micklegarth', (Big City, i.e. Constantinople), where 'King Kirjalax' (a corruption of the Greek usage Kyri-Alexios, or Lord Alexios) gave them a warm welcome.

According to anonymous Byzantine tradition, an unnamed 'noble' Englishman along with many other noble exiles from the fatherland migrated to Constantinople; he obtained such favour with the emperor and empress as well as with other powerful men as to receive command over prominent troops and over a great number of companions; no newcomer for very many years had obtained such an honour. He married a noble and wealthy woman, and remembering the gifts of God, built, close to his own home, a basilica in honour of the Blessed Nicholas and Saint Augustine.

By stages, the English became so numerous in the Varangian Guard as to constitute the majority. Some appear to have entered the service of the imperial household, according to an account by an English pilgrim-monk named Joseph, who claimed to have met them. A later fourteenth century Byzantine account mentions the Christmas celebrations of the *Inglinoi*, which included calling on the emperor to wish him 'many years in the language of their country, that is, English, and beat their battle-axes with loud noise'. Just why Alexios and subsequent emperors preferred the English and others of the Varangian Guard over other ethnic groups as reliable warriors is open to several explanations. One is the obvious need for mercenaries to help conduct the unremitting struggle against the Normans and Pechenegs at a time when local manpower was increasingly scarce. Another reason, and possibly a more basic one, could lie in their simpler, duty-bound north

European mentality that was seen as a factor for reliability in the face of the constant betrayals and intrigues that every Byzantine emperor had to face from his own Greco-Roman class. Whatever the reason, they repaid the imperial trust handsomely, and no doubt many of their intermarried descendants can be found living in Greece and Turkey today.

The Scandinavian Viking element in the Varangian Guard was probably older than the English. It can be traced back to Harald Sigurdson, a Norwegian prince who was just 15 when he had to flee his homeland after being severely wounded in a dynastic battle. He recovered from his wounds in Orkney, where according to a later Norwegian tradition he spent time wondering: 'Yet who knows if I may not win far-flung fame hereafter?' We next hear of Harald in Russia in the early 1030s, serving under Prince Yaroslav of Kiev and fighting the Poles. Sometime during his Russian sojourn he became enamoured with Yaroslav's daughter Ellisif (Elizabeth), but despite his Norwegian royal blood—and very likely because he was a pagan—he wasn't considered quite exalted enough for entry into the Kievan royal family. And it must have been about this time Harald, who had some of the ruthless attributes of Robert Guiscard, took himself off to where he knew there was plenty of money and employment to be had—the 'metal of Micklegarth', or the gold-topped domes of Constantinople.

The emperor at the time was Michael IV. Harald took service in the Byzantine navy and was promoted to command his own Varangian company under General George Maniakes. According to a Norse epic, the *Fagrskinna*, Harald resented being a subordinate to anyone; he hid his royal status to avoid derision and took the name Nordbrikt. Snorri Sturluson, an Icelandic chronicler, described Harald as being nearly seven feet tall, with fair hair and beard, 'grim towards his enemies' but 'very generous to those who were dear to him'. All sources agree that he was greedy for gold and held a magnetic attraction for women. He is said to have attracted Empress Zoe herself, but to have answered rudely when she asked for a lock of his hair. He was not foolhardy in battle but used his wits to figure out the most advantageous tactic. His self-will sometimes brought him into conflict with Maniakes, but not to the point of outright insubordination. It is about this time that Harald Sigurdson acquired the sobriquet by which he is better known to history—Harald Hardrada, or the Ruthless.

For his merits he was promoted to *spatharocandidatus*, a ceremonial post carrying the nominal military rank of the equivalent of colonel, but was ranked sixth in the fourteen grades of court officials. This was a high honour indeed for a foreigner, but to prevent the inevitable anxious grumbling about foreigners 'taking over', the senior commanders were always Greeks. Harald and the Varangian Guard lived in the palace precincts, having assumed some of the duties of the Excubitors. There was some rivalry between the Greeks and the Scandinavians over who should occupy which quarters; lots were drawn and the Varangians got the upper floor, where they sometimes kept the others awake with their drinking parties. Micklegarth was indeed good to them.

It was a fair qualification for him to be appointed (possibly by Zoe's sister Theodora, who succeeded her as empress) to oversee the brutal blinding of Michael V (as related in Chapter 3). But Harald by now may have had enough of Byzantine intrigues, and decided that the time had come to get out. The palace refused to allow him to go, so he slipped out in secret and sailed undetected up the Bosporus and through the Black Sea, ending up in Kiev where he managed to marry Princess Ellisif, essentially buying her with the considerable weight of stolen gold he brought with him. With Ellisif in tow and his 'wealth belonging to the King of the Greeks', he returned to Norway to share rule with his cousin Magnus and live in luxury. He was careful to preserve good relations with Byzantium, which sent Greek priests to Norway and Iceland to preach to the people.

The next stop for this extraordinary man was Jerusalem, where in 1036 he seems to have headed a special Roman military mission to help rebuild the Church of the Holy Sepulchre, which had been burned down by order of Muslim Fatimid Caliph al-Hakim. There followed campaigns in Sicily and then meritorious service against the Bulgars, for which Michael IV rewarded him handsomely. It was now, about 1040 when he was still in his mid-twenties, that Harald was given a senior rank in the Varangian Guard. Yet shortly afterwards we find him behind bars for reasons that remain unclear, but were probably connected with a charge that he misappropriated campaign booty that should have gone to the emperor; resentment by Zoe over the aforementioned slight over her request for his hair may also have played a part. We may discount fantastic tales that circulated in Norse tradition about Harald battling with a dragon in a dungeon filled with the bones of previous inmates; what seems more likely is that he escaped his confinement by taking advantage of the riots and destruction caused by Michael V's banishing the popular Zoe to a convent.

Life as king of Norway may well have been too tame for Harald, as we find him hankering after overseas action when in 1066 William of Normandy was preparing his historic invasion of England. Allied with William was Tostig, the exiled brother of the elected English King Harold Godwinson; Tostig sought the aid of Harald to unseat his brother by promising him the English throne. Perhaps moved by rosy memories of comradeship with the Anglo–Saxons in Byzantium, Harald sailed across the North Sea with an army. Crowned king of England at York (incidentally where Roman Emperor Constantine I was acclaimed in 306 before he began the campaign that resulted in the creation of Byzantium), he collided with Harold's forces at Stamford Bridge and died fighting.

The Varangian Guard can be dated back to at least 911, when the first Kievan Russian soldiers are mentioned in Byzantine documents. As that was several decades before Prince Vladimir of Kiev embraced Christianity and became an ally of Byzantium, those 'Russians' may well have been Scandinavian Vikings. They joined other nationalities such as Germans, Goths, Normans and Pechenegs, and even Turks; the name Varangian could derive from the Pharangians, a contingent of Turkic Central Asians. Thanks to their reliability, these foreign units were incorporated in the *tagmata*, or special battalions reserved to guard Constantinople and especially the palace. Other such *tagmata* included the Scholai, an elite cavalry troop consisting of young higher-class Greeks, whose job included taking part in imperial pageants and who had the privilege of being allowed to live at home. The Excubitors were another crack unit that by the middle of the tenth century had become essentially Constantinople's police force; their military importance, however, seems to have declined as that of the Varangians grew, as their last recorded action was at Dyrrachion in 1081.

The creation of these foreign mercenary units reflected what for the next hundred or so years would be the governing philosophy of the Komnene dynasty. The old theme structure of past dynasties, in which Byzantine provinces (the themes) in the East and West were run by military governors had fallen into disuse. By the middle of the eleventh century almost all of Asia Minor, the traditional Byzantine heartland, was in Muslim hands. The area had accounted for at least fifteen themes, leaving perhaps the nearest Asian theme, the Optimaton just across the Bosporus, still under shaky Roman control. These themes had been the chief source of military manpower that was now being sucked into Turkish service. The only practicable way Alexios could maintain an army worthy of the name, then, was to essentially import a large part of it and pay it directly out of the state coffers. He did not take the decision lightly, and often worried about the mercenaries' loyalty, but he cannot have had any other choice.

In 988 more Russians—perhaps as many as 6,000—had joined the Varangian Guard to help Basil II fight off a domestic revolt. Michael Psellos relates that these mercenaries surprised the rebel leaders 'seated at a table and drinking' and made short work of them. Gradually Scandinavian volunteers came to supplement the Russians and outnumber them. Their fighting qualities, honesty and willingness to instantly obey orders without question were highly valued by emperors constantly preoccupied by intrigues by their native-born upper class. This was probably the reason why Alexios Komnenos, in his seizure of power in 1081, avoided going for help to the Varangian Guard; he knew they would be implacably loyal to Nikephoros III Botaneiates, not because they particularly liked him but simply because their duty was loyalty to the emperor—period. Each volunteer had to pay a stiff fee for the privilege of membership in any *tagma*; few quibbled, as the pay was excellent and there was a guarantee of considerable booty from successful campaigns.

Honour in the ranks amounted to a fetish. Besides the unquestioning loyalty to the throne, internal discipline was strictly enforced. According to one Byzantine account, as early as 1034 a guardsman in the province of Lydia tried to rape a local woman who killed him with his own sword. The reaction of the soldier's unit was to recognize the injustice he had committed and compensate the woman with his possessions; the soldier's body was cast out with no funeral rites, as if he were a suicide. Another story, this time taken from Icelandic sagas, tells of one Thorstein Asmundarson, an Icelander who set out to avenge the murder of his two brothers, one of whom was known as Gettir the Strong. Asmundarson traced the killer, Thorbjorn Angle, to Norway, where he learned that Angle had gone off to Micklegarth to join the Varangian Guard.

Asmundarson followed him there, taking service in the Byzantine navy and then, as it appears, being recruited for the Guard. He probably would not have recognized Angle if he had seen him but, according to the saga, the guardsmen were called for a weapons-check before going on campaign. All the members had to hold out their swords for inspection. We are told that Asmundarson's eyes fell on a rather grand weapon that had a nick in the blade. The owner proudly related that he had taken the sword from Gettir the Strong and cut off his head with it. Asmundarson asked if he could see the weapon; Angle obliged, and in the next instant Asmundarson sliced the man down through the middle of the head to the jaw, killing him instantly in revenge for his brothers' slaying. Thorstein Asmundarson naturally was jailed for his deed, but the Byzantine authorities seem to have understood his motive and were lenient with him. The Icelandic saga goes on to claim that a wealthy Greek lady ransomed him from the dungeon, left her husband and married him, but they eventually separated to 'lead holy lives'.

Other Norsemen in Byzantine service before and during Harald Hardrada's period included the Icelander Halldor Snorrason, who served with him and recorded many of his doings. Bolli Bollason, one of the first Norwegians to make the trek south, was also one of the first to return home with an almost mythic aura about him after serving with Harald in the Varangian Guard. One saga tells of how Kolskegg (Blackbeard) Hamundarson, an Icelandic noble, fled his country after some political reversal and sailed to Denmark, where he is reported to have dreamed of 'a shining figure who commanded him to journey south and become a Christian'. This he did, enlisted in the Varangian Guard and married a local woman. The challenge of Micklegarth could well have become a matter of personal honour for restless young Vikings seeking an outlet for their aggressive urges. Those who fell in battle for the Byzantine emperor were greatly honoured back home in almost Homeric terms. A stone in a Norwegian church contains an inscription for one who 'fell fighting in Gardariki [Byzantium], loved leader of the war-band, among the land's best'. H.R. Ellis Davidson, an authority on the Vikings in Byzantium, cites a 'general assumption that to visit Byzantium was the expected thing for a brave man to do if he wanted to win wealth, the equivalent in the late Viking Age to raiding in the Baltic in earlier times'.

A host of traditions agree that the Varangians' hard drinking often got them into trouble. Attaleiates writes that a band of drunken guardsmen assaulted Nikephoros Botaneiates himself on a staircase. Some Greek troops saved the emperor from severe manhandling, and the offending Varangians expected to be executed; instead, in recognition probably of their military value, they were merely shipped off to distant outposts. In one of his battles against the Pechenegs, Alexios I was reported to have been reluctant to send his Varangians against the stubborn enemy, claiming that his 'wine-bags' (an unmistakable reference to their bibulousness) were too valuable to waste just then. At that point an Icelander named Thorir Helsing said his fellow Varangians 'would gladly leap into the fire if it would please the emperor'. Alexios relented, and his Vikings advanced to victory, calling on Saint Olaf. In fact, the Varangians had long had their own church of Saint Olaf in an annexe to Sancta Sophia (though Greek sources call it the church of the Holy Virgin of the Varangians). Sometime in the reign of Alexios I Saint Olaf's sword, Hneitir, which he had been carrying when he fell mortally wounded in 1030, had found its way to the church; according to Norse legend Hneitir was picked up by a Swede who fought with it and kept it for the rest of his life, passing it down to his descendants, one of whom brought it to Byzantium. Hneitir, possibly via the saintly association, came to the attention of Alexios who is said to have bought it for three times its weight in gold and had it placed over the altar in Saint Olaf. The church and its relic apparently survived for a century and a half until they disappeared when the Fourth Crusaders sacked Constantinople in 1204.

Chapter 9

The 'greedy Latin race': Alexios and the First Crusade

The Vikings and Englishmen of the Varangian Guard were one of the few groups of people whom Alexios could implicitly trust with his life, unlike many of his own senior officers who, in the time-honoured Late Roman style, were ever on the lookout for a chance to boot the emperor off his throne and seize it for themselves. Two of these, according to Anna Komnene, were the Kelt Humbertopoulos and an Armenian noble named Ariebes. The charge against Humbertopoulos surprises us, as he was one of Alexios' most faithful lieutenants and reliable in battle. Perhaps plain human jealousy was at work here, an emotion liable to be aroused whenever a ruler had to act in an imperious manner. In fact, later research suggests Humbertopoulos may not have been involved in a conspiracy at all. But there is little doubt that plots were certainly afoot, and rather more credence can be attached to a story that Alexios' nephew John, the son of the Sebastokrator Isaac, was planning a revolt.

The emperor received his first news of this while at Philippopolis on his way to clear the Balkans of remaining pockets of Cumans. The information unsettled him; this was his own flesh and blood, the son of his beloved brother Isaac, a boy in whom the Komnenos family had great hopes. Isaac, as was natural for a father, wanted to delay the investigation but Alexios could not afford to waste any time. What was worse, John despite his youth was dux, or governor, of Dyrrachion, the city that Alexios and the Romans had spilled so much blood defending against the Normans. The emperor wrote to John ordering him to come to Philippopolis and give him a report on the situation on the Adriatic coast. The messenger, himself a highly placed officer, was given a second letter to hand to the Dyrrachion magistrates with orders to arrest John if he balked at the command.

The faithful Isaac, much perturbed, travelled post-haste to Philippopolis to see if he and his brother could find some solution that would cause the least damage to the Komnene house. Isaac was still only half-convinced of his son's complicity which he was ready to explain away as caused by mere youthful impetuousness. After a two-day ride he arrived at Alexios' camp at night, creeping into his brother's tent and motioning to the astonished chamberlains not to awaken him. Isaac lay down on an adjacent empty bed, dropped off and awoke in the morning to find his brother Alexios staring at him. After Isaac explained what he was doing there, Alexios shook his head, replying that his brother had simply wasted his time.

Isaac retired in despondency to the tent provided for him, but soon recovered his spirits with the news that his son was on his way.

Isaac was determined to let John off the hook. He confronted Alexios angrily, claiming that he was feeling 'rotten' at what was going on, and turning on him, cried, 'And it's all your fault!' The emperor, refusing to be drawn into a shouting match, called in his younger brother Adrian to discuss the issue. But the sight of Adrian inflamed Isaac still more. 'He's a liar!' he shouted, pointing at Adrian, implying that it had been Adrian who had spread the reports about John. Turning to Adrian, he roared, 'I'll tear out your beard!' In Anna Komnene's breathless account, which doubtless she got from her father, at that moment John walked in, apparently having overheard much of the shouting. Alexios, whether convinced of John's innocence or wanting to defuse this potential bomb, said he was ready to forget all the charges against John and send him back to his post at Dyrrachion. A mollified Isaac returned to the capital and a potentially disastrous rift in the Komnene house was averted.

No more threats, real or imagined, came from the direction of John Komnenos. But such was the nature of the Komnene dynasty, based as it was on a network of aristocratic family ties, that it could never rest secure. This was a natural consequence of the aristocratic military clique of which the Komnene house was a part. This elite had a natural opposition in the form of a civil aristocracy that included the intelligentsia, wealthy business people and professionals. Yet the instinct of the mass of people was to back the military aristocracy as a more reliable defender of the realm, and throughout his many crises Alexios could always count on the great bulk of popular support. To their opponents the Komnenes were just one of a number of bossy clans, like the Doukai, who just happened to make the right moves at the right time. Alexios was still technically a usurper, not having any blood or other ties to his predecessor Botaneiates. Everyone knew how dependent he was on foreign mercenaries such as the Varangian Guard. And there were enough nobles, military and civil, ready to probe at that structural weakness, as it were, in their own self-interest.

Alexios had various ways of dealing with threats to his power. One of them, as in the case of Theodore Gabras, was to ensnare the potential rival in a marriage web. Gabras was a noble whose reputation as a man of action rang warning bells in the palace; Alexios sent him off to be dux of Trebizond (modern Trabzon) on the south shore of the Black Sea, which he turned into a fief. To tame this potential troublemaker, Isaac Komnenos betrothed his daughter to Gabras' son Gregory. But as both those children were just that—children—the marriage tie had to wait for a good number of years. Then the Church stepped in with a ban on the proposed marriage on the grounds that the two children were actually distant relatives. This was bad news for Alexios, who feared Gabras' reaction; therefore he kept Gregory in the capital as an essential hostage for the warlord's good behaviour.

It turned out to be the wrong move, as Gabras stormed into Constantinople, demanding his boy back. Alexios flatly refused, so Gabras went to the more pliable Isaac and over a sumptuous wine-fuelled banquet talked his host into letting him be with Gregory for a while. The next thing Isaac knew, Gabras had outwitted the guards and was on his way up the Bosporus with his son. Alexios sent a fast boat which caught up with Gabras when he had entered the Black Sea. The crew delivered a letter from the emperor proposing that Gregory be betrothed to one of his own daughters, accompanied by a clear threat that if Gabras refused, the emperor would feel free to make war on him. Gabras consented and Gregory was taken back to the palace. Young Gregory, though kept in very comfortable circumstances and given a thorough education, made a rebellious nuisance of himself. He in fact intended to escape and rejoin his father, but the plan of course leaked and the elder Gabras was sent to the dungeon. Thus was another conspiracy scotched.

Though kept busy fending off plots, Alexios' main concern was always external security. He was spending far more time in the field than in the capital; hardly had the Gabras threat been seen off than the emperor was back in the saddle, roaming all over the Balkans to make sure the shaky frontiers were kept safe. Once that was done he faced a challenge from Çaka, who in the meantime had made the coastal city of Smyrna into his stronghold from which he hoped one day to launch his bid to capture the capital. According to Anna Komnene, the Seljuk warlord was already wearing the purple and psychologically preparing for the hoped-for day that he would occupy the Constantinople palace. In the spring of 1094 the emperor summoned his brother-in-law John Doukas from Dyrrachion and gave him command as Grand Dux of the Byzantine fleet. The rank of grand dux had recently replaced that of the grand drungarios, or admiral-in-chief. The grand dux was commander of both the army and navy which henceforth were to act in closer concert than before. Doukas' mission was to coordinate a two-pronged offensive against Çaka, with himself marching overland and Constantine Dalassenos sailing through the Dardanelles and down the Asia Minor coast to the island of Lesbos, where they would bring their land and sea forces together for a combined drive on Smyrna.

Doukas landed at the island's main town of Mytilene and began to build a base of operations, but Çaka attacked him there and over several days succeeded in stalling the Roman advance. Alexios was not happy with the news he was getting, and asked a soldier who happened to be on home leave what was being accomplished at Mytilene. The soldier replied not much. 'What time of the day does the fighting take place?' the emperor asked.

'About sunrise,' the soldier replied.

'And which side faces east?'

'Ours.'

That was it. Doukas was foolishly opening the action each day with the sun in his men's eyes. Alexios dashed off a message to Doukas with the sarcastic observation that it made no sense to fight two enemies at once—Çaka and the sun—and ordered the soldier to carry it back to his commander post-haste. As he was leaving the emperor called out to him: 'If you attack the enemy as the sun goes down, you'll win at once.'

Doukas read the message and, we are told, dutifully obeyed. In the following morning the Byzantine troops didn't take their usual place in battle formation; the Seljuks wondered at it for a while and then stood down. Doukas waited until the early afternoon, when the sun was beginning to turn, and launched a massive surprise assault against the enemy lines. Çaka, however, was on his toes and reacted quickly—perhaps he was suspecting just such a move by Doukas—and managed a stiff counter-attack. When the lines clashed, a strong wind blew up great clouds of dust; with the setting sun in their stinging eyes, the Seljuks fell back. The Seljuk army must have suffered considerable losses, as Çaka reacted to the defeat at Mytilene by suing for peace. After hostages for good behaviour were exchanged on both sides, according to custom, a chastened Çaka was allowed to sail back to Smyrna. Only now did Dalassenos turn up with the fleet, and begged to be allowed to carry on the fight. After some persuasion, Doukas agreed and the Roman ships caught up with the Seljuks on their way to Smyrna. In the ensuing action the Byzantine prisoners kept in chains were freed and the crews of the enemy ships executed. The wily Çaka, however, managed to get away and maintain his hold over Smyrna, his wings clipped but still a force to be reckoned with.

Doukas was later sent to oversee operations against rebels in Crete and Cyprus, and scored a signal success. But closer to home, Çaka continued to make a nuisance of himself. This time Alexios tried the diplomatic tack, writing to Kiliç Arslan, the sultan of Ikonion, to try and bring his bumptious rival in Smyrna to heel. Kiliç Arslan obliged—prompting from Anna Komnene the uniquely feminine observation that 'such is every barbarian—constantly lusting after massacre and war'—while Dalassenos sailed through the Dardanelles to confront Çaka who had appeared suddenly at Abydos near the mouth of the strait. But the Seljuk found that his ships had not arrived and that Dalessenos, moreover, had a superior force in front of him. Kiliç Arslan meanwhile had come up in Çaka's rear, and Çaka, blissfully ignorant of the deal between Alexios and Kiliç Arslan, decided to call on his fellow Turk. We leave it to Anna Komnene to tell us what happened next.

> The sultan received [Çaka] graciously with a pleasant smile, and when his table was laid ready in the usual way, he shared it with Çaka at dinner and encouraged him to drink heavily. Then, seeing him in a fuddled state, he drew his sword and thrust it into his side.

Thus with admirable simplicity was the threat from Çaka finally eliminated.

As if on cue, another troublemaker appeared, this time from Dalmatia on what was Byzantium's north-west frontier (corresponding roughly to today's Croatian coast). This was a warlord called Bolkan, who made a habit of raiding Roman territory. Alexios rode out again, but failed to bring Bolkan to heel; the following year, probably 1095, he sent his brother Isaac's son John, the one who had been charged with treasonous plotting at Dyrrachion. Bolkan planned to ambush him, and John had ample warning from a local monk who was a spy. John disbelieved the spy, with the result that Bolkan smashed the Roman army in a night attack, sending John and his staff fleeing in panic. Alexios, hearing of this, donned his armour yet another time and set out. He set up camp at Daphnoution, some miles to the west of the capital, and waited for his staff to catch up. But from one member of that staff, he was about to face a deadly danger.

We have met Nikephoros Diogenes briefly as one of the two young and impetuous sons of the late Romanos IV Diogenes who, 'like lion cubs', were all for charging into action against the Pechenegs at Dristra, and whose impatience may have cost Alexios the battle. Diogenes turned up at Daphnoution 'brimming with arrogance' and proceeded to set up his tent rather closer to the emperor's sleeping quarters than was customary. This was most irregular, and another official went straight to Alexios with a fully justifiable hunch that Diogenes was plotting an attempt on the emperor's life. Diogenes' general insubordinate attitude must have been common knowledge, so it was not especially hard to draw such a conclusion. Alexios appeared to take the threat in his stride, refusing advice to order Diogenes to pitch his tent somewhere else, lest the plotter find a ready excuse for acting. Wondering whether his emperor had lost his wits, the official left wringing his hands.

Despite the warnings, we are told, Alexios and his wife slept soundly that night without the benefit even of a guard outside the tent. According to Anna Komnene's narrative, in the middle of the night Diogenes crept out and approached the imperial tent, sword in hand. He looked in to see a young girl carrying out her task of fanning the slumbering royal couple to keep them cool and drive off mosquitoes. Realizing that he was already compromised, Diogenes skulked off. In the morning the girl told Alexios what she had seen during the night; keeping the information to himself, he resumed the march westward. The next stop was the town of Serrai, where Constantine Doukas, the *porphyrogennetos* son of Michael VII, had an estate; here Alexios could enjoy cool drinks and good food, wash off the grime of days of riding, and relax—while keeping an eye out for Diogenes. But Diogenes was also keeping an evil eye on the emperor, and when he learned that Alexios was having a leisurely bath he walked into the mansion with a short sword strapped on. Tatikios saw him coming and guessed what was afoot. 'What's with the sword?' Tatikios demanded. 'It's now the hour for bathing, not hunting or fighting.' Diogenes drew back, realizing that by now he was under the severest suspicions.

Alexios spent three days in the relaxed surroundings of the Serrai estate, during which he mulled over what to do about Nikephoros Diogenes. He genuinely cared for the young man and was saddened to see it repaid with poisonous jealousy and murderous hostility. But the facts were the facts, and Alexios reluctantly ordered his arrest. Diogenes meanwhile, knowing the game was up, asked Constantine Doukas if he could borrow a racehorse that Alexios had given him, as he planned to flee. Doukas refused, saying he could not possibly lend an imperial gift of that value, and Diogenes found himself forced to resume the north-westward march with the rest. During a stop, Alexios told his brother Adrian, the Grand Domestikos, to play good-cop to Diogenes to get him to admit to his plot, in return for which he would be forgiven. Adrian, very likely shaking his head at what he saw as his brother's overly trusting nature, didn't think it would work, and he was right. Diogenes defiantly kept his mouth shut. The next step was bad-cop torture, and here Diogenes gave in at the 'gentlest probing'. In fact, he sang like a bird, while a secretary took it all down. Letters from accomplices were also found on him; a leading plotter seems to have been Michael VII's widow Maria of Alania, Constantine Doukas' mother, whose motive seems to have been little more than an infatuation with the decisive Diogenes. Alexios kept the information about Maria to himself and kept a close watch on all the named accomplices. Nikephoros Diogenes was put in chains and sentenced to exile.

The sheer number and frequency of the plots against him—one knife-bearing man had tried to get to him while he was playing polo—unnerved Alexios, and reading between the lines of his daughter's account gives us the impression that he couldn't understand why. After Diogenes was disposed of he called a general meeting of his relatives, guard and domestic staff in his headquarters tent. He rightly suspected that among them there might be some foes, possibly armed with daggers, and so decided on a show of force. On the appointed morning he seated himself on his golden field throne, placing the Varangian Guard in a crescent on either side of him. When Tatikios let the others in, the sight of the frowning Vikings and Anglo-Saxons, their great axes resting casually on their shoulders, was enough to cow them into silence. Flushed with nervous tension, Alexios launched into a long complaint that despite his incessant exertions on the part of the Empire, and the consideration he had always shown to such as Diogenes, he had been rewarded with nothing but hostility and threats. 'Indeed, by way of gratitude, he sentenced me to death!'

There must have been many gulps among those present, some of whom wondered whether their own heads were about to roll. They were also intimidated by a rumour spread by Alexios that Diogenes had been blinded. And in their fear they abjectly professed their absolute fealty to the emperor, making a great, if insincere, show of it. Alexios silenced them with a gesture and proceeded to proclaim a general amnesty that received a tumultuous welcome. As for Diogenes, his eyes were put out (though Anna Komnene claims it was against her father's orders). Alexios' reluctance to administer more severe punishment, often praised by Anna as proof of his essential good nature, may reflect an inner security of spirit by which, we are repeatedly assured, he placed his faith in God's will in tight situations. He was realist enough to know that an assassin's dagger could come from anywhere, at any moment, and rather than neurotically worry about it all the time and set up an elaborate security apparatus (which he would not be able to fully trust anyway), he just got on with the job and tried not to make too many enemies. The description of the tent meeting also confirms that the emperor continued to have the utmost faith in his mercenary Varangian Guard of northerners, who repaid that faith amply.

At about this time Bolkan decided that to continue defying the Romans was a losing proposition, and sent out peace feelers to Alexios, who gladly accepted them. The emperor was now in his mid-forties, and the constant campaigning and fending off conspiracies were taking their toll on him. He was relieved to be able to return to a spell of domestic life in Constantinople. There he had to involve himself, as was the fate of almost every Byzantine emperor, in the endless intellectual and ecclesiastical squabbles that every so often made the equivalent of headlines and roiled the marketplaces in that era, 'like a good helmsman guid[ing] his craft safely through the constant battering of the waves'.

He was able during these periods at home to attend to social issues, especially welfare for the poor and needy. Byzantium in this sphere was a veritable beacon of light for Europe. In a society that had no parliament or any means by which the public could press for improvements and rectify injustices, the task of social welfare in the big city depended on the goodwill of the emperor. Alexios, fortunately, had plenty of that. One of the highlights of his reign was the large orphanage and home for the blind which he set up next to a military hospital on the Golden Horn, large enough to care for some 7,000 people. The hospice at the Pantokrator monastery had separate rooms for patients, thick eiderdowns and heating for winter, and face and bath towels. No bed was allowed to remain empty. The patients were given a bath twice a week. Female doctors looked after the women in a separate ward. Each day inspectors would check the quality of the food and take note of any complaints. We are told that an ingenious machine cleaned the surgical instruments.

In the spring of 1095 Alexios was called out briefly to repel an incursion of the Cumans who were moving on Adrianople. The emperor occupied the city, but it took several months of hard fighting, in which Alexios again personally despatched some of the enemy, before the Cumans were decisively repulsed. And at that point, a more formidable, but not entirely unexpected, army appeared over the horizon.

During the years of Alexios' preoccupation with military threats from the north and west, and security threats from within his own ranks, relations with old Rome had been on the upturn. The great schism of 1054 between the Orthodox and what became the Roman Catholic Church was being smoothed over by diplomatic means. Pope Gregory VII, he who had backed Robert Guiscard in his eastern conquests, had never had much use for Constantinople, a sentiment that Alexios heartily reciprocated; but after the pope's death in 1087 his successor Urban II did much to repair the damaged relations, lifting his predecessor's excommunication of Alexios, who in return allowed the Latin churches in Constantinople to reopen and the pope's name to be read out again in church services. In 1095 the pope invited a Byzantine delegation to attend a conference in Piacenza, Italy. The Byzantines seem to have prepared their mission well, as they outlined to their hearers the sad state of Christendom in the east: the Muslim Seljuk Turks were now in possession of Anatolia; the holy city of Jerusalem, once under Roman control, was now in the hands of Saracen infidels; and—this was the clincher—if Europe had any intention of rescuing eastern Christendom from its unbelieving foes, now was the time to act, as the Seljuks were divided and weak. Urban was swayed by these arguments, and it was soon after the conference broke up that the idea germinated in his mind of a great holy war to rescue the east Mediterranean—a crusade.

By 27 November 1095, when Urban attended a church congress at Clermont (now Clermont-Ferrand), he had his plan ready. On that date, after some days of debating church issues, the great pronouncement was revealed. Before huge crowds in open fields, Urban got up from his papal throne set on a high platform, and set forth the Byzantine claims in high tones. Though no clear record of what the pope said has been kept, historians agree that he painted a lurid word-picture of Christians in the East being mistreated and their shrines smashed, of Jerusalem suffering under the Muslim yoke and yearning to be freed. We can trust the version given by Sir Steven Runciman, one of the greatest scholars of both Byzantium and the Crusades:

> Let western Christendom march to the rescue of the East. Rich and poor alike should go. They should leave off slaying each other and fight instead a righteous war, doing the work of God... For those that died in battle there would be absolution and the remission of sins. Life was miserable and evil here, with men wearing themselves out to the ruin of their bodies and their souls... There must be no delay. Let them be ready to set out when the summer had come, with God to be their guide.

'*Deus li volt!*' cried the crowds in a paroxysm, the opening trumpet-blast of the First Crusade.

But if the pope expected the Byzantines to be happy about the result of Clermont, he was mistaken. The last thing Alexios wanted was another foreign army, even if nominally friendly, trampling over his long-suffering domains. He had sent his mission to Piacenza to repair diplomatic relations with the Catholics, not trigger a new war in the Middle East. Besides, the apparent *naïveté* of the westerners disturbed him; if they wanted a crusade, all they had to do was ask the Byzantines, who had been fighting the Saracens on and off for centuries and had first claim on Jerusalem should it ever be ripe for reconquest. The pope's help might be full of good intentions, but the thought of Catholics in Jerusalem was a disturbing one. As news reached Alexios of the first Crusader citizen-armies making their way east, he set up guard posts along their expected route across the Balkan Peninsula to limit the inevitable damage they would cause.

The first reports were certainly ominous. Opening the First Crusade was a ragged and unwashed French monk known as Peter the Hermit, whose 20,000 largely peasant followers killed Jews in the German towns through which they passed like locusts, and thousands of people in the Hungarian town of Zemun that was unfortunate enough to be in their way. It was Belgrade's turn next, burned and pillaged; at Niš they were stopped by Niketas, the Byzantine governor, whose troops decimated them. The survivors and Peter the Hermit himself found their way to Constantinople, arriving on 1 August 1096. Alexios summoned Peter to the palace and was able to get a good look at the sorry figure and his even sorrier followers. The Byzantines soon got to know the campaigner as Cuckoo Peter, indicating they didn't think much of his mental condition. No one in Byzantium could seriously believe that the leaders of this crusade had any genuine Christian motives. 'The Latin race,' observed Anna Komnene, 'at all times is unusually greedy for wealth.' The bulk of Peter's ragtag force was encamped outside the capital busying itself with robbery, rape and murder. Many of the atrocities, it was noted, were carried out by Normans. There was only one thing to do, and that was to send Peter's mob on its way as soon as possible. Five days after its arrival, it was put in boats and ferried across the Bosporus to fend for itself.

In Constantinople it was put about that Cuckoo Peter was taking his revenge from mistreatment at Turkish hands during a previous pilgrimage to the Holy Land. Anna Komnene, who was 13 at the time, must have witnessed the appearance of the Frankish expedition and learned of its outcome. Peter and his force landed at Helenopolis, in the south shore of the Sea of Marmara, to be met by a fierce attack from the town's inhabitants, who had been told of alleged Norman atrocities such as 'babies impaled on spits and roasted over a fire'. Peter's Normans beat back the attack and went to seize another town, only to come up against a Turkish force whose leader employed a mixture of force and disinformation to defeat the Normans in battle and wreck the morale of the rest of the rabble. There followed a massacre of the Franks so complete that their bones piled up to a 'mountain of considerable height'. Peter managed to escape, rescued by a Byzantine ship, and was taken forlorn to Alexios, who uttered the equivalent of, 'I told you so.' Cuckoo Peter's response was to blame everyone else but himself.

Hardly had Constantinople breathed a sigh of relief when Alexios received a letter from the brother of King Philip I of France, Hugh of Vermandois, who took it on himself to follow Pope Urban II's call to fight for the Holy Land. The tone of Hugh's letter, as recorded by Anna Komnene, is revealing:

> Know, Emperor, that I am the King of Kings, the greatest of all beneath the heavens. It is fitting that I should be met on my arrival and received with the pomp and ceremony appropriate to my noble birth.

The first phrase, admittedly, strains credulity. Though the brother of a king, Hugh of Vermandois, assuming he was mentally sound, cannot seriously have viewed himself in the terms of an oriental despot. The second sentence, though, is credible in light of the haughtiness and arrogance that characterized the French knighthood, and it made a thoroughly bad impression on Alexios. Orders went out to John, the Dux of Dyrrachion, and Nicholas Katakalon, the fleet commander in the Adriatic, to keep a lookout for the envoys that were sure to come from Hugh. Twenty-four envoys duly turned up at Dyrrachion, resplendent in golden breast-plates, to suggest in no uncertain terms that the Byzantines should receive 'the supreme commander of the Frankish army' with the requisite pomp and ceremony.

Hugh of Vermandois did indeed land at Dyrrachion, but not in the way he expected. On the crossing from Bari a storm smacked into his ships, all of which went to the bottom except his own. He managed to stagger ashore not far from Dyrrachion and get some much-needed rest and nourishment with Dux John. Under careful guard, Hugh was then escorted overland to Constantinople, where—somewhat chastened by his recent ordeal, we might imagine—'the greatest of all beneath the heavens' willingly took the oath of allegiance to Alexios. Hugh of Vermandois was not the only highly-placed Frankish noble entertaining extravagant notions of crusading; close on his heels came Godfrey of Bouillon and his younger brother, Baldwin of Boulogne, at the head of a 60,000-strong force rather more sophisticated than that of Peter the Hermit. Their march through Europe had come off without incident, though when they arrived at Selymbria on the north shore of the Sea of Marmara they gave them-selves up to an orgy of pillage that was suppressed with some difficulty. Hugh went out from the Blachernai Palace to meet them and ask for their allegiance to the Byzantine emperor. Godfrey haughtily refused on the grounds that he had already sworn fealty to Holy Roman Emperor Henry IV. Distrust was also in the air, as the Crusaders widely suspected Alexios of having sabotaged Peter the Hermit's expedition.

The best-known of the chroniclers of the early Crusades, William of Tyre, wrote that the 'extreme wretchedness of the Greeks and the weakness of their empire' were what struck the Crusaders and fuelled their hostility. But as this phrase reeks of accumulated Frankish prejudice, it should not be taken as reflecting the reality of the time. To be sure, to French and German peasants who knew nothing of the finer things of life, and most of their nobles who cared even less, Byzantium could easily be seen as a den of corruption with a strange language and what the Crusaders' preachers called a schismatic religion. Anna Komnene may be rather closer to the mark when she shuns psychological or doctrinal excuses and simply and repeatedly damns the Franks as arrogant barbarians and leaves it at that.

Any semblance of an alliance between the Franks and the Byzantines evaporated as the former, seething with impatience, began pillaging the countryside north and west of the capital. Alexios was at first reluctant to take hostile measures against fellow Christians, but in the end he had no choice. The last straw was a demonstration of strength by Godfrey and Baldwin on the east side of the Golden Horn that convinced Alexios that these Frenchmen were about to take over the Empire. He was shocked by the fact that these supposed 'Christians' were being aggressive during Holy Week, when the Peace of God banning conflict was in force, and sent them a severe message to desist; if they did not, he warned, he would attack them after Easter Sunday. The reply to this message was a shower of arrows that penetrated even to the throne room of the Blachernai Palace, wounding a courtier.

Alexios sent for Nikephoros Bryennios, the officer to whom his daughter Anna was betrothed, with orders to assemble a force of archers who would make a sally out of Saint Romanos' Gate, approximately at the midpoint of the city wall, and fire at the Franks' horses; the soldiers as far as possible were to be spared according to the Peace of God. Anna Komnene says that the man who was to become her husband deliberately fired over the Franks' heads, but nonetheless they sustained heavy casualties. The issue was decided by Alexios, who sent in a few crack regiments to sweep the Franks off the field. Seeing that Alexios was no pushover, Godfrey and Baldwin very grudgingly gave him their allegiance.

Hugh of Vermandois had by now come round to accepting Alexios as the boss of Byzantium, but Godfrey seethed with knightly resentment, accusing Hugh of lowering himself 'to the level of a slave'. Hugh retorted with good sense that they should have 'stayed in our own countries and kept our hands off other people's'. But Godfrey retained a glimmer of hope in the knowledge that more First Crusaders were on the way and at hand; Alexios knew it too, and had to get Godfrey's mob out of the way as soon as possible. In the end it had to come to another fight, which the emperor's forces won at some cost. The defeat chastened Godfrey who, like Hugh before him, swore seemingly sincere fealty to Alexios in return for being wined and dined and handsomely paid.

The task of ferrying the distrustful Crusader armies across the Bosporus was fraught with difficulty. The incoming waves of men and camp followers seemed endless. The sheer number of them darkening the streets of Constantinople uttering their 'unpronounceable barbaric sounds' was disconcerting, to say the least. What we might today call ethnic racism was in full flower on both sides. The next Frankish noble to arrive was probably Robert of Flanders (or Normandy) with 15,000 more men, and Alexios sent a general, Opos, to get them into Asia before they could do much damage. Robert's proud Franks resisted, and Opos found himself on the receiving end of a fierce charge. At that moment another officer detailed to ferry the Franks across the Sea of Marmara came on the scene and attacked the Franks from the rear, effectively dousing their aggression and taming them enough to get them onto the boats without further incident.

The sheer effrontery of some of the Franks made itself felt in the palace one day when Alexios took the allegiance of their leaders. One French noble named as Latinos, apparently devoid of all ordinary respect, marched up to the unoccupied throne and sat himself on it. Alexios silently fumed, but decided not to create a scene that could easily have turned ugly. Instead, Godfrey's brother Baldwin took Latinos' hand and led him away muttering 'peasant' at the emperor. Alexios later sought out Latinos and asked him quite civilly why he had shown a lack of respect. The Frank's reply revealed him to be something of a thug at home, with a hobby of challenging others to single combat; he boasted that no one so far had dared take him on. 'Well,' said Alexios dryly, 'where you're going you'll get all the fighting you want. Just one piece of advice: stay in the centre, neither in the van nor the rear, for the Turks are wily fighters.'

Two weeks after Hugh of Vermandois appeared in the capital, an old enemy, and far more dangerous, showed his face. This was Bohemond, the son and virtual carbon copy of Robert Guiscard, who ever since his father's death twelve years before nursed a burning ambition to seize the throne Robert had coveted. Bohemond appeared to have thrown in his lot with the Crusaders, not, we may be assured, out of any religious sensitivities but the sheer desire for conquest. The First Crusade was simply a convenient vehicle for him. Nominally the Duke of Taranto, Bohemond had actually no holdings in Italy; his late father had bequeathed them to his stepson Roger Borsa, leaving Bohemond dangerously landless. He turned up in Constantinople on 9 April 1097 at the head of an army and enough noble relatives to populate a hoped-for new realm. Anna Komnene was frankly captivated by his appearance: 'almost a full cubit taller than other men ... of perfect proportions ... and carefully shaved so that his pink face looked smoother than marble.' After his initial audience with the emperor, Bohemond was so pathologically suspicious that he refused all food for fear that it might be poisoned and insisted on preparing his own. When his fears proved unfounded he grudgingly gave Alexios his allegiance which he had no intention of keeping, even when presented with a wealth of costly gifts.

For one Crusader leader, the emperor had great respect; this was Raymond of St Gilles. Raymond was the last to leave when the others had crossed the Bosporus into Asia. He had been detained by Alexios with some sound military advice: don't rush impetuously into battle against the Turks, who will more often than not lay traps for the unwary, and don't pursue the enemy too far and too fast. This was not warfare on the West European knightly model but a tougher proposition where rules of engagement in the West did not apply; the Turks were unscrupulous and crafty fighters, unrestrained by Frankish ideas of chivalry. The emperor also admitted to St Gilles his suspicion of Bohemond, and found that St Gilles completely agreed. 'I will always try to the best of my ability to observe your commands,' were the French knight's parting words to the emperor. Alexios, in fact, decided to go along, if only to make sure that the Crusaders didn't start carving their own states out of the Empire's flesh. If Nikaia was in his hands, he reckoned, it would be a form of insurance against that happening.

Nikaia was in the hands of the Seljuk Turks, but the Seljuk strongman, Kiliç Arslan, was too far away to be of any practical help. The defenders, however, took heart from a report that Kiliç Arslan was on his way to help them, joined battle with St Gilles' Crusaders and were routed. The Seljuk leader re-formed his forces on the plain outside Nikaia, but again was heavily defeated in a day-long bloodbath. St Gilles' men, in the gruesome custom of the time, stuck Turkish heads on spear points, 'carrying them like standards', to encourage friend and frighten foe. Kiliç Arslan advised the defenders to make what peace they could with the attackers, but apparently changed his mind shortly afterwards, as he was able to send supplies into the town. The Franks had built tall, circular siege towers covered in hides and appropriately called 'tortoises', manning them with assault troops to attack the walls while sappers undermined the walls from beneath. A main tower was thus severely damaged in this way, but the proverbially thick walls of Nikaia were another matter entirely.

Alexios, receiving regular reports of the Frankish siege of Nikaia, doubted whether the impulsive and impetuous Franks would manage to breach the walls; their impatience and lack of tactical consistency was already proverbial. He therefore sent other siege engines of his own design to supplement the Franks' 'tortoises' and despatched Manual Boutoumites with a force to gain control of the large Ascanian Lake (now İznik Gölü) to the west of the city, through which Kiliç Arslan were ferrying his supplies to the defenders. Boutoumites and Tatikios with a Frankish force met up and threw their men, plus volleys of arrows and catapult stones, at the walls. The Turkish defence was soon demoralized; Kiliç Arslan was neither seen nor heard from. The inhabitants of Nikaia surrendered to Boutoumites, who gave them generous terms, but there was still resistance on the walls.

The Franks, who we are told were kept ignorant of Boutoumites' achievement in order to keep up their combative spirit, renewed their attack on the walls while groups of leading Turkish officials were led out secretly and ferried across the lake to Alexios. There was a major snag as these Turks, seeing they could easily outnumber their captors, actually seized them in turn. They were about to send them to Kiliç Arslan when the Byzantines talked their way out of their predicament with the realistic argument that if the Turks continued with their plot they might easily by massacred by any Franks or Byzantines in the vicinity, whereas they would be better off surrendering to the emperor and enjoying the benefits he would surely shower on them for delivering Nikaia into his hands. On 19 June 1097 Boutoumites took the formal surrender of Nikaia.

Though Franks and Roman-Byzantines were on the same side, as long as both armies were adjacent to each other the possibility of a clash was always present. Alexios himself had crossed the Bosporus soon after Raymond St Gilles and had set up a vast royal tent at Pelekanos, on the Asian side (about where Karamürsel is today). Seated on a throne in this tent, he demanded afresh the allegiance of the Frankish leaders; all, attracted by the gold promised them, readily assented except one Tancred, a nephew of Bohemond, who flippantly said he would do likewise only if he was given enough money to fill the royal tent, and then some. George Paleologos, on hearing this, shoved Tancred away roughly, and a brawl would have developed then and there had not Alexios got up from his throne and stopped it. Urged on and soothed by Bohemond, a sullen Tancred took the oath. A day or so later, the crusading army set out on the long trek south-east to Antioch, accompanied by a Roman guard under Tatikios.

Considering what he had seen of the Franks, Alexios may well have nursed a hope that what was later to be called the First Crusade would come to grief. Though he respected their fighting qualities, he considered them militarily unsophisticated and easy meat for the wily Muslims. But Godfrey of Bouillon and Baldwin and all the others succeeded beyond expectations, trouncing a Seljuk army at Dorylaion (Kütahya); in that engagement Latinos, the insolent knight who had sat on Alexios' throne, was wounded. A year later, in the summer of 1098, the Crusaders took Antioch. (As for Bohemond, he was captured by the fierce Danishmend Turks and chained in a tower for three years until ransomed by Baldwin.) After a serious setback at Ramleh, the crusade achieved its ultimate aim on 15 July 1099 when the Franks burst into Jerusalem and waded into a fearful massacre of Muslims and Jews that has conditioned Muslim attitudes to the West to this day. Baldwin became Baldwin I of Jerusalem, inaugurating a 192-year Latin occupation of Palestine and Syria that did little, if anything, to enhance the reputation of Christendom in that part of the world.

While the Crusaders were occupied in trying to take Antioch the emperor wanted to help them but couldn't risk an expedition so far overland when there were plenty of Turkish enemies closer at hand, such as along the east Aegean coast and on large islands such as Chios and Rhodes. Anna Komnene informs us that her father did ride as far as Antioch but, seeing that the weight of enemy opposition was considerable and having little faith in the Franks' powers of endurance, decided to return to Constantinople with as much of Antioch's Christian population as was willing to go with him. This withdrawal of the emperor has been a source of dispute ever since. Until recently western historiography, informed by Crusader sources, painted Alexios as implicitly deceitful or worse, for not making more of an effort at Antioch, and for being absent at the triumphal moment when the Crusaders, heartened by the alleged discovery of the Holy Lance that had pierced Christ's side, seized the city in a grand assault. Anna Komene takes pains to exonerate her father from this charge, claiming that with so many Seljuk potential foes between him and the capital, plus the ever-present threat of being deposed by some rival for the throne, made it unwise for Alexios to stay in the Antioch theatre for too long. In historical terms, the jury is still out.

Alexios must have been still pondering the strategic implications of a rival Christian state operating out of Jerusalem when in 1101 four more Crusader armies materialized out of the West, expecting to receive rest and recreation in Constantinople. Alexios advised them to take the longer but safer coastal route to get to Palestine rather than attempt the straight overland route through the Turk-ridden heights of Anatolia. But the expedition's leaders thought they knew better—either that, or they distrusted the emperor's advice—and got as far as Ankyra (now Ankara), which they took on 23 June. From there on, however, the troubles began. The summer heat was unbearable, made even more so by the fact that the Turks had poisoned all the wells and were burning crops. At one place some local Christian clergy had come out, 'in their sacred vestments and carrying the gospel and crosses,' to naively greet and help the Crusaders. They and their flock were thanked by being promptly massacred. Retribution soon came at the hands of the Turks, who fell on the Crusaders at Amaseia (Amasya) and routed them. Their women and children were carried off as slaves. A lucky few nobles with horses managed to make it to Jerusalem, but Hugh of Vermandois died of wounds sustained in a clash near Herakleia.

By 1103 Alexios was still feeling no securer. Part of him wanted to encourage the Frankish kingdom to do its part towards keeping the Turks away from the Empire; but could he trust the Franks themselves? It was a dilemma from which he never managed to free himself. Moreover, Bohemond was free again. As the area around Antioch was still shaky, he sent Boutoumites with a picked force of Byzantines and Kelts (some probably from the Varangian Guard) to clear Kilikia in what is now south-east Turkey. Since ancient times Kilikia had been the gateway to Palestine and the Middle East and anyone holding the latter had to have the former. Almost at once Boutoumites had problems with Bardas and Michael, two young nobles barely out of their teens and prone to the arrogance that had been bred in them as privileged protégés of the emperor's household. They were also used as imperial commissars of sorts, tasked with informing the emperor on what was happening in the army through secret messages. But young Bardas and Michael appear to have exceeded their authority, triggering resentment among the troops, with the result that Boutoumites demanded their recall. The pair were transferred to Cyprus.

The Crusaders' difficulties in Anatolia gave Alexios and the Byzantine Empire a breathing space in which to recover territory in Kilikia, as we have seen, and down the north Syrian coast. The Muslims were harassing the Kingdom of Jerusalem, diverting energy that might otherwise have been used against Byzantium. But Bohemond, ever the energetic activist in his drive to eliminate the Byzantine Greeks, crossed to Italy in early 1105 for reinforcements. Anna Komnene, retelling a tale that must have been common currency in the capital, says that Bohemond, disguised as a corpse, was smuggled over the sea in a ventilated coffin together with a dead rooster to provide a convincing stench, but most authorities discount it. Once in Italy Bohemond stayed eight months raising volunteers and talking Pope Paschal II into believing that Alexios I Komnenos was a worse foe than the Muslims. It was a wake-up call for Byzantium. Writes Lord Norwich:

> The entire Crusade was now revealed as having been nothing more than a monstrous exercise in hypocrisy, in which the religious motive had been used merely as the thinnest of disguises for what was in fact unashamed imperialism.

In the autumn of 1107 Bohemond was poised to launch his new papal-blessed fleet across the Adriatic to seize Dyrrachion, that old objective of his father's, preparatory to marching over the Via Egnatia to seize Constantinople from the 'schismatic Greeks'. The Holy Land was forgotten. The mask was off.

The Dux of Corfu, Alexios Komnenos, nephew and namesake of the emperor, had received intelligence of the plan as early as the spring of 1105 and passed it on to the emperor. At about this time, according to Anna Komnene (whose timescale accuracy here is not to be trusted), Alexios appealed to the Fatimid caliph of Egypt, al-Afdal, to free scores of high-ranking Frankish knights who had been captured and kept in stinking dungeons in conditions of near-starvation. The caliph obliged, and the knights found themselves in Constantinople and free to go home—and hopefully counter Bohemond's propaganda that Alexios was a pagan. Alexios himself felt he could not remain in the capital while another Norman threat was gathering, and rode west to Thesssalonike to see to the defences and raise new levies. Generals Monastras and Kantakouzenos were recalled from Kilikia and Syria, though at the cost of losing some Kilikian towns to Tancred, Bohemond's bumptious nephew who was proving to be a formidable warrior.

Alexios, in this as in other campaigns, was careful to take his wife Irene Doukaina with him. Described by her daughter as a retiring and saintly character, ill at ease in public and a model consort in every respect, Irene was nonetheless a quiet pillar of strength to Alexios. He was barely 50 but rapidly passing his prime, and in constant severe pain from gout. His wife's care was probably more effective than that of his doctors. Irene served also as a second mother in a way, as she was a valuable pair of eyes and ears in view of the plots and conspiracies that Anna assures us were being constantly hatched. She is reported to have policed the imperial kitchen to make sure that no poison would enter her husband's mouth. She did not like roughing it on campaign, preferring the comfort and safety of the palace, but appeared not to complain, and rode in a plain litter drawn by two mules so as not to attract attention. Her daughter describes how she managed in the wilds of the Balkans:

> [W]hen she arrived at the tent set apart for her and went inside, it was not to lie down at once and rest, but to open it up and all the mendicants were allowed access. To such persons she was very approachable and showed herself ready to be both seen and heard. Nor was it money alone that she dispensed to the poor; she also dispensed excellent advice... this empress could be seen every day mixing her pity for others with food and drink.

If Anna Komnene's portrait of her mother is largely authentic (and there is no reason not to consider it so), it is that of the classic military wife, the consort whose family duty has become conflated and identified with her husband's duty to country and faith. His hardships, physical and mental, are her own; her morals are unimpeachable if rigid, and though she pities and helps the poor she urges them, if they are able, to get jobs and give themselves some of the dignity that she takes for granted in her own upper military caste. It's a lesson that could well be relearned in our own time.

While the army and nobles were assembling at Thessalonike a comet appeared and stayed in the sky for more than a month, unnerving everyone. Though the emperor was sceptical of any supernatural explanation, he consulted one of his experts; this man, finding himself at a loss to explain the phenomenon after tiresome astrological calculations, is said to have dreamed of Saint John the Evangelist, who told him the comet heralded the coming of the Franks. It was not exactly news to the army, but this imperial astrologer had to explain the comet somehow, and this would have seemed the most convenient way. But Bohemond had still not appeared over the Adriatic horizon, so Alexios and the army moved on westwards to Dalmatia, where he remained for a year and a half pacifying Dalmatia before moving back to the capital at the beginning of winter 1107.

It was soon afterwards that the Anthelion statue in the Forum of Constantine was blown down, filling the superstitious with dark thoughts, followed by the plot of Michael Anemas and his brothers. We have seen, at the start of the first chapter, how young Anna Komnene was so impressed by Anemas' bearing in chains that she successfully lobbied her parents to be lenient with him, merely jailing him instead of blinding or beheading him. Then there was Gregory Gabras, the young man who found life in the palace too restrictive and escaped with his father, and now headed a serious revolt around Trebizond. As there were increasing signs that Gregory was not quite sane, Alexios sent his nephew John to bring him to Constantinople by force. The emperor's first impulse was to have Gregory's eyes removed by the standard method, but John talked him out of it and Gregory was imprisoned in the same tower where Anemas lan-guished. By now Gregory appears to have been quite mentally unbalanced and to be sliding into a severe depression that rendered him, in the emperor's view, quite harmless, so he was eventually released and compensated with honours and gifts.

Anna Kommene does not go into the possible root causes of all these conspiracies against her father except to assume that they were triggered by mere aristocratic jealousy. There were surely other causes. Alexios' militarization of public life and centralization of power deprived many proud local warlords of their own feudal powers. Despite the efforts of eight centuries of Roman-Byzantine emperors, these provincial fiefdoms retained a fierce independence that at times only paid lip and manpower service to the throne. The Komnenes had also been one of these houses, which made Alexios' ascent to absolute power intolerable for many. Add to this the administrative camarilla that any emperor inevitably had to employ to do the state work, and the possibility for serious grudges was endless. There were also domestic economic reasons for discontent, such as taxation and inflation. It was no doubt one reason why Alexios was generally lenient to those who crossed him, knowing that needless severity would only worsen the threats.

In the west, Isaac Kontostephanos, the newly-appointed Megadux of the Fleet, had already sailed across the Otranto Strait and laid siege to the Italian coastal town of the same name, hoping to forestall Bohemond's move. Kontostephanos took the town, but didn't figure on the resourceful woman who headed the negotiations with the Byzantine admiral. We are not given her name; Anna Komnene passes on a rumour, never verified, that she was Tancred's mother (which might make her Bohemond's sister). She stalled for time, enabling a Frankish force to come up and defeat the Byzantines. Bohemond took six Pecheneg prisoners with him to Rome where he made his case before the pope. A chastened Kontostephanos sailed back to Dyrrachion, where he braced for Bohemond's onslaught, ordering Landulph, his fleet commander, to keep patrolling the coast.

Intelligence in the Roman camp seems to have been good, as there was no lack of informants crossing the Adriatic, including traders and perhaps a soldier of fortune or two, who could brief Kontostephanos on the state of Bohemond's preparations. When invasion seemed imminent, a frisson of apprehension ran through the army. By now Bohemond had become, like his father before him, something more than human. He was rumoured to be indestructible, a veritable malign superman. Many an ordinary Byzantine soldier quaked in his boots at the thought of measuring swords with this man and his fierce Frenchmen. Suddenly many soldiers decided they were unwell and needed some leave to go to the healing baths at Chimara (now the Albanian town of Himarë) a short sail to the north. Landulph frowned and kept his own crews where they were.

On 9 or 10 October Landulph duly spotted Bohemond's invasion force bearing down, and a formidable sight it was: hundreds of oars raised up great sprays of water over which the shapes of large transports loomed, a southerly breeze filling their sails all along the horizon. The fleet was probably made to look and sound bigger than it actually was, but Landulph figured that there was no way of prevailing against it head-on, so he moved smartly out from the approaches to Avlona. Bohemond's Franks, Kelts, Germans and Iberians, plus one English contingent that would normally have been fighting for the emperor but probably found itself dragooned by Bohemond, hit the shore and began to lay waste the country. The main target, of course, was Dyrrachion, the gateway to the Balkans, the necessary first objective for anyone to advance over the Via Egnatia to Constantinople.

The Byzantines were positioned at Elissos, a naturally strong defensive height some miles to the north-east. The nearby Drymon River gave them access to fresh water and supplies. Alexios heard of Bohemond's landing as he was returning to the palace from a hunting trip. A courier ran in, prostrated himself, and delivered the news in dramatic tones. If we are to believe Anna, while everyone reeled with shock and awe, the emperor continued calmly to loosen his leather shoe-straps. 'For the moment let's have lunch,' he said with a studied casualness that he did not feel. 'We'll attend to Bohemond later.' It was clearly time to set off again. Irene grumbled, but her husband insisted she go along as usual.

Alexios sent messages to Kontostephanos instructing him to keep the Adriatic clear of any reinforcements that might be on their way to Bohemond. At the Evros River a bored Irene wanted to go home, but Alexios would not hear of it. It was lucky for him, as it was Irene's solicitous presence at night that thwarted an assassination plot that was in its advanced stages. The plotters, frustrated, vented their spleen by slipping scurrilous notes into the emperor's tent at night—one wonders how efficient or otherwise his personal guard was—with warnings to Irene to leave, so that her husband could be vulnerable. The writers were detected and severely tortured. But the menacing messages didn't stop. One day after lunch Alexios found one right under his couch; whoever wrote it must be close by, he figured, perhaps even in the very tent. The note read at the end: 'I, the monk, write this. For the moment, Emperor, you do not know me, but you will see me in your dreams.'

The identity of this sinister 'monk' was soon revealed, and then purely by chance. One night when almost everyone was asleep, a senior courtier of Irene's was awake, having just said a prayer, when he overheard a voice in a nearby tent, raised as if in argument, and threatening an unseen hearer to 'tell him everything about your plans and denounce the letters that you keep on throwing at him'. It must have been clear to the courtier that 'him' referred to the emperor, and forthwith sent a servant to see who the speaker was and bring him out. It turned out to be Strategios, a servant of a senior officer named Aaron, of half-Bulgarian origin. Strategios promptly spilled all he knew and was led straight into the imperial sleeping quarters, where Alexios was woken up to personally listen to Strategios' account fingering Aaron as the brains of the conspiracy and a Pecheneg slave who was to be the hit man.

Alexios knew enough about human psychology not to automatically accept Strategios' story at face value; for all he knew, Strategios could be inventing the whole thing as a personal vendetta against his master Aaron. But Strategios insisted he was telling the truth. A senior eunuch was deputed to escort him to Aaron's tent to seize evidence. By that hour Aaron was asleep; a search of his quarters turned up a soldier's pouch that was found to contain a host of scurrilous messages of the kind Alexios had been receiving. Dawn was breaking when the evidence was presented to the emperor, who lost no time in exiling Aaron. Alexios could finally strike camp and continue on to Thessalonike, delayed for five days by the hunt for the mystery poison-pen wielder.

The reader at this point may justifiably wonder at the apparent amateurishness of these plots against Alexios, especially the Aaron plot. Would not the emperor, by now the veteran of countless life-threatening situations on and off the battlefield, have put in place an effective personal security apparatus? Was this man whose immense talents were spent in essentially militarizing the Roman-Byzantine administration really so careless of his own safety and that of the royal family? It certainly appears so through the vivid pages of his daughter, who attributes Alexios' lack of security-consciousness to a rock-solid faith in God and a conviction that whatever happened or did not happen to him would be God's will, period. He was thus able to sleep soundly with the minimum of protection, whatever the shadowy threat hanging over him. But Anna was not too far off the mark when she wrote, long after the events:

> Of all the emperors who preceded [Alexios], right down to the present
> day, not one had to grapple with affairs so complicated, with the wicked-
> ness of men, at home and abroad, of so many types as we have seen in the
> lifetime of this sovereign.

Yet that assertion also hides a good deal. The whole truth was probably a good deal
murkier. We know from other chroniclers of the period such as Niketas Choniates
that relationships within the emperor's immediate family were not of the best;
indeed, they were positively poisonous. Anna was doing a slow burn, as we shall
see later, over her father's obvious grooming of her little brother John for the succession. Backing her to the hilt was Irene, who did not exactly regard her husband as a saint; the two women are reported to have tried to put the skids under
Alexios wherever possible. Would that have been to the point of fomenting open
conspiracy? Probably not. Anna was too devoted to her father to wish him any
real harm. But to fulfil her dreams of ruling alongside her husband Nikephoros
Bryennios she had to derail John's prospects, and to do that she needed to diminish
her father's political influence. And what was Alexios' desire to have his wife close
by him on campaign, say Anna's critics, if not get her away from the vipers' nest of
intrigue in Constantinople?

Alexios managed the war from Thessalonike, from where he could oversee
the defence of the Balkan passes through which Bohemond would have to come.
Recruits flocked to his banner. As 'emperor, general and instructor,' he had them
trained and drilled and honed to sharp competence, promoting 300 of the most
promising men in their late teens and early twenties to officer rank; the cream of
these were appointed battalion commanders and sent to guard the passes. The
defence of Dyrrachion was left to his nephew and namesake, Dux Alexios, who
put up a strong resistance to the Norman-Frankish depredations. Bohemond had
ordered his ships destroyed, ostensibly to give his soldiers no choice but to keep
moving forward, but also to keep the vessels from being sunk by Landulph. By
the spring of 1108 he had built some formidable siege engines, but in his fury and
haste had typically neglected the finer points of warfare, such as logistics and provisions, of which the Byzantines were masters. Dux Alexios' stranglehold on food
and water supplies told on the besiegers, who began to starve to death, first the
horses and then the men. Then dysentery struck, decimating the army yet further.

Bohemond, however, was not to be beaten by these misfortunes. He ordered
a massive battering ram to be built and employed it against the stout wall of
Dyrrachion. But instead of butting a hole in the masonry, the ram merely
rebounded after each hit. The defenders on the walls, beefed up by a contingent
of Seljuk Turks sent by Sultan Malikshah, laughed at that, and according to Anna
mockingly opened the gates with the words: 'You'll never make a hole with that

thing, so why not just come in through here?' It testifies to the demoralization caused by famine and disease that the Franks were unnerved at this and abandoned their ram to be burned by the defenders. Even now Bohemond refused to give up but sent sappers to tunnel under the north part of the wall, where the soil was softer. But the Byzantines cottoned on to that, too, digging a counter-tunnel that intercepted Bohemond's and squirting the feared Greek Fire into the attackers' faces. Attempt number two thus came to grief.

Bohemond's third attempt came in the form of a siege tower so big that it appeared to the defenders like 'a giant moving above the clouds'. It must have been many dozens of feet high, able to telescope upwards by the use of levers, and topped by a drawbridge-type platform from which the attacking force could swarm over the wall. The defenders were no less ingenious, setting up a framework tower just as tall as the one outside the wall. From the top platform they launched jets of Greek Fire at the Franks' tower, but the fireballs fell short. The defenders then filled the distance between the opposing towers with combustible material that was set alight and reinforced by judiciously-applied doses of the Fire. Many Franks perished in the blazing tower, either consumed in the undousable flames or hurling themselves off it in panic. So much for the third attempt.

Alexios the emperor now turned up to take matters in hand. As he appeared to be safe for the time being, Irene had returned to Constantinople. He encamped at Diabolis (probably near Tirana, the present-day capital of Albania) in the mountains, some distance from the coast. Knowing Bohemond's persistence, he decided to use guile instead of sheer force to bring the Norman to heel. He assigned a senior Frank in his service named Roger, Peter Aliphas and Marinos Neapolites (as his name suggests, a native of Neapolis, or Naples today) the secret task of spreading disinformation among the Frankish ranks and undermining morale. Their weapons were a series of carefully-forged letters purporting to be from the emperor to some of Bohemond's key commanders. These letters said, totally fictitiously, that those commanders had contacted him expressing dissatisfaction with their leader and that he warmly thanked them for their consideration, offering rich rewards if they would defect to him. Each letter was personally delivered to its recipient by special messenger. That was just half of the scheme. Ahead of the messengers Alexios sent an unnamed soldier whose orders were to pretend to be a deserter and, when brought before Bohemond, reveal the commanders' supposed treachery. The unsophisticated Norman leader fell for this ruse, had Alexios' messengers detained, and opened their messages. He almost swooned at what he read. But we are told that after six days sulking in his tent he decided, or was told, that the letters were faked, and dismissed the matter.

The Franks launched frantic attacks on the Byzantine mountain outposts, which sustained considerable casualties. Alexios sent his General Kantakouzenos, a veteran of the wars against the Cumans, to stem the Frankish advances. His attempt to seize the castle of Mylos was repulsed, and he staved off mass panic only by ordering his men to burn their siege engines before they ran. An attempt by Kantakouzenos to hold the line at the Charzanes River looked at first like it would be another disaster, but he and his second-in-command, Rosmikes, rallied the troops in a spirited counter-attack that smashed the Frankish formation. Among the high-level prisoners taken, along with a variety of Frankish heads on spears as trophies, was Hugh de Pol, who had marched to Jerusalem with the First Crusade nine years before.

Kantakouzenos won the next encounter at the Bouses River, killing more of the enemy and sending more nobles to the emperor in chains. One of them was a mountain of a man, Bohemond's second cousin. For a laugh, Kantakouzenos sent off the gigantic Frank to the emperor under the guard of a diminutive Pecheneg soldier.

> When the sovereign heard that they had arrived [Anna writes], he took his seat on the imperial throne and commanded the prisoners to be brought in. In came the [Pecheneg] leading this tremendous Kelt on a chain, barely as tall as his waist. Of course there was an instant outburst of laughter from all.

The mirth was short-lived, however, as news arrived of more Roman reverses in those inhospitable mountains of what is now Albania. Then a message arrived from Landulph, keeping watch on the coast; Kontostephanos, he said, was being negligent in guarding the Otranto Strait. His so-called blockade was full of holes, with the result that Bohemond's forces were receiving plenty of reinforcements and supplies by sea. Alexios fumed, but could do little except send Kontostephanos written lessons and diagrams on naval tactics; in the end, Kontostephanos was sacked and replaced by Neapolites, who put an end to the illicit commerce.

But the emperor's army was by no means united in spirit. Anna hints at 'would-be deserters' who had to be thwarted from going over to the enemy. The reasons for this are unclear, though Anna's own underground efforts to reduce her father's clout probably had something to do with it. Could it reflect possible defects in Alexios' leadership? We have no way of knowing. No leader, of course, is ever perfect, and Alexios' constant preoccupations and painful gout may well have led him at times to rub some men the wrong way. We must also remember that the Byzantine-Roman army was not a national army in the modern sense, owing allegiance to a flag and nation. There were many disparate elements in Alexios' ranks united only—and often very shakily—by nominal allegiance to the emperor's standard. Many units saw the emperor as a mere paymaster rather than a figure to revere for his own sake. If after a string of imperial defeats Bohemond was rumoured, rightly or wrongly, to pay more, and seen to be on the 'winning side', then many imperial soldiers were quite prepared to switch sides at any moment. The compulsory military service was also greatly resented by men forced to leave their farms and harvests. By the same token, it says much for Alexios' leadership qualities that the great mass of the Byzantine army, not to mention the allied Seljuk Turkish units, remained faithful to him throughout.

Neapolites' effective blockade stopped provisions from reaching Bohemond by sea, forcing him to send more foraging parties inland, where they came under attack by Byzantine patrols and lost many men and horses. Bohemond himself appears to have realized the increasing hopelessness of his situation, made worse by renewed hunger and more disease. When Count William Claret, a Frankish noble, deserted to the imperial army with fifty horses, Alexios generously plied him with gifts and gave him senior *nobilissimus* rank. Word came from Dux Alexios in Dyrrachion that Bohemond was putting out peace feelers. The emperor decided to accept, concerned that if the war was prolonged, some of his own officers might turn against him. But could he trust the duplicitous Norman warlord? He penned a cautious message to Bohemond that read in part:

> You know perfectly well how many times I have been deceived through trusting your oaths and promises... But it is better to be deceived than to offend God and transgress His holy laws. I do not therefore reject your plea. If you do in truth desire peace, if you do indeed abominate the impossible and absurd thing you have attempted, and if you no longer take pleasure in shedding the blood of Christians... then come in person with as many companions as you like.

But Bohemond, too, was suspicious and demanded hostages from the emperor as a guarantee of sincerity. One of these was Neapolites, who met Bohemond and his entourage outside the latter's camp. Neapolites gave the Norman the emperor's assurance that any of his men who wished to go on to the Holy Sepulchre would enjoy a safe conduct through Byzantine territory. After a day or so of difficult negotiations Bohemond agreed to visit the emperor; he was escorted to Diabolis by Constantine Euphorbenos Katakalon. Alexios greeted Bohemond cordially and seated him near the tent throne. After some introductory small talk Bohemond balked when Alexios demanded that he become an imperial subject and that he tell his nephew Tancred to hand back Antioch. The talk was getting nowhere fast, so Alexios loudly called for the horses to take Bohemond back to Dyrrachion—a signal that he was breaking off the negotiations. Bohemond sulked a while in his own tent, until persuaded by Anna's husband Nikephoros Bryennios to relent and accept the emperor's terms. It was the badly weakened state of the Frankish army rather than Alexios' cordiality that made up his mind.

The resulting Treaty of Diabolis (or Devol), as it is called, was a signal diplomatic success for Alexios and quite remarkable for the circumstances. It shelved past grievances by both sides and removed at a single stroke the western menace to Byzantium. Bohemond formally pledged (the state of his forces must have been parlous indeed) to serve and defend the emperor at all times. Some of the terms, as recorded by Anna, sound melodramatic to us:

> I [Bohemond] shall be, from this moment, the loyal man of Your Majesty... I undertake to arm my right hand against all who oppose your power... and I will be your liegeman, sincere and true, as long as I breathe and am numbered among the living... And if there should be any ill-disposed to your power, unless they be the like of the immortal angels, impervious to wounds inflicted by our weapons or endowed with bodies hard as steel, I will fight them all for Your Majesties... To guard your life I shall be under arms, like a statue hammered out of iron.

There were several pages in much the same exaggerated strain, which most likely reflected formal diplomatic usage that was not to be interpreted too literally. This could explain why the ordinarily indomitable Bohemond signed the treaty without reservation, almost abjectly. Certainly the sweeteners in the deal—that Bohemond would be amply compensated and allowed to carve out a feudal domain of his own in and around Antioch—made it easier for him to accept. But was he, even now, sincere? No one could be sure. But the question soon became academic. After signing the treaty he sailed back to Italy. He must have been either ill or broken in spirit, for he died not long afterwards, either in 1109 or 1111. As for Alexios, his military and diplomatic triumph was complete.

Chapter 10

A fighter to the end

The Treaty of Devol that Bohemond signed contained an interesting clause inserted among its flowery terms: he had to pledge loyalty to Alexios' son, 'the much-loved Emperor Lord John'. This could be the first time the name of Alexios' firstborn appears in a recorded history, and it was added to ensure that the terms would not expire with Alexios. In his father's campaigns John had stayed in the palace holding the fort, as it were. Later, however, when they were old enough, Anna and John accompanied their father on some expeditions—'we did not,' she stresses, 'lead a pampered and sheltered existence.' Alexios doubtless wished to toughen up the two children who would become his heirs, to accustom them to difficulty and hardship.

At the time when Alexios gained a military and diplomatic breathing space with the Treaty of Devol, John was 22 and making it quite plain that he was next in line for the throne. That was precisely why Anna never had much use for him—we recall her upturned-nose reaction to the birth of her 'dark-complexioned' sibling—and neglected no opportunity to denigrate him. John Zonaras, another historian of the time, takes a wider view, regarding the whole extended royal family as a self-serving clique, where favourites such as Anna's husband Bryennios were given large estates at public expense. Nepotism certainly was practised on a wide scale, but given Alexios' fluctuating popularity and constant insecurity, it seemed justifiable in that way to preserve the dynasty that was expected to continue unbroken with John.

But domestic discontent simmered, and one main reason was the unstable state of the Byzantine economy. Alexios' constant campaigning had made huge demands on the treasury, which in turn taxed the people heavily. The nobility and the monasteries bore the brunt of the taxation, providing plenty of upper-class motivation for the conspiracies that seemed to sprout like mushrooms after a rain. The result was a debasement of the currency and inflation that fuelled economic chaos until 1109, when Alexios established the gold *hyperpyron* (super-refined coin) that stabilized exchange rates and enabled commerce to continue. A clergyman wrote to Dux John in Dyrrachion that many of his flock had left their homes to live rough in the woods in order to escape crushing taxation and compulsory military service: 'In the church the people no longer sing, the candles remain unlit.' Conditions were similar all over the Empire. Whatever popularity Alexios had earned in his active and heroic youth, by his mid-fifties was evaporating fast.

Though the Treaty of Devol had put paid to the threat of Bohemond, Tancred was breathing defiance down in Antioch. Moreover, the Turks had resumed their raids on Attaleia. The emperor despatched Eumathios Philokales, a man of no military training but otherwise competent enough, to pacify the restive regions in west Anatolia, from Smyrna to Philadelphia (near present-day Sarayköy in Turkey). He did this with rather more severity than was warranted; Anna reports that he ordered new-born Turkish babies boiled alive. Militarily, Philokales (whose name, ironically, means lover of good) the non-soldier, succeeded in his task, eliminating Turkish pockets between Philadelphia and the coast.

But Tancred was another matter; Alexios could not quite decide whether to cultivate him as a fellow Christian fighter against the Turks or to bring him to heel as a clear violator of the treaty his uncle had put his name to. In late 1111 he sent envoys to Tancred with a list of complaints, the chief of which was Tancred's perceived treacherous contempt of the emperor's orders. According to Anna's account, Tancred, the 'barbarian lunatic', flew into a rage and roared his defiance of Alexios and the whole world; he would hold on to Antioch 'even if his adversaries came with hands of fire', and dismissed 'all Romans' as 'nothing more than ants, the feeblest of living things'. It was a fine act, but when it was reported to Alexios he decided he'd had quite enough of this mad Norman; he wanted to make straight for Antioch to put him in his place, but the Senate advised against hasty action. Better, the senators said, to first sound out the other Frankish potentates in the region, including King Baldwin I of Jerusalem, to see if they could be enrolled in the effort.

Manuel Boutoumites was detailed to head the mission, which took along bags of money to meet the expected bribery requirements. Philokales, who for his successful Anatolian campaign had been rewarded with the governorship of Cyprus, provided a dozen ships for transport. Landing at Tripoli, Boutoumites gained (or more accurately bought) the support of Bertrand of St Gilles, the son of the Raymond of St Gilles who had helped Alexios handle the first waves of Crusaders. Baldwin, as soon as he heard that Byzantine gold was being handed around, invited the envoys south. At the time, he was in the process of besieging Muslim-held Tyre, but was soon routed and retreated as far as Acre, where Boutoumites met him. The meeting did not go well, as the Byzantine envoy naively tried to fool Baldwin into thinking Alexios himself was on the march which Baldwin, thanks to his own intelligence, knew to be untrue. Boutoumites was persuaded to accompany the king to Jerusalem. There Baldwin asked for money but Boutoumites, probably suspecting that the king was secretly sympathetic to Tancred, delayed handing it over.

With negotiations at a stalemate, Boutoumites returned to Tyre, to find that Bertrand of St Gilles had died and his successors refused to hand back the money deposited there. Cajolery and threats proved unavailing, and thus some bribery had to be resorted to, after which Boutoumites was able to regain the gold but return empty-handed to Constantinople. This diplomatic failure of Alexios' came on the heels of bad news from Philadelphia, where Sultan Malikshah of Ikonion (Konya) was raiding as far as the coast. The emperor donned his armour once more and sailed across the Sea of Marmara where he set up a headquarters, issuing instructions to his military governors. He must have made the move reluctantly as, apart from his ill health, he was receiving dismal reports from the West: the Italian maritime states of Genoa, Pisa and probably Venice were flexing naval muscle in the Aegean Sea at the expense of Byzantine rule.

For the next five years Alexios fended off one threat after another, from both east and west, with a mixture of force and diplomatic bribery. It is something of a miracle that he managed it, beset as he was by problems of a domestic, political and religious nature. Whenever he could he tried to reconcile the eastern and western churches, but he stoutly refused to abandon his basic Orthodox position, and thus failed to come to any agreement with Pope Paschal II. After hearing of Bohemond's death he nursed hopes of clawing back south Italy, but papal opposition thwarted that plan. The Italian naval states were also an issue, as he needed them for aid against the Turks but distrusted their own expansionist aims. He was able to deal with them by awarding the Pisans a trading colony in Constantinople, reserving seats for their top traders at the Hippodrome and in Sancta Sophia.

At home in the palace, Alexios made himself readily available to anyone, high or low, who wished to speak to him. This especially applied to the Franks in the city, who had to be placated in case their arrogance morphed into a real security threat. He would take his seat on the throne at daybreak and listen to these 'brazen-faced, violent men, money-grubbers' who seemed to have no sense of decorum. Such sessions might last all day, during which, Anna tells us, her father never lost his patience at their effrontery, and always gave measured replies. Night brought little respite. As we have seen, Alexios was blessed with the ability to require remarkably little sleep; through most of the night, despite his debilitating gout, he would analyse the issues and formulate policy as his aides and attendants dozed and nodded off and grumbled, or slipped off somewhere to snatch a little nap. After the briefest of rests he would be on his feet again at sunrise, ready to plough through another exhausting day. Small wonder, one feels, that he was often eager to escape the palace life by going on campaign.

This heavy schedule worsened his gout. When he talked about it, which was not often, his attitude was that it was divine punishment for his sins. Anna implicitly blames the stress of dealing with difficult people for aggravating the malady. In fact, in the summer of 1112 Alexios' condition became more serious than his daughter admits, and he was bedridden for weeks. It was during a painful interlude at his camp at Damalis, sometime in 1113, when Irene was tending his foot and sweetening his drinks with honey, that word arrived of a Turkish attack on Nikaia. Ignoring his pain, Alexios took up a whip and climbed into a chariot—he was now too crippled to ride a horse—flanked by columns of cheering, spear-wielding soldiers. The route he took is unknown; we are told the ride took him three days, after which he reached Kibotos in the Gulf of Nikaia, which means he must have gone along the south shore of the Sea of Marmara. Once there he messaged the defender of Nikaia, Eustathios Kamytzes, and his 500 men to avoid any engagement if possible while monitoring the enemy's moves.

Kamytzes either misunderstood the emperor or thought he knew better. Against orders he attacked the Seljuks who at first were driven back, but he bungled the rest of the operation badly. The Seljuks regrouped and attacked in force, briefly capturing Kamytzes, who was wounded in the legs but managed to escape to the emperor's camp on a borrowed horse. Going on to Constantinople, Kamytzes received a warm welcome from Irene and the courtiers, and then, still wearing his stained Turkish-style campaign apparel, rode to the Forum of Constantine with full military escort. There he regaled the crowds with none-too-accurate reports of Roman victories, but reassured them that the emperor was well and still in control of events. A few days later Alexios himself returned, his head crowned with a laurel wreath, to the public acclamation that Kamytzes had prepared for him.

Back in the palace Alexios resumed his daily duties, reading and studying scripture in his spare time, and taking the occasional ride or hunting trip as exercise for his gout. He was now pushing 60 or just past it, and his family fretted that he was wearing himself out with matters of state. But the prodding and probing of Byzantium's external foes did not allow him any prolonged rest. In November 1114 the Cumans crossed the Danube into Bulgaria; the emperor set up his field headquarters at Philippopolis, where he tried to convert a potentially subversive sect of heretic Manichaeans to Orthodoxy, with mixed results. It was a time when theology and national security were tightly intertwined. 'Freedom of religion' as we understand it today was unthinkable; Byzantium's very political essence, as we have noted, was not based on a flag or a set of physical frontiers but on Orthodox Christianity. Any deviation from official doctrine was thus by definition treasonable. Such people as the Manichaeans, Paulicians and a Balkan sect called the Bogomils, which preached a minimalist version of the faith, were all assumed to be dangerous microbes that must not be allowed to survive in the body politic. Muslims and Roman Catholics enjoyed a measure of tolerance (though Jews had precious few rights), but they knew it could be withdrawn at any time at the whim of the emperor or patriarch.

After dealing with the heretics Alexios hurried on towards the Danube, to find that the Cumans had received word of his coming and had dashed back across the river. Returning to Philippopolis, he appears to have converted some more

Manichaeans before going home. Sometime in early 1116 an aggravation of his gout immobilized him for days and perhaps weeks. His agony was made worse by the knowledge that his enemy Malikshah was on the warpath again in central Anatolia; he fumed as he received reports of Muslim jesters making fun of his illness, and Malikshah putting it about that it was an excuse for cowardice. During a partial recovery Alexios struggled out of bed and put himself at the head of an army that marched to Nikaia and routed a Turkish force. The emperor decided to stay for the summer at Lopadion (possibly today's Mustafa Kemalpaşa), as to ride back to Constantinople meant a long trek through dry country in the intense heat. Lopadion was easily reachable from the Sea of Marmara, and Alexios sent for Irene to join him.

Irene had been there just a couple of days when a messenger arrived at dawn saying the Turks were close at hand. She took the message, thinking her husband was asleep, but he heard everything. He rose at the normal hour, outwardly calm but inwardly worried; a second messenger arrived later in the morning with the news that the Turks were getting closer. The imperial couple were just sitting down to lunch when a third courier, stained in blood, ran up and sprawled at Alexios' feet. Irene, for her own safety, was ordered back to Constantinople. Alexios led the army to Nikaia, on the way meeting Irene who had been held up by rough seas, and then to Nikomedia, easily suppliable from the capital. The Turks, hearing of his advance, had withdrawn but were ever watchful.

With the onset of cooler weather, and apparently relieved from the worst of the gout, he made straight for Malikshah's lair at Ikonion. On the way he stopped at the plain at Dorylaion, where he drilled his soldiers and instructed them in tactics, including what to expect from the Turks. His tactical plan—what his daughter described as 'a battle order inspired by angels'—was to position the army so that it would fire obliquely at the right of the Turks, where their shields left them unprotected. Presumably he intended to march on Ikonion with that formation, and was approaching Philomelion when he found that the Turks had burned all the crops in the approximately 100 miles between there and Ikonion. To proceed through that smoking wasteland without food would be risky in the extreme, so he once more had recourse to faith.

> He therefore decided... to inquire of God whether he should follow the road to Ikonion, or attack the barbarian in the area of Philomelion. He wrote his questions on two pieces of paper and placed them on the Holy Altar. Then the whole night was spent in singing the hymn of the day and addressing to God fervent prayers. At dawn the priest went in; taking up one of the papers from the altar he opened it in the presence of all and read aloud that the emperor should choose the road to Philomelion.

Alexios rode ahead in the vanguard, with his son-in-law Nikephoros Bryennios on the right. After some skirmishing he occupied Philomelion and took under his wing the Christian non-combatants who flocked to him for safety. As the army was withdrawing, keeping the refugees in the centre for protection, it set upon by a large, yelling Turkish force. The emperor bucked up his men with his own courageous example, saying he was not afraid to die for them all, and the attack was eventually beaten off. The following day, at dawn, the attack was renewed, this time on the Roman rear; Bryennios heard the din but didn't turn back to intervene, fearing to disrupt the marching order. On the left however, the commander of that sector, the *porphyrogennetos* Prince Andronikos, who 'had just reached the most wonderful period in his life, a daring soldier in war, but prudent too, with a quick hand and a fine intellect', wheeled round and counter-attacked, to quickly meet his end in a brutal hand-to-hand encounter. Now Bryennios turned round and routed the attackers. On the third day the Turks made yet another attempt, which likewise came to grief.

Sultan Malikshah, who had been coordinating the attacks on the Byzantines, decided that Alexios could not be beaten in daylight, and put out peace feelers which the emperor at once accepted. The whole Roman army remained in position, their weapons and armour gleaming in the sun, as Malikshah and his entourage rode up to Alexios who was also on horseback, flanked impressively by his nobles. Malikshah wanted to dismount out of respect but Alexios told him to stay in the saddle. The sultan nonetheless jumped down and kissed the emperor's purple-clad foot. Alexios helped Malikshah mount a Byzantine horse and rode with him for a short distance; Alexios slipped off his cloak and put it round the sultan's shoulders. This was the good-cop gesture. When they reached the place of negotiation, Alexios, with his characteristic skill, offered to let the Seljuks live in peace in their own domains as they had been before Romanos IV Diogenes had suffered his 'notorious and unfortunate clash' nearly half a century before as long as they swore allegiance to emperor and Empire. Otherwise—and here he switched to bad-cop—'you can be sure of this—I will exterminate your race'.

Malikshah readily assented, whether willingly or not no one can say. No doubt the gold that Alexios piled on him helped make up his mind. The emperor also knew that Malikshah was in danger from his own side, namely his brother Mesut, who was plotting to eliminate him. Alexios advised Malikshah to wait a while before leaving, until more could be learned about the plot. But the sultan, either suspicious that Alexios wanted to detain him as a semi-prisoner or refusing to take the threat from Mesut seriously, insisted on taking his leave. On the way, a conspirator in his entourage speared him, but not fatally. Bleeding, Malikshah spurred his horse to return to the Byzantine lines, but other plotters caught up with him and blinded him. He was led back to Ikonion where Mesut, furious that his brother was still alive, had him strangled with a bowstring.

The march back to Constantinople was slow, held back by the multitude of refugees, many of whom were ill or pregnant. For each death and birth the army would stop and perform the required burial and baptism, not moving on until the rites were completed. The old and infirm were privileged to sit at the emperor's table. At Damalis, on the south shore of the Sea of Marmara, Alexios crossed to the capital in a small boat ahead of the rest, to prepare to handle the influx of refugees. Having banned any triumphal procession, he at once set about personally seeing to their welfare, allocating orphans to noble families and monasteries for adoption; those showing promise were enrolled in the imperial orphanage to receive an education. An entire quarter in the palace district (in the environs of today's Topkapı Palace) was turned into a refugee town, where what must have been hundreds of disabled and destitute people were housed and fed at imperial expense. It was one of the greatest acts of mass charity in history.

Alexios, as we have seen, was as much a fighter for the Orthodox faith as he was on the battlefield, and in 1117 he had to take on the latest doctrinal foe. These were the Bogomils (Slavic for 'Beloved of God') who originated in Bulgaria and whose austere form of worship included elements of Manichaeanism. Thanks partly to their simplistic, no-frills teaching, the Bogomils became a kind of fad in Constantinopolitan society, which in turn aroused the imperial concern. The leading light of the Bogomils was a monk named Basil, who was brought to the capital to explain himself. Alexios rose politely from his throne when Basil was ushered in. Present was the Sebastokrator Isaac, who put some leading questions to the cautious Basil, hoping to get him to say something heretical. When the emperor pretended to be intensely and favourably interested in whatever Basil had to teach, the monk let his guard down and 'vomited out' (in Anna's words) the hated heresy. Hidden behind a curtain was a scribe who took everything down. Alexios had what he needed. In a prefiguring of the later Catholic Inquisition, Basil was arrested and tortured, yet refused to recant. The emperor visited him in jail to try and talk him out of his Bogomilism, but to no avail.

Basil's sympathizers near and far were arrested and once those wrongly seized had been weeded out, a group of Bogomil hardliners were hauled before the emperor, the Senate and the patriarch in an ecclesiastical trial. Some recanted at once; the others stubbornly refused, and the emperor's expression was thunderous as he set out the penalty: two pyres were to be erected, with a cross set in the ground next to one of them. The defendants were given a choice of pyres; those who pledged allegiance to Orthodox Christianity were to mount the pyre by the cross, while the Bogomil holdouts would get on the other. Both were to be set on fire, which presumably would not matter, as any true Christian ought to be prepared to die for his faith. As more defendants moved towards the flaming pyre by the cross than to the other, the crowd called for clemency, outraged that innocent

Christians should be put to death in this way. What the people didn't know was that Alexios had no intention of carrying out this gross injustice; it was one of his renowned tricks, a Solomonic ruse to see how many of the defendants were true Bogomils. No one was burned that day, but the unrepentant were jailed. Basil, however, would not escape the fire, and Anna gives us a dramatic account of his demise in the Hippodrome before an audience of thousands.

The monk was led into the arena where a huge bonfire for him had been prepared and lit. A cross was set up nearby; Alexios had given him the option, even at this late stage, of walking over to the cross in symbolic recantation and thus saving himself. Basil was led in, jaunty and smiling and chanting an Old Testament psalm, fully confident in his belief that angels were about to swoop down and lift him to safety. But when the crowds parted and his got his first view of the flaming inferno awaiting him, with crackling sparks shooting out, his cockiness evaporated.

> For all his boldness he seemed to flinch before the pyre, and appeared troubled. He darted his eyes now here, now there, struck his hands together and beat his thighs, like a man at his wits' end...

The emperor appears to have sent some kind of message to the condemned man to give him a last chance at saving himself, but Basil, despite his discomfiture, declined them. Even the official execution squad were beginning to wonder whether angels or demons would indeed descend and whisk away their victim.

> So there stood this Basil, despicable, helpless before every threat, every terror, gaping now at the pyre, now at the spectators. Everyone thought he was quite mad, for he neither rushed to the flames, nor did he altogether turn back, but stayed rooted to the spot where he had first entered the arena, motionless.

By now the crowd, which we might liken to that at a modern football match, was getting impatient. What was holding up the spectacle? Then someone, perhaps the chief executioner (we are not sure), took Basil's cloak and threw it on the fire to see if it would burn—if it didn't, it would be proof that Basil was under supernatural protection. The robe was instantly consumed, but Basil, either hallucinating or desperate, cried out that he saw his robe rising unscathed into the sky. Then:

> They seized him and threw him, clothes, shoes and all, into the fire. The flames, as if in rage against him, so thoroughly devoured the wretch that there was no odour and not the slightest change to the smoke.

All that was left of Basil was 'one thin wispy plume rising from the centre of the flames'. We are not told explicitly whether Alexios was present on that grisly occasion, but Anna's account strongly indicates that he was, and very likely she also was an eyewitness. As we have seen in the case of Michael Anemas, the Hippodrome backed on to the palace, and all the royal family had to do was step out of a back porch to enter the royal seats for the spectacle.

If, as all our sources assure us, Alexios was a kindly and forbearing character, then a question mark can be raised over why—albeit reluctantly—he ordered a brutal act such as the burning of a heretic. Anna hints, probably correctly, that it was a combination of illness and stress. Alexios' gout, despite the ministrations of Irene and his doctors, never left him; indeed, as he aged it became worse. The emperor may have exposed himself to a chill wind while watching a race at the Hippodrome, with the result that the pains extended to his neck and one of his shoulders. Nicholas Kallikles, a renowned physician who was treating the emperor, suggested purgatives to get rid of the 'humours' which, in the medical theory of the time, were believed to be responsible. The suggestion horrified the rest of the medical team, and Kallikles was overruled. After several days the symptoms subsided.

We are not told which of Alexios' shoulders was afflicted, but if it was the left shoulder it could indicate heart disease. Reinforcing this speculation is the fact that six months later, in early 1118, Alexios complained to Irene of severe shortness of breath and 'a deadweight of stone lying on my heart'. More medical tests showed an irregular pulse, and the diagnosis was an 'inflamed heart' brought on by stress and overwork. But a remedy seemed to be out of reach as the emperor's condition became progressively worse. His illness 'was throttling him like a noose'. Mere breathing became an excruciating ordeal, possible only when he was sitting up. Sleep was almost impossible. He could barely eat and drink. He found some brief respite after ingesting a medicine containing pepper, but soon he relapsed. Irene would sit up with him all night, the tears streaming down her face, clasping his hand and willing him to keep breathing.

The only thing that gave Alexios even slight relief was movement. Thus he was taken from his usual sleeping quarters to a southward-facing room, which presumably had a view of the sea. Courtiers and servants were detailed to carry him around on a luxurious litter in relays. Eventually he was moved for more privacy to the Mangana monastery a short distance up the coast, towards the entrance to the Bosporus. Irene decreed that churches and monasteries throughout the realm should conduct incessant prayers for the emperor. By now 'his stomach was visibly enlarged to a great size, and his feet also swelled up, and fever laid him low'. An oedema afflicted his mouth and pharyngeal cavity, blocking the oesophagus; Anna was able to feed him only liquefied food. Then came bouts of diarrhoea. The doctors were throwing up their hands in complete despair.

On 15 August the doctors anointed the emperor's head to mark the feast of the Dormition of the Virgin Mary. Irene by now was in a bad way, sleepless and unable to eat, keening and fainting at Alexios' bedside. But in one sense she kept her wits about her, and that was to deter her son, the Kaisar John, from making any moves to seize the throne once the emperor had gone. What Anna guiltily does not mention in her otherwise gripping memoir, and which Choniates has preserved for us, is that Irene and Anna made their hostility to John quite plain when he hurried to his father's bedside. John went off to consult with his younger brother Isaac and other allies within the family to decide what to do; by now it was clear that Anna, with her mother's backing, sought the throne for her and her husband Nikephoros Bryennios. Though it was assumed that an emperor's eldest *porphyrogennetos* son would succeed him, as in any ordinary monarchy, it appears not to have been an ironclad rule in Byzantium, where it was in fact up to the emperor to decide whom he wished to succeed him; Anna therefore considered herself a fully legitimate candidate, primarily on the grounds that she believed she had more innate ability to rule than John, whom she despised as a loose-living heavy drinker, among other inadequacies.

After talking to Isaac, John returned to the Mangana. Somehow, when his mother and sister were temporarily absent, he slipped into his father's room and embraced him. Choniates hints that father and son had a brief communication, during which John took Alexios' signet ring and put it on his own finger. Whether Alexios asked him to do it, or John removed the ring secretly under cover of an affectionate embrace—as Anna charged—will never be known. Wearing the imperial ring, John rode with his retinue to the main palace through crowds already acclaiming him emperor. Irene, outmanoeuvred, urged Bryennios to seize the throne before John could move, but Bryennios, probably seeing that public opinion was already rallying to John's support, did nothing.

While this struggle for power was in full spate, Alexios was weakening rapidly. Anna's younger sister Maria was giving him sips of water; Irene in despair sobbed to her husband that John was treacherously 'stealing the throne'. According to Choniates, the emperor smiled weakly, and told his grieving wife not to bother herself about earthly matters in the face of 'his imminent departure from this life'. Anna's version of Alexios' words runs: 'Why do you give yourself up so to grief at my death and force us to anticipate the end that rapidly approaches?' He followed with some advice for her to start looking out for herself as from now on she would be in danger. Irene's rather churlish response was to snap back that Alexios had been a master of deceit all his life, and wasn't changing now. Anna herself kept taking her father's pulse and checking his breathing while he slipped in and out of consciousness. Inevitably, that pulse faltered and stopped. Realizing that the end had come, Anna stepped back, sobbing. Irene let out a loud, tragic wail.

Alexios I Komnenos was barely into his mid-sixties when he passed away, worn out by constant warfare and domestic administrative problems. He was a workaholic, an attribute that worked wonders when he was young but in the end hastened his death. The verdicts of history have generally been generous to him. He assumed power when Byzantium was under threat by a variety of foes from all points of the compass, and over thirty-seven years gave himself to his Empire tirelessly and with incredible courage, and all without resorting to the temptation to tyranny. He left the Empire still under threat, but much stronger and better-organized, after it had often seemed that it was on the verge of extinction. 'No emperor,' writes Lord Norwich, 'had defended his people more courageously, or with greater determination, or against a greater number of enemies.' His handling of the First Crusade was nothing less than inspired.

Not all judgements of Alexios have been so favourable. Before Byzantine studies became rehabilitated, as it were, in the West, Oxford scholar C.W.C. Oman, writing at the close of the nineteenth century (and perhaps influenced by Gibbonian cynicism), could conclude:

> Alexios was a man of great courage and ability, but he displayed one of the worst types of Byzantine character. Indeed, he was the first emperor to whom the epithet 'Byzantine' in its common and opprobrious sense could be applied... [He was] the most accomplished liar of his age... he could fight when necessary, but preferred to win by treason and perjury... [he was] a strange mixture of moral obliquity and practical ability.

One feels that Irene Doukaina would have endorsed the 'accomplished liar' description, but in the light of what we know of Alexios, Oman's verdict is not quite fair. All great historical figures are in a way mysteries, compounds of contradictory elements. But there can be no doubt that Alexios I Komnenos, for all his faults, was one of the greatest statesmen the Christian world ever knew.

Chapter 11

John the Good: A soldier's soldier

When John rode up to the palace while his father was breathing his last, the guards were at first reluctant to let him through. They appeared to be under orders to admit no one not authorized by the emperor, and not even the sight of Alexios' ring on John's hand could change their minds. At this, John's armed escort physically levered the palace doors off their hinges, and surged inside. Some of John's supporters among the people slipped through as well, and according to Choniates began pilfering some of the valuables. Soon, however, the news broke of the emperor's death and John II Komnenos began his reign.

Even now, he was not unchallenged. Anna could not bear the thought of losing the fight for the throne and might well have connived at a plot to assassinate her despised brother during Alexios' funeral. John probably got wind of something afoot and stayed away. Several months later Anna apparently decided that the time had come to act. Her husband Nikephoros Bryennios had placed himself at the head of a conspiracy against John, to strike when the new emperor was outside the city walls running his horses. But at the last moment Bryennios lost heart; he was not by nature an impulsive or particularly energetic man, and may well have felt that trying to topple the legitimate emperor was just plain wrong. We have already mentioned the possibly apocryophal story that Anna pointed to her husband's genitals and said: 'I should have those things and you should have mine!' Apparently, she could hit back with whatever sexual equipment she did have. Choniates gives us a startlingly explicit account that describes Anna, 'disgusted at her husband's frivolous behaviour, and being a shrew by nature,' exercising a certain set of muscles during sex and causing 'great pain' to him. Whether this is pure gossip or not is impossible to determine, but it would be sexual politics taken to extremes.

Bryennios was right to be cautious; the plot was discovered and the plotters taken before John. They were not physically punished, and John took a philosophical attitude to his sister's treason. 'How the natural order has been inverted for me!' he marvelled. 'Kinsmen have become the enemy, and strangers friends.' On the advice of his Grand Domestikos, he decided to let the issue against Anna drop, but he barred her permanently from the palace. Humiliated and without allies, Anna, still only 35 and with plenty of potential before her, retired to the Theotokos Kecharitomene (Mother of God Full of Grace) convent where, embittered, she waited a quarter of a century more to begin writing the memoir which has preserved her name through the ages. Irene, to her credit, did not approve of the conspiracy. Thus with Anna's departure the domestic scene was tranquillized enough for John to be able to embark on his first military campaign.

He was 21, rather on the short side like his father, but not terribly well-favoured in facial features. The dark complexion that his sister had sniffed at when he was born carried over into his maturity, enough to make it noticeable to his lighter contemporaries. His character, however, was benevolent enough to earn him the sobriquet John the Good (*Kaloioannes*). He was as devout as, or even more than, his parents, to the point of enforcing a puritan regime in the palace; entertainment and merriment were banned, and anything but serious conversation frowned on. Meals were kept as simple as possible, and any noble appearing in sumptuous dress was severely reprimanded. Like his father, he had a forgiving nature, almost to a fault. He could have quite justifiably meted out severer punishment to Anna and his other adversaries, but considered it better to simply distance himself from them. Conscious perhaps that he was expected to be worthy of his father, he made sure he was his own man. He picked his own counsellors, chief among them an ethnic Turk named John Axuch; this man had been captured by the Roman army while an infant and brought up in the palace. Such appears to have been his ability that John promoted him to Grand Domestikos, commander of the armies.

In one sense John saw his mission as surpassing that of Alexios, who had spent all of his long reign battling external foes in what was essentially a defensive military policy. The imperial territory had shrunk, so John wanted to resume the offensive, clawing back what his father had lost. Like Alexios he was a born soldier and remained faithful to his wife, the Hungarian princess Piriska (renamed Irene to make her more 'Byzantine'). Assessing the strategic situation, John figured that with the west and north relatively quiescent, he would concentrate his first thrusts against the Turks in Anatolia who were becoming aggressive. There was no single Turkish tribe to fight against, as the border between the Byzantine and the Turkish territories was maddeningly fluid. In the spring of 1119 John decided to march south into Phrygia, where he pushed back Turkish advances. He took the field again a year later, moving on Sozopolis in Pamphylia (now south-central Turkey). Paktarios, the emperor's cavalry commander, carried out a clever manoeuvre that bamboozled the Turks occupying Sozopolis who were decisively trounced. It was John's belief that 'an army, like a red-hot iron dipped in water, is tempered by the sweat of blazing battle'.

In 1123 the Pechenegs, supposedly eliminated by Alexios, made their reappearance in Thrace, ravaging the countryside. John rode out to confront them; he proved to be an able pupil of his father by resorting to bribery and public relations to win over some of the disparate Pecheneg tribes. But the rest proved recalcitrant, and at Beroe the emperor took them on in what Choniates describes as 'one of the most frightful and terrifying battles ever fought'. In the uncertain first phase, John received a minor wound. The Pechenegs re-formed arranging their wagons in a circle, inside which they formed a network of passages which an enemy would find impossible to penetrate. John's response to this was to:

> [L]ook upon the icon of the Mother of God and, wailing loudly and ges-turing pitifully, shed tears hotter than the sweat of battle. It was not in vain that he acted thus; donning the breastplate of the power from on high, he routed the [Pecheneg] battalions just as Moses had turned back the troops of Amalek by raising his hands.

It probably wasn't quite as easy as Choniates makes it sound. Several Byzantine attacks were, in fact, beaten back until the emperor ordered everyone to dismount and advance on foot; the horses were probably proving to be too vulnerable. Alongside him marched the Varangian Guard, whose battleaxes hacked the enemy wagons to pieces and deprived them of their prime defence. Captured Pechenegs were resettled in Balkan villages, and not a few were enrolled as imperial troops. That same year John inflicted a similar defeat on the rebellious Serbs, resettling a part of that nation in Asia Minor.

The West, meanwhile, was not proving to be as peaceable as John hoped. True, the threats posed by the likes of Robert and Bohemond Guiscard had long since gone. But competitive trade now replaced military aggression as the western threat to Byzantium, and its instruments were the Venetians, now growing into the chief naval power in the Mediterranean. Venice, like other Italian maritime cities, was quick to take advantage of the First Crusade and the establishment of the Latin kingdoms in Syria and Palestine. But as early as 1082 their presence in the east Mediterranean had made inroads into Byzantine trade. Alexios I, barely a year into his reign, had granted the Venetians a trading colony at Pera on the north side of the Golden Horn opposite the capital proper (now the Karaköy and Galata districts). Forty years later, however, as the colony grew so did the wealth, privileges and arrogance of its inhabitants, who made themselves thoroughly despised by the locals. In 1122 Doge Domenico Michiel of Venice wrote asking John to routinely confirm the status and rights of the Pera colony, and to his surprise and rage, John refused. Thenceforth, John said, the Venetians would have no more rights than anyone else.

The emperor was no doubt acting out of the highest principles, and no doubt was well aware of what the average Byzantine thought of those haughty Catholic Latins. But being young and strong-minded, may have failed to think out the consequences, and whether the Empire could handle them. In August Doge Michiel sailed from Venice with seventy-one ships to teach the schismatic Greeks a lesson.

The fleet besieged Corfu for six months; fortunately for the Byzantines, an urgent plea to the Doge arrived from Latin King Baldwin II of Jerusalem, who had been captured by the Turks. In order to sail to the rescue of Baldwin the Venetians lifted the siege of Corfu, but harassed other Greek islands such as Rhodes, Andros, Chios and Lesbos. With the Byzantine navy largely powerless to halt such incursions, John reluctantly restored the Venetians' privileges in Pera in 1126, and in some measure the rivalry ceased. The emperor could never have imagined the appalling price his Empire would pay for this climbdown in less than 100 years.

At about this time John's first child was born, a boy who was named Alexios after his grandfather, and who from the outset bore the expectation that the Komnene dynasty would endure with more than one member bearing that honoured name. The expectation took enduring symbolic form when the infant was formally clothed in a purple robe, shod with the purple slippers, and entitled to be acclaimed along with his father. While the royal infant was being suckled in the palace John moved against his wife's people, the Hungarians, whose King István (Stephen) was angry that his brother had thrown in his lot with the Byzantines. In the spring of 1128 he sprang a two-pronged attack on the Hungarians from land and sea. The navy sailed round into the Danube from the Black Sea. John raided Hungarian territory, bringing back rich spoils. Barely was that adventure over than he swung east to deliver a stinging attack on the Turks. All this took several years, and in 1133, after fifteen years on the throne, John celebrated his string of victories in Anatolia with an old-style triumphal procession into Constantinople, the first the city had seen in more than 160 years. A special silver-plated chariot was made for the occasion. The scene is well described by Choniates:

> [A]ll manner of gold-embroidered cloth decorated the streets... the framed images of Christ and the saints... one would have said were not woven figures but living beings... The splendid quadriga was pulled by four horses, whiter than snow, with magnificent manes. The emperor did not himself mount the chariot but instead mounted upon it the icon of the Mother of God, in whom he exulted and entrusted his soul... ordering his chief ministers to take hold of the reins and his closest relations to attend to the chariot, he led the way on foot with the cross held in his hand.

John rested for some months, along with his soldiers who were able to get some home leave; he made sure he was seen regularly at public events in the Hippodrome.

In the autumn of 1134 events in Anatolia called him out again. Mesut I, the Seljuk sultan of Ikonion, was under pressure from a Turkish rival and gained the alliance of the Byzantines, who saw a chance to fish in the troubled Muslim waters. John marched into Kappadokia, but on the way his wife Irene, the former Piriska of Hungary, sickened and died, forcing him to return to the capital briefly. In the meantime he found himself undermined by the slippery Mesut who had made his peace with his rival. Back in the field, John set up camp near Turkish-held Gangra in the north. Repeated attempts to breach the walls of Gangra ended in failure, so John brought his large mangonels into action, hurling stones 'which seemed to be flying rather than being shot from engines of war'. The bombardment was aimed not at the walls but at the buildings inside the city, causing considerable casualties. Morale in the town collapsed, and John took the surrender. It was, however, a brief triumph. Months after John had returned to the capital, the Turks returned to Gangra in force and starved it into submission.

John by now had learned what every Byzantine emperor since Romanos IV Diogenes had to learn the hard way: that the Muslim Seljuk Turks would stop at nothing to subdue the entire Christian Middle East, the south Byzantine Empire included. More than half a century had passed since Manzikert, and despite (or perhaps because of) the efforts of the Crusaders, the Turks never seemed to run out of expansionist steam. As soon as one tribe was beaten, another would take its place, taking advantage of the irregular and indefensible Anatolian heartland to thrust here and feint there in an endless series of pressures that could never let the emperors rest. Alexios I had performed superhuman feats against threats in the west and east, having to fend them off sometimes almost simultaneously. The Turkish drive was clearly a long-term one; though the Turks themselves had originated in central Asia, and their Muslim religion was a fruit of Arabia, they appeared to genuinely consider home as far westward as they could get. Islamic fanaticism probably played only a small part in this relentless drive; the main motive was a desire to elbow in on the luxuries, trade and temperate climate of the Greco-Roman world.

Typically for the region, the Muslims were not the only foes of Byzantium in that part of the world. Apart from the Latin kingdom of Jerusalem, Christian Armenia never looked kindly on the pre-eminence of Constantinople. Their King Leo in 1133 launched a war of conquest right down to the borders of Syria, whereupon John set out to thwart him. The Armenians had a new military invention in the form of red-hot pellets of iron that did some damage to the Roman siege engines, but in the end John's persistence paid off and the Armenians ran out of resolve, leaving John to proceed to a far more important objective. That was Antioch, the key to Syria and the Holy Land, the possession of which was crucial to anyone wanting to control the land route from Europe to the Middle East. Antioch was in the hands of Raymond of Poitiers, a Frank who had come in the wake of the First Crusaders. Having meanwhile secured his northern borders by a treaty with Lothair III of Germany, John pressed on to the south-east, overcoming a Muslim army at Shaizar and reaching the walls of Antioch in August 1138.

Though as a Frankish Catholic he distrusted the Byzantines, Raymond could hardly refuse a request by the Christian emperor to ride into the city. John did so, as Raymond walked by the side of the emperor's horse in an act of formal vassalage. After a service in the cathedral, John told Raymond in no uncertain terms that he had expected more support from him against the Turks; going further, he said he was personally taking control of Antioch as the Empire's main south-east operational base. At this, one of Raymond's officials ignited a false rumour that the Greeks were about to expel all the Latins; the resulting bloody rioting in the streets, however, failed to incite John to anything rash. He decided to return to Constantinople with Raymond's simple assurance, sincere or not, that he would remain an imperial vassal. He left, says Runciman, 'with an outward show of friendship and complete mutual mistrust'. At the best of times the rude and unsophisticated Normans were no match for Byzantine diplomacy. As for Raymond, who had been living a comfortable life in England in the court of King Henry I before being shipped east, he was utterly bored in Antioch and was prepared to do anything the emperor told him. As long as the Turks were prowling around as a check on Frankish ambitions, John could expect no serious trouble from that quarter.

We know very little of John the Good's private life and character, except that everyone agrees he inherited his illustrious father's military and diplomatic talents, as well as his generous and easy-going nature. No scandal of any sort appears to have been attached to his name. He is assumed to have been a serious family man before his wife's death, and faithful to her memory after it. He was a fastidious stickler for decorum and neatness, constantly checking his family members' hair to see that it was properly cut, and whether their shoes were made to the appropriate high standards. Choniates writes:

> He would avoid the commotion of large crowds, turning a deaf ear to their babbling and jabbering; his speech was dignified and elegant, but he did not spurn repartee or in any way hold back or stifle laughter... depriving no one of life nor inflicting bodily injury of any kind throughout his entire reign.

John's campaigns in Anatolia were bedevilled by treason on the part of none other than his uncle the Sebasokrator Isaac, the late Alexios' brother and faithful confidant. According to the story, Isaac broke from Alexios while the latter was still alive over 'some trifle' that is not described. Anna Komnene mentions nothing of the kind in the *Alexiad*. But it would be reasonable to conjecture that this 'trifle', whatever it was, may have had something to do with Irene's and Anna's consistent contempt of John, a feeling that would have been intensified after John became emperor and began scoring triumphs in the field. They may, in short, have 'got to' Isaac. Also, the entrenched civil servant class, which had never really warmed to the military Komnene, could have seen a chance to stir up trouble in the household.

Isaac's discontent with his nephew's rule got so bad that he fled Constantinople along with his eldest son John, the one who had been accused of disloyalty at Dyrrachion, and to whose defence his father had rushed. Isaac by now must have been in his seventies. For eight years they canvassed Byzantium's foes, seeking funds and forces to overthrow John, and were not above trying to enlist the aid of Mesut of Ikonion. They found few takers. Either John's diplomacy had succeeded in tarring father and son with the taint of treason, or they simply weren't taken seriously. Eventually Isaac realized that 'it was for nought that he was separated from his family, and that he was suffering an evil existence'. John bore no grudge against the rebellion, embracing Isaac and taking him back to Constantinople.

The emperor did not quite feel secure with the situation in Antioch. He knew that the city was under constant threat from the Arabs in Syria and was none too confident that Raymond of Poitiers was strong enough to keep it in Christian hands. He decided it would be worth enlisting the Crusader kingdoms in a joint offensive against the Arabs, to secure the overland route to the Holy Land once and for all. His health was not of the best, but he was still quite capable of campaigning. Yet something in him changed; he never stopped being a first-rate soldier, but now took on an imperious, autocratic stance. Many of his troops resented being driven hard year after year—and forbidden to do any looting in compensation. Those whose homes were in Anatolia and near the line of march were not allowed to visit their families. Horses perished from overexertion, while provisions were sometimes scarce. True, the emperor was ever-ready to listen to his soldiers' grievances, but instead of trying to rectify them he would try to persuade them to keep on marching and fighting. He himself provided the supreme example of the fighting man, conspicuous in his glittering gilded helmet, appearing anywhere and everywhere in the heat of battle, unafraid of anything the enemy could throw at him. So they stayed.

Before striking east, John had to deal with a foe in the north-east. The Seljuks were just one of several tribes of Turks swirling around Anatolia; another was the Danishmends, whose current emir, Mehmet, controlled the northern part of Kappadokia and thus was in a position to threaten any imperial army marching to and from Antioch. John's first attempts to subdue Mehmet in late 1139 fared quite badly. The emperor had unwisely chosen to campaign in a harsh Kappadokian winter; horses and pack mules perished, and the lack of supplies and extreme discomfort eroded the Byzantines' energy. On at least one occasion the Danishmends sent their foes flying 'as though they had been picked up and blown away by the wind'. The imperial cavalry, already decimated by cold and hunger, was hit especially hard in these encounters. John made up for this by collecting the few able horses that were left and forming them into a compact cavalry corps manned by skilled lancers; many infantry standards were raised among those of the cavalry, to give the impression of a large force. With this he checked further Danishmend advances.

At Neokaisareia, some distance farther east, John came up against constant Turkish attacks. In one fight his youngest son Manuel levelled his lance and, entirely without orders, charged the enemy alone; his courageous move inspired the rest of the army to overcome the enemy, but his father was definitely not pleased. He had not brought his four sons—Alexios, Andronikos, Isaac and Manuel—with him on campaign for them to needlessly risk their lives. He may well have had a preference for Manuel as being the most aggressive, and his son's wild charge shocked him. The punishment was severe: Manuel was made to lie face down on the ground, where his father flogged him with a willow-twig whip. Rather more of a problem was the emperor's nephew John, the son of the Sebastokrator Isaac, who after his eight-year defection was still not reconciled to the emperor. During one battle the emperor noticed that 'a distinguished knight from Italy' had lost his horse; John ordered the younger John to give up his; the latter disdainfully refused, but complied in the face of his uncle's fury. Mounting another horse, the nephew picked up his lance and rode off—right to the enemy's ranks, where he doffed his helmet and defected to them. (He later embraced Islam and married into the sultan of Ikonion's family.) The loss of the younger John to the enemy filled the emperor with alarm; the defector would surely tell the Turks all he knew of the Byzantine plans and dispositions. The wisest course at this stage would be to withdraw, which he did, returning to Constantinople in January 1141.

After only a few months' rest he was on the way east again, but the autumn brought with it the usual cold Kappadokian conditions—'snowflakes as large as boulders and sleet like javelins'—that drove him back again. In the spring of 1142 he felt he had to make the decisive push. We may surmise, from Choniates' vague mentions of previous ill-health, that John may not have been in the best shape for yet another gruelling campaign. He was now around 55, and his hesitation in the face of harsh weather indicates that his endurance had begun to flag. We learn that when John set out this time, his daughters Maria, Theodora and Eudokia wept. His immediate goal was Attaleia on the south coast of Anatolia with its milder climate, where he intended to set up his base of operations and pacify the surrounding countryside.

During the slow advance towards Syria John suffered a severe double blow: his eldest son and heir-apparent Alexios, who bore the name of his revered grandfather, died after a brief illness that seems to have been a particularly virulent fever. Barely had he time to mourn this loss than his second son, accompanying

Alexios' body back to the capital, sickened and died also. Stunned, John wondered whether his sons' deaths portended military disaster. But, true soldier that he was, he resisted what must have been a strong temptation to return home and committed himself to 'unite Antioch to Constantinople and then to visit the holy lands trodden by God... [and] clear away the barbarians round about'. The main premise of Roman-Byzantine foreign policy was still there, unchanged since the time of Heraclius, the ultimate supreme duty of every emperor. He also nursed a plan to give Antioch to his youngest son Manuel, who had distinguished himself in combat and was seen to possess the mettle to be a governor.

By late September John was approaching Antioch, where in the meantime Raymond of Poitiers had made himself thoroughly unpopular by his incompetence and misrule. He was also under subtle blackmail from supporters of his teenaged wife, the Princess Constance, who officially was the sovereign of Antioch. When John demanded the surrender of the city, Raymond's coterie of vassals disingenuously argued that it really wasn't up to him. John felt he had no choice but to attack, yet cold weather was again coming on and he withdrew to Kilikia, a short distance north-west of Antioch, where he could prepare for a fresh offensive in the spring. To keep Raymond and his ilk on their toes, and his own men in morale, he ravaged several isolated Frankish estates and maintained operational preparedness by raiding Turkish outposts.

John's pressing desire to visit the Holy Sepulchre in Jerusalem never wavered. He planned, when he arrived there, to talk the Latin King Fulk into joining his planned sweep of Muslim-held lands. On receiving the imperial envoy who bore the proposal, Fulk had a disturbing thought of legions of Byzantines overrunning the Kingdom of Jerusalem and bringing the Frankish domains into Byzantium's orbit. Jerusalem's Catholic clergy fanned his fears; his reply was to send a Templar knight named Geoffrey to John to explain that he would be welcome as long as he brought with him a 'small escort'. For some reason, John decided to delay his pilgrimage; perhaps the preparations for the coming campaign were taking up all his time.

On 1 April 1143, with the weather improving, John took a day off to go hunting. In Choniates' account he came on a wild boar and thrust his javelin into it; but it seems to have been a rather strong animal and pushed back, forcing the emperor's right hand back, where it hit his arrow-filled quiver. The quiver overturned, spilling its razor-sharp arrows, one of which grazed his hand. To stop the bleeding he applied a piece of shoe leather and presumably continued with the hunt. It wasn't until the following morning that the wound began to swell painfully, and the emperor must have suspected why—the arrow had been one of those specially poisoned for hunting. Doctors removed the provisional piece of leather and attempted to cauterize the swelling with hot irons, but within a short time the infection had spread up John's entire arm. The doctors considered amputating the arm, eventually deciding against it, while John lay in pain ignoring them. The wound developed into septicaemia, and on Easter Sunday, three days after the fateful hunting trip, he called together into his tent his family members, close friends and officials.

As the rain poured down outside, and with Manuel present, John sadly acknowledged that he had been thwarted in his attempt to reach 'Palestine where Christ did raise our fallen nature', not by any human agency but by God's will. Going on, he summarized his own twenty-five-year reign: 'nearly my whole life was lived out of a tent.' He voiced a hope to those present:

> [God] should then grant you a sovereign who is not a devourer of the people, giving the lie to his name, capricious by nature, bent forward over the table with his hands ever on the wine ladle, and never tearing himself away from the palace like those portraits on the walls in coloured mosaics.

So who, then, should the successor be? Here was a delicate issue, a potential political minefield. The deaths of Alexios and Andronikos had left John with two surviving sons, Isaac and Manuel. By tradition, Isaac as the eldest surviving son would inherit the throne; but the emperor didn't want him, and had to explain that to those assembled solemnly before his sickbed. He had recourse to the Old Testament and its example of Jacob, who obtained the birthright by outwitting his elder brother Esau, proving himself to be the cleverer brother and hence more deserving of the father's inheritance. Isaac was ruled out, he said, because he was emotionally unstable: 'provoked by some cause he flies into a towering rage, a fault which ruins the wise.'

> It is pretty obvious to me [John continued] that my last-born son Manuel would be the better administrator of the empire... Manuel is not a stranger to meekness, readily yielding to what is useful and willing to listen to reason. Since... we humans, furthermore, prefer to be led by a hand clasping the sword and by a temperament which subtly searches out the trespasses of subjects, I have chosen Manuel to be emperor.

A question mark hovers over what Isaac thought of this decision. He had been left behind in the palace while his father and brothers were on campaign. Almost certainly he had his favourites in the administration who would have preferred to see him wearing the crown and who, John suspected, were capable of working underhandedly towards it. At any rate, the reaction in the tent was overwhelmingly positive, while John called Manuel to his side and put the imperial diadem on his head and the imperial purple cape around his shoulders. There followed the traditional Roman army acclamation, plus the individual allegiance of the nobles present. John II Komnenos, the Good, passed away a few days later aged 53, mourned by his people as 'the equal of some of the best emperors of the past'.

Chapter 12

Manuel I and the Second Crusade

Manuel was about the same age as John had been when he succeeded
Alexios, 21 years old or thereabouts. But to confirm his power he had to
move fast; for all he knew, informal messages bearing the news of John's
demise could well be hurrying over the miles to the capital, where Isaac was in a
perfect position to get himself crowned long before Manuel could show up. While
Manuel presided over the time-consuming funeral rituals, which included founding a monastery in his father's name, he sent John Axuch, the Grand Domestikos,
to the capital post-haste. Making excellent time, he found that he was the first to
deliver the news; when Isaac protested at Manuel's elevation to the throne, Axuch
had him locked up. Convincing the powerful Church, however, was another matter; for this purpose Axuch had 200 pieces of silver with him if bribery should
prove necessary, and 200 gold pieces in case the priests held out. It so happened
that the Church at the time had yet to elect a new patriarch in place of the last, who
had recently died. Axuch called the senior clergy together and showed them the
silver which would be theirs, he said, if they endorsed Manuel. They needed no
urging; Axuch didn't even need to use the gold. The only real resistance came from
Kaisar John Roger, a Norman who had married Manuel's sister Maria; unsurprisingly, it was Maria herself who informed on her husband and had him arrested.

Meanwhile, Manuel had put his father's body on a ship for transport to
Constantinople and had set out for the same destination overland. He had to leave
the situation in Antioch unresolved for the present; the priority now was to make
himself seen in Constantinople and become officially crowned in Sancta Sophia.
The East could wait. In July Manuel rode into the capital to public adulation.
At the ceremonial palace gate, which only emperors were allowed to go through,
Manuel had a job controlling his skittish Arabian stallion before he could enter.
People who saw him for the first time noted that he was tall, slightly stooped in the
shoulders and handsome, with 'a gentle smile'. He had inherited the swarthiness
of his father enough to make it stand out among the generally fairer Byzantine
population.

The reign of Manuel I Komnenos began with favourable auspices. His irasci-
ble brother Isaac was reconciled with him (though we are in no position to know
whether the fence-mending was genuine) and dollops of gold promised to the
Church made sure of the allegiance of that influential institution. With the home

front thus secured, Manuel was called out to inaugurate his own imperial service in what by the middle of the twelfth century had become Byzantium's perennial battleground—Asia Minor and Syria. Such was the pressure of the aggressive Turkish tribes, backed by the deeper threat of Islamic expansionism, that no emperor could afford to neglect that theatre of operations even for a moment. In the months that Manuel spent in Constantinople consolidating his rule, Raymond of Poitiers was ravaging Byzantine communities in Kilikia while Mesut, the sultan of Ikonion, had never stopped raiding Byzantium's eastern provinces.

Manuel set out against Mesut in 1144 but an attack of pleurisy forced him to break off the operation and return home. He sent his nephews John and Andronikos Kontostephanos, of the military family that had distinguished itself against Bohemond under Alexios I, plus a fleet under Demetrios Branas to discourage Raymond, reserving for himself the more important fight against the Turks. Manuel pursued them into west Kappadokia; in an encounter at Philomelion he lanced a Turk who, while falling backwards, managed to fire an arrow into Manuel's foot. The wound seems not to have been serious, as he was able to continue the battle. Meanwhile, Mesut had abandoned Ikonion, leaving it apparently in the hands of Manuel's own cousin John, the troublesome son of the Sebastokrator Isaac. John, as we have seen, had joined his people's enemies by becoming a Muslim and marrying Mesut's daughter. Manuel and the army reached the walls of Ikonion but probably judged them too stout to attack at once. His withdrawal, however, drew fanatical attacks from the Turks from which he extricated himself with great difficulty.

Back in the capital Manuel had to concern himself with finding a wife who would give him the required Komnene heir. He would have been considered a supreme prize for any high-born damsel; good-looking, intelligent, witty and fun-loving, a skilled debater and brave in war to the point of foolhardiness. But we learn also that he was, quite unlike his puritanical father, a keen and most accomplished womanizer. When in the capital he spent much of his time partying in one of the palaces or royal villas fronting the Bosporus. We should therefore not be surprised that he was distinctly disappointed with the first noble wife found for him; she was a German princess, Bertha of Sulzbach, described with rueful diplomacy by Choniates 'not so much concerned with physical beauty as with her inner beauty'. Bertha had been promised to Manuel by his late father as part of a diplomatic deal with the Holy Roman Empire, but that counted for nothing with the young Don Juan now on the throne. To make her unattractiveness worse, the German Bertha disdained make-up and eyeliner and other aids natural to southern women. She also is reported to have been Teutonically blunt in her manner, an alien trait in Mediterranean Byzantium.

Nonetheless, John's agreement with the Holy Roman Empire had to be honoured, and Manuel and Bertha were wed in January 1146. The marriage was consummated at least once, as it produced a daughter. But 'in matters of the bed,' Choniates writes, 'she was wronged.' Manuel made sure he had plenty of sex—but with other women. Even his niece Theodora did not escape his amorous conquests. He may well have contracted a sexually-transmitted disease from all this, as our chronicler—perhaps drawing on a hostile Church source—claims that his hand-some face became disfigured by 'warts or pustules of dull white leprosy'. Whatever Bertha (officially renamed Irene on her marriage) thought of this is unknown. To her credit, she continued the duties of official consort without apparent complaint; on at least one occasion, in 1148, she brought a certain diplomatic talent to bear by helping cement a political alliance between Manuel and her brother-in-law Conrad of Germany. For the remaining twelve years of her life, through her husband's myriad infidelities, the neglected and devout Bertha devoted herself to good works, earning a fulsome encomium at her funeral.

In his more serious moments Manuel turned his attention to internal admin-istration, employing a cohort of learned men. One of them was John of Poutze, a stern and incorruptible taxman who squeezed the emperor's subjects to the groan-ing point with merciless exactions and was not above tearing up even an imperial instruction when he thought it wrong. In fact, the power that Manuel allowed this economic tsar was extraordinary. Choniates rolls out a long list of Poutze's greedy and abusive practices, such as enriching himself and his family at the taxpayers' expense, physically checking visitors to see if they had any gold on them, sending food given him as bribes to be sold in shops for his own profit, gobbling down the fare on display at street markets and paying for it all with a single bronze coin—from which he demanded change. 'He was attached to Wealth,' writes Choniates, 'which held him permanently fettered in unbreakable and indissoluble bonds.' When Poutze died after being disgraced, 'he was found to have storehouses teem-ing with money.'

Had Poutze been less rapacious he might have helped head off one of the great mistakes of Manuel's reign—the neglect of the navy. For centuries the basis of the Byzantine Empire's power and prosperity had rested on seaborne trade. Constantinople stood at an ideal geographical crossroads, where Asia meets Europe and where the Black Sea meets the Mediterranean. The Sea of Marmara, the gate-way to the Bosporus, had become in fact one huge port area. From the main naval base on the Golden Horn fleets could set out for wherever the Empire's outposts were in danger, receiving the blessing of the emperor as he stood at his palace window seeing them off. 'Domination of the world is mine,' Nikephoros II Phokas could boast to a visiting Italian prelate in the middle of the tenth century, 'because I am the master of navigation and the sea.'

But in the eleventh and twelfth centuries the Italian maritime states such as Venice and Genoa had been gradually muscling in on Mediterranean trade, especially in the Aegean area right on Constantinople's doorstep. They were able to do this partly because they developed new shipping and financing techniques, but also because Byzantium became preoccupied mainly with land wars against foes such as the Pechenegs and the Turks. A navy was not much use, for example, in the wilds of Anatolia or Syria. Under a military dynasty such as the Komnenes, the army took pride of place. As long as hostile ships and pirates did not directly threaten the main naval bases in the Golden Horn and Sea of Marmara, Constantinople could remain complacent. Then, inevitably, the Turks began to acquire naval expertise, taught them by the Arab corsairs. Why, in the face of this menace from the sea, the Byzantine navy was allowed to waste away for lack of funds remains something of a mystery.

Manuel Komnenos' fun-loving and adventurous character was a façade that masked a strict and imperious administrator. He no doubt approved of Poutzes' harsh tax regime, being of like mind himself. Much of the revenue was, of course, spent on his own enjoyment, and when it was slow in coming 'he treated his ministers as slaves'. Such conduct must have seriously eroded his once-great popularity, further sullied by a Church distrustful of his apparent indifference to ritual and by his occasional attempts at diplomatic reconciliation with the Roman Catholic Church. On the other hand, the conspiratorial tendencies that had bedevilled Alexios I's reign, and to a degree John II's, seem to have been absent.

The Frankish domains at the time had their hands full, as the Atabeg of Mosul, Imad ed-Din Zengi, had established control over all of north Syria and was planning to swallow Antioch and Jerusalem as well. Zengi, the son of a Turkish slave, had the backing of both the decaying Abbasid caliphate in Baghdad and the Fatimid caliphate in Cairo, and was able to mould the Muslims, both Arabs and Turks, into a single striking force. This 'tamer of atheists and destroyer of heretics' ruled his army with a harshness and cruelty remarkable even for the time, and hostile sources tar him with the sins of drunkenness and unbridled lust. The kingdom of Jerusalem was in a weakened state, with Baldwin III, just 13, on the throne and effective power wielded by his mother Melisende. Manoeuvring his way towards his ultimate goal of eliminating the Frankish element, in 1144 Zengi captured Edessa, which had been a Frankish state since the First Crusade.

News of the fall of Edessa sent a great shock wave through Christendom. The symbolic repercussion of the event was probably greater than its actual strategic significance, as Edessa had been the very first Crusader state to be set up. In the half-century or so since the First Crusade Western Europe had pretty much left Outremer—the name for the Frankish realms of Palestine and Syria, meaning 'over the sea'—out of its immediate attention span; it was a convenient destination for pilgrims and a continuing source of revenue for the Italian maritime powers who transported those pilgrims and dominated trade with the east Mediterranean.

But militarily Outremer was weak, depending for its defence on the military orders of the Knights Hospitaller and Templar, and heavily outclassed by the Muslims. Western and central Europe were in throes of a mighty power struggle between the papacy and secular governments, where doctrinal issues were elevated to high visibility. Popes and kings and princes vied with one another over who could best uphold Christian policies (though they almost all resorted to decidedly un-Christian means to do so). Add to this a new generation of feudal nobles in France and Germany who had grown up listening to romanticized tales of the First Crusade and who longed to follow in its footsteps for some God-sanctioned action, and the stage was set for a new surge towards the Holy Land.

Like all crusades, the Second Crusade needed an emotional spark to get it going. This was provided by a fanatical Cistercian monk, Bernard of Clairvaux, whose preaching was of such power that it hooked Louis VII of France and the Hohenstaufen Emperor Conrad III who personally undertook to lead their armies eastwards. As for Raymond in Antioch, the fall of nearby Edessa rattled him enough to travel to Constantinople to personally plead for help from the emperor. Manuel at first snubbed Raymond, agreeing to see him only after the Frenchman had abjectly knelt before the tomb of John II. Manuel was generous with gifts and money, but held back any military aid on the grounds that he could not spare any troops from the continuing raids on the Turks. Raymond returned despondently to Antioch, but his visit to Constantinople had one unexpected result in that Zengi, sobered by the thought that Raymond could bring Byzantine power on his side, temporarily shelved his plans against Antioch. Meanwhile, a Latin prelate travelled from Jerusalem to Rome to request a new crusade.

Byzantium did receive some advance notice about what was to come. In 1146 Louis VII wrote to Manuel to enlist his aid in the coming campaign. There were many older people in Constantinople who must have remembered the coming of the First Crusaders and the costly upheavals they had caused before being packed off into Asia. Anna Komnene, from her privileged position, might have regarded them with a mixture of admiration and trepidation, but to the average Byzantine Greek, crusaders were bad news: not only were they Catholics but they had displayed a shocking hostility to anything 'eastern'. Manuel's response was to flash a yellow light, as it were: the crusaders were free to come as long as they paid for what they consumed and their leaders pledged allegiance to him as sole legitimate Christian emperor. But he had no great faith in their promises, and he was right.

The first appearance of the Second Crusaders in Byzantine territory would have confirmed the locals' worst fears. These 'Germans' were, according to Choniates, 'a death-dealing pestilence'.

Females were numbered among them, riding horseback in the manner of men, not on coverlets sidesaddle but unashamedly astride, and bearing lances and weapons as men do, dressed in masculine garb, they conveyed a wholly martial appearance.

These women presumably belonged to the nobler class of crusader, but the great mass of campaigners can be fairly described as ne'er-do-wells of every stripe who 'exulted more in the spilling of blood than others do in the sprinkling of water'. They left a bloody and smoking trail through the Balkans and up to Constantinople, where the emperor had stationed defensive garrisons; some troops were sent around the rear of the crusaders as a precaution. When Conrad and Louis arrived with their armies they were duly ferried over the Bosporus; the sheer number of men defeated the efforts of officials sent to count them and monitor the crossing. However, any discontent on the part of the crusaders was at least partly justified; Choniates alleges that Manuel himself give them a debased currency to use to buy provisions; perhaps on his instructions, the Byzantine communities on the Asian side did everything to harass the crusaders, including cheating them and even selling them poisoned provisions. And, in what seems to be a striking departure from Christian solidarity, Manuel is reported to have actively encouraged the Turks to attack the crusaders whose German section on 26 October suffered serious losses in a battle near Dorylaion.

We may in hindsight wonder why Manuel connived at these practices when he expected that the inexperienced westerners would come to grief anyway in the wilds of Anatolia. Moreover, he himself admired many of the nobler western chivalric traditions and hoped to transplant some to Byzantium. Since we have no way of judging whether Choniates is accurate or not, the safest course would be to presume that Manuel's inconsistent actions were motivated by confusion and some panic at the strength of the French and German forces, not to mention the unhappy political memories of the First Crusade, no doubt embellished in the retelling. In 1146 it would have been hard to tell which was the greater threat— Turk or crusader?

In September 1146 Zengi had unexpectedly met his end at the hands of one of his eunuchs in Aleppo. The assassination was the signal for Zengi's many foes to take advantage of the inevitable period of confusion; Seljuks and Raymond's Franks joined forces to move on Aleppo, but while Zengi's body was yet unburied his younger son Nur ed-Din removed the ring of office from his father's lifeless finger—rather as John II reputedly did with his father Alexios—and quickly rallied his forces who within a year had wrested much of Syria from Frankish hands. Heroic efforts by the young King Baldwin III of Jerusalem could not stem the Muslim advance. Nur ed-Din, just 29 but already displaying at least as much ability as his father while proving himself a rather better character, was free to face the bigger enemies in the west.

From the standpoint of Byzantium, the story of the Second Crusade can be briefly told. From the moment the German and French hordes had vanished over the eastern horizon, Manuel did not concern himself with them overmuch. He would most likely have received regular reports of their progress down the Anatolian coast through Byzantine territory, and of the stubbornness of Louis VII who insisted on taking the far riskier route through the hinterlands, despite Manuel's sage advice. Eventually, in the spring of 1148, after a nightmarish trek through snow and ice and attacking Turks, what was left of Louis' and Conrad's armies straggled into Antioch. Louis' queen, the strong-minded Eleanor of Aquitaine (who was to become the mother of England's Richard I), had become quite fed up with the whole business. On the gruelling march she had been particularly chilled mile after mile by the sight of months-old German corpses at the roadside. She made a vow never to be dragooned into such an ordeal again.

The Byzantine inhabitants of the communities through which the crusaders passed had the worst of both sides, suffering Turkish raids (which might well not have materialized had the crusaders not been there) and earning the contempt of the westerners for not having enough food in their ravaged fields to feed them. If the local Greeks did sometimes ally with the Turks, it was simply because the crusaders were the more serious threat to their lives and livelihoods. The French and Germans, even though fellow Christians, were viewed as far cruder and far less cultured than the average Turkish Muslim. It is fair to say that Manuel I on the Christian side, and Nur ed-Din on the Muslim side, were statesmen of a much higher calibre than either Conrad or Louis. Manuel could not have been surprised when after a series of missteps and disasters, by the end of 1148 the Second Crusade was all but finished, with nothing to show for it except two humiliated European kings and the bones of thousands of their subjects whitening in the Anatolian mountains and in the parched wilderness of Syria.

With the East now temporarily inactive, Manuel could concentrate on something that had been an official aim of all Byzantine emperors since Justinian I. Though south Italy and Sicily had long since been lost to the pope and the Normans, Constantinople had never given up its long-term aim of recovering those lands to reconstitute the Roman Empire. Politically and militarily the idea may have been highly unrealistic, but ideology is rarely a slave to realism. In April 1147, while the Second Crusaders were still milling around Anatolia, Manuel's attention was forcibly brought round to the west when Roger II de Hauteville, the Norman ruler of Sicily and descendant of Robert Guiscard, sailed against the west coast of Greece. Commanded by a renegade Greek, George of Antioch, the fleet attacked Corfu whose inhabitants, suffering under a rapacious Byzantine tax-collector, had initially welcomed the invaders. Three hundred Sicilian knights occupied the island's citadel. Moving on down the Greek coast and rounding the Peloponnese, the fleet attacked the fortress-citadel of Monemvasia but could make no headway against its Gibraltar-like natural defences. George of Antioch then raided as many points on the Greek coast as he could, robbing the historic town of Thebes of its wealth and carrying off many of the eminent citizens along with the best 'comely and deep-bosomed' women. Many of these latter were weavers in the Theban silk industry, which at one blow was forcibly transferred to Palermo. The same treatment was meted out to another historic Greek city, Corinth.

Those raids, plus the fact that they were led by a Greek no less, stoked the emperor to red-hot anger. In February 1148 he decreed that Roger II, 'that dragon [and] common enemy of all Christians and illegal occupier of the land of Sicily,' be cleared from the face of the sea. He knew it would be a tall order. The manpower and naval power required would be considerable. The neglected navy, especially, had to be rebuilt; the yards along the Golden Horn echoed to the construction of new triremes while older 50-oared vessels and horse transports were hastily repaired and put back into commission. Choniates puts the strength of the new fleet at some 1,000 sail, many of them armed with the feared Greek Fire. Complementing the fleet was an infantry force of perhaps 30,000 men plus cavalry. Just weeks after the imperial edict the whole force was ready and placed under the command of Manuel's brother-in-law Stephanos Kontostephanos, with Axuch as Grand Domestikos.

Manuel himself was in the fleet as it approached Corfu. Before ordering an attack on the Sicilian defenders he sent envoys to see if they were prepared to surrender; they were not, and so a mutual bombardment began. The Byzantines, on low coastal land, were at a disadvantage from the projectiles fired from the Corfu battlements. A fragment from a stone missile hit Kontostephanos in the groin, mortally wounding him. Axuch took over as overall commander and continued the battle. Manuel, feeling he ought to do something while his officers were in the thick of the fight, boarded his flagship to sail around Corfu to reconnoitre possible points of attack. Apparently finding none, he pondered the problem of the well-nigh impregnable citadel. His way of tackling it was to order the construction of a great ladder made of spare ship timbers and reaching the height of the cliff on which the citadel rampart stood. But when he called for volunteers to be the first up the ladder with the words, 'He who loves the emperor and is eager to distinguish himself in the face of danger, let him ascend,' no one stepped forward. The operation seemed suicidal.

Eventually four brothers of the Petraliphas family, said to be of Norman descent, dared climb the steps, preceded by Poupakes, one of Axuch's bodyguards, who by his original name (Abu Bakr) appears to have been a Christianized Turk or Arab in Byzantine service. As often happens in such cases, the raw courage exhibited by a few shamed the rest, and before long the emperor had to hold back the more experienced troops whom he could not afford to lose. To those going forward he addressed heartening words intended to reassure them in case they didn't survive:

> [S]hould you lose your lives, winning honour for your fatherland and glory for yourselves, I shall not neglect your affairs, but I will so dispose of those things pertaining to your homes, children and wives that they who survive must deem these fortunate and worthy of emulation, and this great solace will follow you down to Hades.

This pep talk is worth examining for a moment. There is a certain echo of the famous funeral speech of Pericles, the fifth century BC Athenian leader, when the dead of the first year of the Peloponnesian War were brought into Athens for burial. Pericles had been perhaps the first to broach the idea that death in battle for one's country somehow ennobled the soldier who suffered it, ensuring that his name and family name would live on. Manuel went one step further, hinting that death might not after all be the end, that those in Hades might nonetheless have 'a certain perception' and would be able in some way to know of their fame.

The references to Hades sound odd in the mouth of a Christian emperor who was fully expected to uphold the purity of the Christian doctrine of everlasting life for the believer. Here—assuming Choniates records his words more or less accurately—he must have sounded like a pagan. We have seen how he was always rather indifferent to Church ritual and, unlike his father and grandfather, had few if any soul-searchings. He was also seeking ways to reconcile the eastern and western churches, apparently having little use for the doctrinal minutiae that were used as excuses for their separation; after all, if he were to realize his dream of getting back south Italy and Sicily, the last thing he needed was the enmity of the popes. But apart from these practical situations, where exactly Manuel stood in the matter of Christian doctrine remains unknown.

Not so for the bodyguard Poupakes who made the sign of the cross before starting up the ladder ahead of the rest of the picked squad who held their shields above their heads against the rain of projectiles from above. They seemed about to make it to the top, and Poupakes had already jumped off to engage the enemy, when the ladder collapsed, throwing those still climbing into the sea; many who survived the fall itself were drowned. As for Poupakes, he fought his lone way through the first line of defenders and got through into the citadel. With the help of the Venetians, Manuel was able to drive off the Sicilians, but brawling between them and the Byzantines threatened to upset the alliance; the Italians surely went too far when, Choniates tells us, they stole the imperial galley, got hold of 'a certain black-skinned

Ethiopian' and dressed him up on deck and 'crowned' him as mock-emperor in full view of the Byzantines—a crude jab at Manuel's dark colouring, for which the emperor never forgave them.

But with Roger II still a menace, Manuel swallowed his anger and continued the alliance with Venice. Repeated attempts to storm Sicilian-held Corfu came to nought, but the defenders eventually were worn down to the point at which, despairing of aid from Roger, they sent out peace feelers to the emperor. At first he took a tough line, which duly softened up the Sicilians, after which he could be more accommodating. In early August 1149 Corfu surrendered to the emperor. A contingent of his Germans was stationed in the citadel. From here Manuel saw his way clear to a counter-invasion of Sicily as the first step towards reclaiming south Italy. According to Choniates, he could rest for a while in the knowledge that,

> [T]hose who shun warfare for peace utterly forget that, as a consequence, a multitude of enemies burgeon as though planted in a fertile piece of farmland, destroying their dominion and making it impossible for them to enjoy any stable peace.

Manuel had uprooted one set of enemies, and in summer was on the point of crossing into Sicily to uproot some more when bad weather forced his fleet to stay on the east shore of the Adriatic Sea. He spent the early autumn suppressing the rebellious Serbs and as winter approached returned to Constantinople to an adulatory welcome by people and Senate.

In the autumn of 1151 Manuel was forced to show himself in the Balkans once more, this time against the Hungarians as well as the Serbs. At the Sava River (somewhere in modern Croatia) he is reported to have felled a 'giant' Hungarian who charged him, thrusting his sword through the man's eye. The campaign was successful enough to earn Manuel yet another triumphal procession with droves of captives in tow. But the Sicilians still needed to be discouraged from venturing eastwards, so Alexios Bryennios, the son of Nikephoros Bryennios and Anna Komnene, and hence the emperor's cousin, together with John Doukas, a scion of that noble house allied to the Komnenes, sailed to attack the island and adjacent toe of Italy.

Manuel was able to do this in part because he had gained a powerful ally in the person of Conrad, head of the Holy Roman Empire, who had benefited from the emperor's medical skills after the fiasco of the Second Crusade and whose position was now under threat from Roger of Sicily's intrigues. But at the same time, Louis VII of France and Roger were setting up their own league and seeking the blessing of Pope Eugenius III for a planned third attempt on the Holy Land which could be accomplished, they believed, by eliminating untrustworthy Byzantium. Conrad was most put out by all this; if anyone had the moral right to drive the Muslims out of Palestine and Syria it was the Holy Roman Empire, acting if need be in concert with the Byzantine Empire. What business did the despised Frenchmen and Sicilians have elbowing in on this right? In part thanks to Conrad's steadfast support, the Byzantine expedition against Sicily, scheduled for the autumn of 1152, had considerable chances of success.

Conrad did not see the result, for he died in February, to be succeeded by Frederick I, known as Barbarossa for his reddish-brown beard. Frederick, an impressive-looking man with ample ability, itched to go after Roger in Sicily but his pride didn't allow him to accept the Byzantine Empire on equal terms with his own. To him Manuel was as illegitimate as the German emperors were to Byzantium. It was this that prompted him to sign an accord with the pope to allow no Byzantines anywhere on Italian territory. Then Eugenius himself left this world in July 1153, followed by Roger of Sicily seven months later. Succeeding Roger was his son William I, nicknamed the Bad, less because of his character than of his appearance; a western source describes him as having 'a thick black beard [that] lent him a savage and terrible aspect'. William was much less a diplomat than his father, and revealed his weakness by offering to send back to Manuel all the spoils his father had taken in the expedition against Greece plus the Greek prisoners. Manuel spurned the offer and kept the planned offensive on the cards.

He was encouraged by the policies of the new pope, Adrian IV (the Englishman Nicholas Breakspear), who had as little use for the Normans of Sicily as Manuel had. The emperor despatched the capable Alexios Axuch, son of Grand Domestikos John Axuch, to Ancona to raise a corps of Italian mercenaries and join the pope in attacking the Norman domains. At about this time (the chronology is uncertain) Alexios Bryennios and John Doukas set sail. At first they did well, beating William I's forces in several naval encounters and laying siege to Brindisi. But William rallied, gathering a large number of mercenaries, and decisively defeated the Byzantines, capturing both their commanders. The news hit Manuel hard, 'as though he had drunken deep of wormwood.' His furious reaction was to fit out another fleet under Constantine Angelos. This is the first appearance of the rising family of the Angeli, which aspired to join the military aristocracy to which the Komnenes and Doukai belonged. Hailing from Philadelphia (near what is now Sarayköy in west Turkey), the Angeli had married into the Komnenes when Alexios I's elder sister Theodora wed the Constantine Angelos who in the spring of 1157—and though 'robust in stature' by now getting on in years—found himself commanding an imperial naval campaign. Manuel ordered the fleet to sail, but a day had scarcely passed when he frantically sent signals to order it back again. What had happened?

We have seen how indifferent Manuel was to the ritualistic aspects of the Christian doctrine that every emperor was expected to uphold by setting a personal example. We have also seen how in the Corfu campaign he made repeated references to Hades and other pagan concepts in his exhortations to his troops. It therefore comes as no surprise to learn from Choniates that the emperor was prone to a most un-Christian belief in astrology and other forms of mysticism. True to form, he had consulted his stars and planets before ordering Angelos to sail, but almost at once his astrological advisers fell into confusion about what exactly was portended, so to be on the safe side, Angelos was recalled. The 'signs' were duly and painstakingly read again, and this time they endorsed the expedition. Choniates drips sarcasm:

> So advantageous was the determination of the exact moment to the success of Roman affairs, or in redressing the failures of preceding commanders, and in redeeming every adversity, that forthwith Constantine Angelos was delivered into the hands of the enemy!

Angelos never even got to Sicily. He was intercepted by William's ships and delivered in chains to the Norman king. So much for the merits of astrological warfare. Manuel had apparently learned nothing from the fate of the Athenians in Sicily in 413 BC, where their General Nikias, terrified by an eclipse of the moon, abandoned all common sense and led his army to annihilation. Sobered by the fate of his kinsman but also by the mounting expenses of the war, Manuel sought a diplomatic solution. He had probably heard enough about Frederick Barbarossa to estimate him as a potentially greater enemy than William who, for the same reason, deemed it wiser to reach an accord with Byzantium in 1158.

This left Manuel to pay more attention to a running sore within his own wider family that had revealed itself during his campaign in Serbia a few years before. This was his cousin Andronikos, the youngest son of John II's brother Isaac. Andronikos for some time had been making a notorious reputation for himself. As a sexual predator, we are given to understand that he far outstripped Manuel's own early accomplishments in that sphere. That, indeed, was his stated aim, he would say when criticized, and engage in playful banter with the emperor on the subject. One of his conquests was Eudokia, the widow of his cousin and namesake Andronikos who had perished during John II's campaign before Antioch. On campaign in Serbia, and while Andronikos was serving as governor of the Belgrade area, they were in bed in his tent when a group of Eudokia's relations and a posse of armed troops surrounded it. The quick-witted Eudokia suggested that her lover disguise himself as a chambermaid and escape, but he would have none of it

– cowardice was not one of his vices. Drawing his sword, he slashed open the tent and bounded through the tear. Arrested, he was dismissed from his post.

Andronikos spent three miserable years in the palace dungeon at Constantinople, chained in stout iron stocks and suffering abuse by the guards. Yet he refused to be broken, and in the autumn of 1158 succeeded in tunnelling his way under the dungeon floor with his bare hands, being careful to reseal the hole after he left. When the guards brought in his dinner, they found an unaccountably empty cell. He appears to have hidden underground for a while before making the break for freedom, as his wife was arrested as a suspected accomplice, and somehow—the narrative here is contradictory and unclear—the couple managed to meet fleetingly and 'engaged at length in sexual intercourse beside the prison'. After a hue and cry throughout the city Andronikos was soon recaptured and consigned to the dungeon with double fetters and a sadistic guard. But Byzantium certainly had not seen the last of him.

Manuel was probably not so much concerned with Andronikos' erotic life— though it put the palace in a bad light—as with his bumptious cousin's more politically sinister motivations. While governor of the Belgrade area Andronikos had been suspected of conspiring with the Hungarians to topple Manuel, which was one more reason for his incarceration. Choniates, our chief source for the period, hints strongly that Andronikos indeed aimed for the throne, but also indicates that Manuel was not at first willing to believe it. Conspiracies in his reign were not as common as they had been with his father and grandfather. Now, with his cousin in chains, the emperor was free to turn his attention to what he considered the great unfinished business of his reign so far, the taking of Antioch.

Manuel and his army reappeared before the city in April 1159, but the welcome was by no means cordial. Antioch was now in the hands of one of history's more unsavoury characters, the Frenchman Reynald of Châtillon, an ex-crusader who had stayed on and married the widow of Raymond of Poitiers, thus gaining control of the city without a single sword-stroke. The news of Châtillon's escapades in the region, which included an invasion of Cyprus where he ordered Greek priests' noses cut off, gave Manuel plenty of incentive. The Latins, seeing they could not prevail against the mass of Byzantine steel arrayed against them, decided for the moment to submit. Châtillon offered to surrender Antioch at once, but Manuel wanted to make it a bit more humiliating for the Frenchman who in the end had to walk a considerable distance, barefoot and bareheaded, out to the emperor's camp. In the royal tent and surrounded by heavily-armed imperial troops, Manuel at first made a show of royal indifference, and then laid down his terms: immediate surrender of Antioch, which would provide a contingent for the Byzantine army, and replacement of the Latin patriarch by a Greek Orthodox one. Châtillon, overwhelmed, agreed at once. The message was clear: if anyone was going to be the boss in the Christian East, it would be the Byzantine emperor.

On Easter Day 1159 Manuel made his triumphant entry into Antioch. He must have harked back to a similar occasion twenty-one years before, when he had accompanied his father over the same ground. He knew, however, that much if not most of the public adulation was false and that he was in constant personal danger; in fact, before his procession he had ordered the disarming of all the Frankish and Latin troops. His own formations were the more impressive for that: first the burly Russians, Scandinavians and Englishmen of the Varangian Guard, with their famed battleaxes on their shoulders, then Manuel himself, clad in a magnificent purple robe over his coat of mail. Walking at his side, most tellingly, was Reynald de Châtillon himself, humiliatingly on foot holding and fiddling with the emperor's stirrup strap. Baldwin III of Jerusalem, who had come up for the occasion, was relegated to a similar subsidiary role. Meanwhile, Manuel had made one concession to the Latins, agreeing to keep on the Latin patriarch of Antioch, who officiated at the welcome mass in the city's cathedral.

During the week of celebrations that followed, the emperor noticed some Latin troops boasting about their prowess with the lance and suggested a joust between the Greeks and Latins; the challenge was accepted, and on the appointed day Manuel, grinning confidently, rode out to the field on 'a war-horse with a magnificent mane and trappings of gold'. He told his own contestants 'to wear the most splendid armour possible'. Châtillon, for his part, rode up in similarly splendid array and wearing 'a cap like a sloping tiara, embroidered in gold'. The ensuing mock battle between the opposing teams was a rough one; several times a knight on one side or the other, 'pale with fear,' would cower behind his shield or turn tail and run. The pennons flew back and forth, rippling in the stiff wind. Manuel himself, to the despair of his staff, heartily joined the fray, felling two knights at once with his lance. Afterwards, Manuel was able to apply his medical skills to Baldwin III, who broke his arm while out hunting. In this way Manuel was able to improve relations with the rulers of Outremer while keeping his longer-term attention on the Turks, and felt confident enough soon afterwards to return to the capital.

At about this time Manuel's German wife Bertha, who had been living in the palace in unbedded and saintly obscurity for the past fourteen years, passed away. Manuel seems to have genuinely grieved for her, yet her death came as a relief in a way. But the vital son and heir had not been produced, so therefore, on cue, the matchmaking was set in motion. Offers came from all points of the compass. The choice came down to two attractive Frankish princesses, the blonde Maria, the daughter of the late Raymond of Antioch, and Melisende, a cousin of Baldwin III of Jerusalem. A flurry of shuttle diplomacy ensued, as here was an excellent chance for Byzantium and Outremer to forge ties of blood and provide, at last, a united front against the Muslims. For a time it appeared that Melisende was the front runner, and all of Outremer prepared frantically for the royal wedding. But Manuel had been hearing vague rumours that Melisende's health was not of the best, a factor that would militate against her producing an heir. Abruptly he switched his preference to Maria, triggering a diplomatic firestorm, but there was nothing the Frankish rulers could do about it. Manuel and Maria were wed in Sancta Sophia in December 1160 by no fewer than three patriarchs. As for Melisende, she never recovered from the shock and disappointment and seems to have fallen into a terminal depression.

Manuel probably allowed himself a minimum time to become familiar with his new bride, as we find him campaigning again in the east against Sultan Kiliç Arslan II of Ikonion. This time he was aided by the Serbs, a contingent of Reynald of Châtillon's Franks, one of Pechenegs, one of Danishmend Turks and Nur ed-Din from Iraq, all of whom homed in on Ikonion from different directions. Hopelessly outmatched, Kiliç Arslan threw in the towel. He was rewarded with a state visit to Constantinople. The emperor, sporting 'a ruby the size of an apple' around his neck, treated the sultan with elaborate generosity. Kiliç Arslan was allowed to keep all the gold and silver plates and cups in which his food and drink were served. The flamboyant public entertainments lasted for several days. Choniates describes what happened one day before thousands of spectators in the Hippodrome when one of the sultan's 'conjurers' announced that he would fly through the air by launching himself from a precarious wooden tower erected for the purpose.

> He stood on the tower as though at a starting post, dressed in an extremely long, white robe... It was [his] intention to unfurl the upper garment like the sail of a ship, thus enveloping the wind in its folds.

As he stood there perched, swaying in the wind, the crowd was getting impatient. The shouts of 'Fly! Fly!' became louder. Manuel, looking on with concern, sent someone to talk the man into abandoning his foolhardy stunt, but to no apparent effect. The sultan, too, was worried. The man high up on the swaying platform began playing with the spectators' suspense.

> Many times he raised his arms, forming them into wings and beating the air as he poised himself for flight. When a fair and favourable wind arose, he flapped his arms like a bird in the belief that he could walk the air. But... instead of taking wing, he plummeted groundward like a solid mass pulled down by gravity. In the end, he plunged to earth, and his life was snuffed out, his arms and legs and all the bones of his body shattered.

The spectators, and the rest of the city, just laughed; shopkeepers jeered the sultan's entourage in the streets, their prejudices about the Turks fully confirmed.

On the Empire's north-west front the Hungarians were becoming restive. Hungary, lying between the Byzantine and Holy Roman Empires, and hence of vital importance to both, was interested in extending its influence into Dalmatia, which meant that the Hungarians had to be brought 'on side', through marriage alliance if necessary. An opportunity arose in 1154 when István, a brother of King Geza II, had fled to Constantinople to escape a palace intrigue. Manuel, delighted, gave him the hand of his niece in marriage; shortly afterwards, envious of István's luck, his younger brother László followed him. Relations with Hungary appeared to be on a smooth path when Geza II died in 1162 – as Choniates extravagantly puts it, 'the taut strings of his mortal frame were slackened by nature, dissolving into those elements of which it was composed'—to be succeeded by his son István III (not to be confused with the brother István). But the Byzantines didn't count on the ordinary Hungarians, who resented Constantinople's influence over their affairs and threw out the Byzantine envoys sent to attend István III's coronation. Manuel therefore set out to chastise them.

The chastisement proved more difficult than expected, partly because Andronikos had again managed to escape his palace jail by what was probably a makeshift rope ladder and hiding in tall grass for a few days. The most bizarre luck was on his side as he managed to get on a fishing boat; the boat was intercepted but Andronikos (helped no doubt by the shackles still on his feet) successfully pretended to be a foreign boat slave who couldn't speak Greek. He briefly reached his home and family, but Manuel's agents caught up with him. Escorted under guard back to Constantinople, Andronikos made a convincing show of suffering tummy trouble and often asked to be allowed to go into the bushes to supposedly relieve himself. One night, as he was engaged in this deception, he wrapped his cloak around his staff and arranged it in such a way as to resemble, in the dim light, someone squatting. By the time the guards realized that the act of nature was taking rather too long and went to investigate, Andronikos was well away. Manuel's wrath fell on Poupakes, the one who had led the charge up the siege ladder at Corfu, who seems to have been complicit in Andronikos' escape. The former hero was publicly flogged and led around the city with a rope round his neck as an example.

The problem of Andronikos, who ended up living the good life as a guest of the governor of Galitza province and was suspected of stirring up the Cumans against Byzantium, hindered Manuel from giving his full attention to the Hungarians. The Byzantines were crushed in one battle, but with some difficulty he took the strategic town of Zevgminion. Choniates preserves the story of a noble Hungarian defender who saw his attractive wife being dragged off by a Byzantine soldier and, unable to bear the thought of her being used by someone else, ran her through with his sword. The historian gives us another vignette from the occasion:

> A Hungarian, still wearing his native hat and dress, was being led away captive. A certain Roman [Byzantine] fell on him, struck a blow with his knife and killed him; he put the Hungarian's hat on his own head and without further ado proceeded on his way... From among the troops in the rear, another even more violent Roman came on the scene with sword in hand and, believing him to be a Hungarian captive, smote a mortal blow upon his neck.

Constantine Angelos was put in charge of rebuilding the walls of Zevgminion and fortifying Belgrade and Niş.

By the start of 1166 Manuel and Maria had been married for at least four years, but the coveted son was nowhere in sight. Wicked tongues in Constantinople attributed the lack to a sinister 'curse on the empress' womb' uttered by a deposed patriarch a quarter of century before. That had applied to Bertha, who had given Manuel a daughter, Maria, but that was all. Was the same curse applying to his second wife as well? Manuel, now in his forties and never knowing if he would return alive from his next war, reluctantly proclaimed his daughter as heiress and arranged for her to marry a Hungarian prince when she came of age. This way, at least, there would be a male to give the throne some backing when he was gone.

But Manuel hadn't reckoned on Andronikos, who by now seems to have returned to the capital, possibly through a pardon, and was developing into a serious pain in the imperial neck. Andronikos noisily objected to the succession arrangement, no doubt because he eyed the top job for himself. He especially opposed designating a Hungarian as royal consort, a view which found a good many supporters. Perhaps to get him out of the way, Manuel sent Andronikos to Antioch as governor. Once there he besieged Philippa, the daughter of the late Raymond of Poitiers, who was totally bowled over by his roguish virility and 'forsook both home and family' to be his lover. He would strut through the city in tight-fitting robes slit along the thighs and hips; even the highly critical Choniates concedes that he was devastatingly handsome. Around him would be a squad of bodyguards 'tall in stature and [with] blond hair tinged with red', carrying silver bows.

Hearing of all this, Manuel decided to deal with his aggravating cousin once and for all. A clumsy attempt to detach Philippa from Andronikos' embraces by sending a rival suitor came to nothing, earning the emperor only embarrassment. To save himself, Andronikos fled Antioch and moved on to Jerusalem, where he continued his sexual predator habits. One of his willing victims was Theodora, the widow of Baldwin III, who was still only 21. Though Theodora was a Byzantine

Komnene like Andronikos, and their union was denounced as incestuous, they lived together in Beirut. Manuel wrote to King Amalric I of Jerusalem demanding Andronikos' arrest and extradition. But the letter fell into Theodora's hands. Andronikos again judged it wise to make himself scarce; he and Theodora vanished into the Muslim world and were excommunicated by the Church. Little that Andronikos cared, as he and Theodora had two children, living the good life in the Seljuk domains.

While all this was happening Manuel was continuously preoccupied with the Hungarian threat. His campaigns between 1166 and 1169 make tedious reading and can be passed over. They fuelled his suspicions of his daughter's betrothed, Alexios of Hungary, who was seen as not terribly reliable. But the emperor's attention, possibly prompted by Andronikos' escapades, was turning south to Egypt, an important source of grain, that he wanted to wrest from the Fatimid caliphs. In this he had the consent of Amalric of Jerusalem and the descendants of the Crusaders, especially the Military Orders of the Hospitallers and Templars, whose *raison d'être* revolved around the constant struggle against the Muslims. Manuel sent sixty warships under Theodore Mavrozomes to inform Amalric that as many as 200 more were on their way. But in the meantime, Amalric was having second thoughts, and it wasn't until late October 1169 that the main Byzantine fleet under Admiral Andronikos Kontostephanos joined Amalric and the Franks in the siege of Damietta on the Nile.

The Byzantine fleet ferried the Franks across the Nile, but when Amalric saw how formidable the defences of Damietta were, he quailed. It was now late in the year, and the attack had to go ahead now, Kontostephanos argued, or not at all. Moreover, the fleet's supplies were dwindling. Weeks passed as Amalric agonized over what to do, weeks which the Muslims used to strengthen their garrison. In December Amalric gave up; as his knights trudged disconsolately back to Jerusalem, a storm damaged Kontostephanos' fleet on its way back to Constantinople. (The admiral himself chose to return overland via Jerusalem.) It was one more defeat for Manuel and another wedge in the perennial distrust between the Byzantines and the Latins.

But in the meantime, the emperor had cause to rejoice, as on 14 September Maria gave birth to the longed-for male child in the Purple Chamber. Manuel himself attended the birth, along with one of his stargazers; the old 'vagina curse', it seemed, had at long last been broken. As Manuel threw parties for the people of the capital, he named his son Alexios after his fabled grandfather. As the boy grew 'like a flourishing and luxuriant young plant', he was designated heir to the throne, displacing his daughter Maria and the Hungarian noble she had been joined to. Whether the pair were in fact wed or merely betrothed remains vague. Choniates hints at the latter, as the arrangement was easily annulled, which no doubt satisfied many in Byzantium who were anxious for the throne not to fall into foreign hands. In 1171 the Hungarian Alexios himself succeeded to the throne of Hungary as Béla III, so there were no complaints from that quarter. But what to do with daughter Maria, who now must have been about 30 and anxious for some domesticity? Thanks to her *porphyrogennete* status, the only course open to her was to wed some foreign prince or king. Choniates, who served in the palace staff, describes her as 'stately as a white poplar wet with dew, longing for the marriage bed'. Maria seems to have been presentable enough, and before long a husband was found for her in the person of Renier of Montferrat who it seems was still in his teens.

In March 1171 a sore that had been festering in Constantinople for decades burst open. The city's Italian commercial colonies, thanks to favoured trade treatment, had flourished and with wealth came arrogance. The two most numerous colonies were those of the Venetians and Genoese, together numbering about 80,000 people, clustered mainly in and around the Galata and Pera districts on the east side of the Golden Horn. Though the Venetians and Genoese were keen rivals, with little love lost for one another, both were uniformly despised by the local Byzantine Greeks for their obstreperous behaviour. One day the Genoese settlement was attacked and seriously damaged; the perpetrators were never identified, but Manuel found a convenient excuse to blame the Venetians. Squads were sent through the city and provinces to arrest leading Venetians and confiscate their assets. Security considerations also could have played a part, as the Italians in Constantinople almost certainly harboured Venetian spies. Some 10,000 Venetians in the capital found themselves behind bars; a few managed to board a ship that eluded a Byzantine flotilla sent to stop it.

The Venetian Republic fumed. The doge, Domenico Michiel, taxed his subjects viciously to raise a fleet of 120 ships which by the autumn had sailed into Greek waters, with himself in command. The Byzantine fleet under Kontostephanos shadowed the Venetians but did no more, as Manuel appears to have repented of his harsh actions and sought an accommodation with Venice. Putting in at Euboia (now Evia), Michiel met imperial envoys who suggested that he send a peace delegation to Constantinople where they were confident the issue could be ironed out. The doge agreed and sailed on to winter at the island of Chios to await the result. There, plague struck, carrying off thousands of men. Barely had Michiel absorbed that shock than another awaited him: his returning envoys reported that far from being accommodating, Manuel was intransigent and had treated the mission miserably. It was a broken doge who sailed back to Venice with the surviving remnant of his force, the bearer not only of bad news but also of plague germs. Shortly afterwards, he was knifed to death in the streets.

With the Italian threat seen off, Manuel could turn his attention—after an interval of at least ten years—back to the East. We don't know if he still harboured an ambition to reclaim Italy. But the Muslim Turks of Kiliç Arslan II were closer to home and a perennial threat to the link between Byzantium and Outremer. The sultan had eliminated his Muslim rivals and his Sultanate of Ikonion was stronger than ever, extending its diplomatic tentacles even into Germany. Besides, Anatolia was familiar campaigning ground for him. Manuel deemed that the Turks were trespassing with their crops and herds on the Dorylaion Plain. As for Dorylaion itself, he decided to rebuild its walls and reinstall a Byzantine garrison with the aim of regaining the fertile land. Manuel rode there with his army; while there he received a letter from the sultan politely asking him why he was rebuilding the fortifications. Manuel, his lip curled in contempt, read the letter and ignored it. To set an example to his men he carried the first stones for the new wall of Dorylaion on his own back. The Turkish attacks were incessant. One of them occurred while Manuel was peeling a peach with his knife; he was in such a hurry to don his armour that he had to throw the fruit away uneaten.

In the summer of 1176, after praying in Sancta Sophia, Manuel again set out eastwards 'intent on destroying the Turkish nation and holding captive the sultan whose neck he would trample as a footstool'. It was hard going, as Kiliç Arslan had laid waste the countryside in the emperor's path and poisoned the wells. The sultan also called on considerable reserves from Mesopotamia and elsewhere in the Muslim world, at the same time trying to stay the emperor's progress with peace feelers. With men and horses suffering from privations, the emperor's senior advisers urged him to make an accommodation with Kiliç Arslan. But he distrusted the wily sultan, who had often broken his word before. Moreover, younger noble officers who had never seen combat, contemptuously described by Choniates as favouring 'beautiful hair styles and bright and cheerful faces and [wearing] around their neck collars of gold'—a type common to the start of all wars in all ages—favoured action. These impatient high-born youngsters, some of them of the Komnene house, had the emperor's ear.

The imperial army passed a derelict fortress at Myriokephalon (Place of a Thousand Heads) and headed into the long Çardak defile on the way to Ikonion. From what we know, here the emperor appears to have abandoned all military common sense. He and every soldier in his army could see the Turks lined up on the heights overlooking them on either side, yet Manuel seems to have taken no preventive action. Instead, as the Turks raided his flanks, he plodded on. On 17 September the van of the army, led by the sons of Constantine Angelos, surprised the Turks at the end of the ravine and scattered them. But a gap opened up with the rest of the army, including the emperor, who were still in the ravine. Into this gap the Turks poured down from all sides. The contingent commanded by Baldwin the Frank, the emperor's brother-in-law, took the first hit, whereupon Baldwin himself and a few knights rode madly into the enemy's midst and were killed.

The rest of the army was now trapped. Pack animals, orderlies and soldiers milled about, jammed tightly together, dying without being able to defend themselves. Oxen pulling the supply wagons were killed along with their drivers; the immobilized wagons blocked the troops of the rearguard from coming to the rescue of the centre. Choniates writes:

> The hollows were filled with bodies. The groves were glutted with the fallen. The bubbling, rushing streams flowed red with blood. Blood commingled with blood, human blood with the blood of pack animals. The horrors that took place there defy all description.

Manuel was stunned; his despair deepened when he looked up and saw a head raised on the point of a Turkish lance, recognizing the head as that of a nephew, Andronikos Vatatzes. Nevertheless, he at first tried to order the rear and centre to press on and break the Turkish vice. Seeing that it would be hopeless to dislodge a superior Turkish force from higher ground, he appears to have decided that the battle was lost. Choniates, however, claims that he made one supreme personal effort to allow what remained of his army to escape, personally charging the enemy. Manuel, the story goes, fought with extreme courage, pierced with wounds, his helmet askew and dozens of arrows stuck in his shield. But in the end, blinded by a dust storm that had blown up, he had to fall back.

Exhausted, Manuel dismounted and sat down under a pear tree to get his breath back. A Turkish soldier ran up and tried to grab the emperor's horse; Manuel had nothing in his hands but the stump of a lance, and swung at the Turk with it, knocking him down. Other Turks rushed up but Manuel, having seized one of his cavalrymen's lances, ran one of them through. Choniates' account indicates that the emperor still had hopes of prevailing against the Turks and gathered up a couple of dozen soldiers to try and break through the enemy and join the advance echelons of the army that had emerged from the defile. An elite Turkish cavalry squad, mounted on splendidly-caparisoned Arabian stallions, headed for him but his men beat them off. Eventually Manuel reached the van of his army; on the way he asked an orderly to bring him a pitcher of water from a nearby stream, but took only a few sips before he saw that the water was fouled by blood. He groaned aloud at the realization, but one of his men rebuked him: 'Get along with you, O Emperor! Often in the past you have drunk unto intoxication from a wine bowl of Christian blood, stripping and gleaning your subjects.' The soldier's words are a startling indication of the unpopularity of the Komnenes after nearly a century of rule, and show that the taxes levied to maintain the militarization of the Byzantine state were becoming unsupportable for many.

But the soldier was not finished. Manuel saw Turks ripping open the captured imperial treasure bags and scattering the gold and silver pieces on the ground in their haste. Manuel wanted the men around him to fall on the enemy and get the money back, but the cynical soldier had a ready response: 'That money should have been given to [us] earlier, not now, when it can be retrieved only with great difficulty and bloodshed.' He insolently challenged the emperor, who he suspected of being in the grip of 'sour wine', to go and fight for the money himself. Too exhausted to discipline the insubordinate man, or perhaps perceiving the bitter truth of his words, Manuel made no reply.

At nightfall Manuel gathered together what remained of his army amid general despondency. Fear did not let them sleep, as Turks could be heard in the darkness shouting that everyone in the camp would be dead in the morning. No doubt Manuel had in mind the fate of Roman IV Diogenes at Manizikert. There was no way, however, he was going to allow himself to be captured like Romanos. The only answer, he told those assembled in his tent, was flight under cover of darkness, but a soldier eavesdropping outside the tent (perhaps the same one who had berated his emperor at the bloody stream) was horrified at what he heard. 'Are you not the one,' he shouted, addressing Manuel, 'who has squeezed us into these desolate and narrow paths, exposing us to utter ruin, the one who has ground us as though in a mortar between these cliffs falling in upon us? And now will you deliver us over to the enemy, like sheep for the slaughter?' Manuel's planned flight would come at the inevitable cost of leaving his surviving troops to their fate. He realized this and shamefacedly abandoned the plan. But these instances of insubordination present a striking picture of the decline in the prestige of the emperor at war. It is impossible to imagine Alexios I or even John II being similarly challenged from the ranks.

At daybreak the Turks, yelling 'their barbarian war cry', resumed their attacks on the perimeter of the imperial camp, beating back feeble counter-thrusts by the Byzantines. It appeared to be the end for Manuel and his staff when without warning the enemy attacks ceased, and in their place came an emissary of Kiliç Arslan named Gabras bearing a truce proposal along with a superb parade horse and two-edged sword for the emperor. It is unclear why the sultan was being so accommodating. He must surely have known that he had all but eliminated the Byzantine army in the Çardak defile, and that the helpless Manuel was his for the taking. The consensus among scholars is that he was thinking in the long term: given the constant rivalry among Muslim rulers, he might well need Byzantine support in the future and wanted to give Manuel a face-saving way out. Gabras, no doubt acting on the sultan's orders, praised the emperor fulsomely for his courage in adversity and generously tried to relieve Manuel's gloom by suggesting that his gold-embroidered yellow surcoat, an unlucky colour for battle, was the real reason he had lost; the implication was that the emperor ought not to blame himself or his courageous troops for the disaster. It was an ingenious stroke of diplomacy. Smiling grimly, the emperor doffed his surcoat and handed it over to Gabras. A truce was then drawn up, to include the surrender of the fortresses of Dorylaion and Souvleon. Manuel signed on the spot.

He wished to withdraw by a route other than the corpse-strewn defile of Çardak, but his guides forced him through it anyway. The sight that met his eyes was horrifying:

> The slain had their scalps torn from their heads, and the phalluses of many had been cut off. It was said that the Turks took these measures so that the circumcised could not be distinguished from the uncircumcised and the victory therefore disputed and contested since many had fallen on both sides. No one passed by on the opposite side without bursting into tears and calling by name his slain companions and close friends.

The march westwards was not without its problems as the Turks, shadowing the imperial army, picked off stragglers and walking wounded. At Philadelphia the troops could finally relax and Manuel could receive treatment for his wounds. He ordered that each man in his army receive a financial bonus for any treatment he might need. Contrary to the terms of the treaty he had signed with Kiliç Arslan he left the Dorylaion fort untouched; the sultan heard of it and demanded an explanation. Manuel said he just hadn't had time, but Kiliç Arslan didn't buy that excuse and launched raids on all the Anatolian territories as far as the Aegean Coast. Several hard rearguard actions were fought as Manuel slowly progressed towards Constantinople. Near Nikomedia he received news that the Turks were investing Klaudiopolis and turned back to deal with it. He left behind his tent and bed and took with him just his gold-adorned horse and the armour he was wearing; though Choniates does not mention any companions, he must have taken with him a basic staff. He slept rough, whenever he could sleep at all, soaked to the skin whenever it rained. When he reached Klaudiopolis the besiegers saw his standards and fled, making the imperial ordeal worthwhile.

It was lucky for Manuel that at this time the West was absorbed in its own troubles. Frederick I Barbarossa of the Holy Roman Empire was moving on Rome, itching to be formally crowned by Pope Alexander III, but the pope was reluctant. Manuel threw his weight behind the pope, warning him not to give his blessings to what was essentially a counterfeit Roman Empire. Alexander agreed, and Barbarossa was shut out of Rome. But the emperor could not totally alienate himself from western Christendom, and in the spring of 1178 he had the chance to mend an important fence when Count Philip of Flanders passed through Constantinople on his way back from a pilgrimage. In the palace Manuel introduced to Philip his

9-year-old *porphyrogennetos* son Alexios and proposed that he be betrothed to one of the daughters of King Louis VII of France. The king agreed, and thus at Easter 1179 Princess Agnes of France, also 9, set out for her new life in the Queen of Cities. The children were wed on 2 March 1180 and the imperial succession was therefore buttressed.

The summer of 1180 saw a surprising arrival at Constantinople—that of Manuel's troublesome cousin Andronikos Komnenos, whom we last saw in self-exile with his mistress Theodora, an honoured guest of the Seljuk sultan. The emperor was unwell, and Andronikos likely saw a chance to aim for the throne; he had written to Manuel begging for forgiveness and a safe conduct back to Constantinople. Manuel, his judgement possibly impaired by illness, had consented. Andronikos returned to the capital in July; an elaborate welcome was laid on for him and to all appearances it seemed that the emperor and his cousin were reconciled. The appearance suited Andronikos down to the ground, for he had never ceased his diabolical cunning. His play-acting when he met Manuel was most convincing:

> Andronikos... hung around his neck a heavy iron chain which reached down to his feet; he secured it close to his body, concealed inside his cloak... He exposed it before the emperor the first time he appeared before him. Stretching himself out on the floor, mighty in his mightiness, and holding forth the chain and shedding tears, he pleaded fervently, begging forgiveness for his alleged misdeeds.

Whether Manuel believed him or not is not known, but perhaps he was too unwell to resist. Andronikos, restored to favour, took up residence at Oinaion near the capital.

Manuel's illness may have owed something to that harrowing rough ride to Klaudiopolis in bad weather when he was pushing 60. It may have been as much psychological as physical as after Myriokephalon he had been unable to recover his spirits. His mental state became quite precarious, as he sought refuge in all manner of soothsayers. He panicked when they forecast a devastating earthquake, ordering deep shelters to be dug and supposedly shaky parts of the palace pulled down. But the dreaded quake never materialized. In September, six months after his son Alexios' marriage ceremony, Manuel seems to have realized the end was near. He wept when he considered the bleak future his young son would face on his accession. He realized that his astrologers for years had been feeding him nonsense and consented to absolution by the patriarch. He then doffed his robes and put on a simple monk's habit (taking his pulse while he did so). On 24 September he died. Placed over his tomb in the church of Pantokrator near the north-east wall was a heavy stone slab on which, according to tradition, Christ's body had been placed after being taken down from the cross. Manuel himself had carried the stone on his back from the port to the palace when it had been shipped from Ephesos.

The death of Manuel I after a thirty-seven-year reign found the prestige of the Komnene dynasty at a low ebb. Gone were the glory days of Alexios I and John II, whose unceasing efforts kept the Empire alive and created legends of military prowess. Manuel was at least as capable and as courageous as his forebears, as his record shows, but during the latter part of his reign a fatigue had begun to set in. The wars against foes east and west seemed endless; the taxation to support them became more and more onerous. Much of the money went to pay the mercenaries who by now probably made up the bulk of the Byzantine army and were despised wherever they were billeted. Manuel himself was a man of many parts, impulsive and overgenerous with state money, whether to bribe diplomatic adversaries or to hand perks to his friends. Families of the military aristocracy were in general not good money managers and the Komnenes were no exception. Ordinary Byzantine Greeks were put off by Manuel's predilection for the trappings of western knighthood and preference for the ways of Western Europe over the East; they resented his belief that somehow his fellow Byzantines were behind the times and needed to mimic the West—a cultural conflict that persists in the Greece of today. He was not mourned to the extent that his father and grandfather had been, and left the Empire in a worse state than he found it.

Chapter 13

Bloodstained finale: Andronikos I

Manuel's son by Maria was barely 11 when he found himself the ruler of the Byzantine Empire as Alexios II Komnenos. Worryingly, there was little in the boy's character that suggested he might grow into a wise and able sovereign. With his father away on campaign a great deal of the time, we may assume that Alexios was brought up by his mother and what Choniates describes as 'nursemaids' who still attended him. In short, he had lived in a totally protected, womb-like palace environment where his sole activities, it seems, were going along on hunting trips and watching the chariot races in the Hippodrome. Apart from his tutors, there was no one in his wider family who cared enough, or made the time, to take a hand in forming the character of the youth who would one day be emperor. The immediate family environment, it must be said, was not one to inspire maturity of outlook. Choniates notes acidly that Alexios' mother Maria, still young, blonde and attractive, and now the regent, was the object of constant wooing and outright sexual harassment from high-born men in the palace entourage; she is reported to have given herself to one of them, a nephew of her late husband's called Alexios Komnenos who ranked as Protosebastos (First in Respect), and to have carried on a regular affair. The state mechanism, too, was in disarray, with corrupt and venal officials taking advantage of the administrative confusion attendant on a change of emperor to fill their pockets with public money.

The close relationship between the Protosebastos Alexios and Maria naturally ignited strong suspicions that he might be after the throne himself. He was an unlikely candidate for Maria's favours; Choniates describes him as advanced in years, spending most of his day lazing in bed with the curtains drawn and in his spare time cleaning other people's bad teeth, so we may take reports of a sexual liaison with a rather large grain of salt. If Maria was indeed erotically attached to him, it might well have been a purely practical arrangement to secure protection from his and her Frankish family in the face of anti-western hostility by the populace. And there was no lack of challenges facing the regent Maria, whose stepdaughter, also named Maria, led an attempted uprising in the city in early 1181. For a time it seemed as if the attempt would prevail, and there was some nasty street fighting before it was bloodily suppressed. The incident stained the image of empress-regent Maria and her consort even more in the eyes of the people, who rose up when the patriarch was exiled for supposed involvement in the plot. Maria was forced to repeal the order and the clergyman was brought back in triumph on the shoulders of his flock. They had never taken the Frankish Maria to heart anyway; to them she was always the *Xene*, the foreigner.

And there was an unpredictable joker in the pack in the person of Manuel's notorious cousin Andronikos Komnenos, who had recently returned to Constantinople and can be imagined rubbing his hands at reports of young Alexios' immaturity plus the disorganization and corruption of the administration. He seems to have kept a copy of the oath he had sworn to Manuel and his son Alexios; he seized on the clause that obliged him to act if he should 'see or perceive or hear anything bringing dishonour to you [Manuel] or inflicting injury to your crown'. There was plenty going on, he reasoned, that could be interpreted precisely as bringing about such dishonour or injury. Choniates is bitter in his denunciation of the 'filthy deeds' of venal officials all over the Empire who 'rolled about... rooting like swine after every evil gain'. It was a situation ripe for someone like Andronikos, despite his sordid record, to present himself as a terrible sword of vengeance. Therefore he set in motion his plot to get rid of Alexios II as well as Maria's alleged lazy lover and seize the throne.

His first move was to write to boy-emperor Alexios and others who had been close to Manuel, bemoaning the sad condition into which the state had fallen and warning that a takeover of the throne by Maria's elderly boyfriend was in the works. It was a correct first step, as later no one could say they had not been warned. Andronikos in fact made sure he was thoroughly briefed on what was going on in the capital. His next move, in August 1182, was to set out from Oinaion for Constantinople. Throngs turned out to cheer him on; he must have been an impressive spectacle, over six feet tall and even in his mid-sixties maintaining a suppleness and vigour that made him look twenty years younger, though he had probably lost most of his hair. His reckless and womanizing reputation may well have lent him an added aura of attractiveness and power, as so often happens with such figures. There was a universal yearning for a Komnene strongman to drain the massive swamp of corruption and incompetence, and few cared how he planned to do it.

In Constantinople the ever-watchful Protosebastos Alexios 'clung to the palace apartments like an octopus clamping its suckers on a rock'—and mostly horizontal, as we have seen. But few in the royal entourage were taken in by reports of Andronikos' new-found humility and supposed purity of intention. When Andronikos approached Nikaia he found the city resolutely closed to him, but farther on, found considerable support around Nikomedia. But there he also came on his first military opposition under Andronikos Angelos. The forces clashed at Charax; Angelos was defeated and barricaded himself in his house with his wife and six sons. But seeing that Andronikos had by far the superior numbers, and perhaps that he had strong support among ordinary people, Angelos and his family decided to join him. Andronikos exulted when he saw Angelos and jocularly quoted the Bible: 'See? It's just as the Gospel says: "I shall send my Angel, who shall prepare the way before thee."'

Andronikos continued his progress 'as though he were making his way to the land of the Philistines'. Biblical metaphors abound in this section of Choniates' narrative. Byzantine emperors, would-be emperors and generals tended to view themselves as avatars of Old Testament heroes such as Moses, Joshua, Saul, David and Solomon. These heroes' exploits in leading the tribes of Israel to the promised land and keeping them there were likened to Byzantium's own travails and triumphs. The Roman Empire (as the Byzantines still called it) was the Christian promised land, and just as the Jews had to fight hard and long against the Philistines and Egyptians and other foes of the true God without let-up, so the Byzantines, too, were bound to constant warfare against Muslims and where necessary, heretical westerners.

When Andronikos and his force reached the Bosporus and were within sight of the capital, the city was thrown into confusion. People looked across the strait at night and saw what appeared to be a huge number of watchfires, lit deliberately to give an impression of overwhelming strength. A good number of imperial troops were quite prepared to go over to Andronikos and did so. The young Emperor Alexios—or more accurately his regent mother and her consort the Protosebastos—decided to fight Andronikos by sea. For this they recruited the Genoese and Venetian maritime traders in the city, paying them more than handsomely, to provide most of the ships that arrayed themselves in the Bosporus to block Andronikos' crossing. At the same time an imperial envoy was sent to Andronikos with letters from Alexios promising him great honours and rewards if he would desist from his attempt. Andronikos' reply was to contemptuously reject the offers, but he pledged to desist only if Maria was packed off to a convent, the Protosebastos banished and young Alexios allowed to reign 'without being choked by weeds'.

It was a clever, if insincere, reply, and could have been taken at face value by Kontostephanos, the fleet commander, who promptly defected to Andronikos with the Byzantine crews. This was the signal for more defections, and soon the Protosebastos found himself first without an ally and then a prisoner, as the German contingent of the Varangian Guard seized him in the middle of the night. A few days later he was put on a pony and led down to the shore, where he was 'thrown aboard a fishing boat'. The boat took him to Andronikos, who had his eyes gouged out. That was one weed taken care of. But there were others in Andronikos' view, personified by the Latin Italians who had done so much to make themselves despised in past years and had been identified with the misrule of Maria and her lover. Enthusiastically joined by the great majority of local Greeks, he launched a fearful pogrom of the Italians in Constantinople; many thousands perished, butchered in the streets and in their plush homes that were burned down. Several boatloads of Venetians and others managed to escape after losing all their wealth. It was an ominous foretaste of the methods that Andronikos would henceforth employ in the defence of the realm.

Not surprisingly, in these troubled days many believed they saw portents of disaster in the heavens and skies. One of them was a supposed comet whose tail at times looked like a coiled serpent, terrifying all who saw it over two days. Another was a hunting falcon that out of the blue swooped down onto Sancta Sophia; eluding attempts to catch it, the bird winged its way to the palace, alighting on the roof of the chamber where newly-crowned emperors were presented to the people. At this point the falcon was snared and taken to Alexios, who was easily persuaded that the bird stood for Andronikos, who was sure to be likewise apprehended.

The great majority of the city, however, thought otherwise. By now Andronikos had been joined by Patriarch Theodosios, the head of the powerful Church and keeper of the people's pulse. Andronikos had greeted the priest in an extravagant show of humility that included prostrating himself and licking the sides of the patriarch's feet. But Theodosios was not to be deceived.

> The patriarch looked upon Andronikos for the first time and perceived his vicious glare as he scrutinized him, his insidious effrontery, his self-serving and affected manner... his strutting and his supercilious leer.

If Theodosios saw the ruthless calculator for what he was, one might well ask why he had gone over to him in the first place. Choniates, who describes the meeting, does not give a reason. We therefore assume that the patriarch saw which way events were going and that Andronikos' progress was unstoppable, and therefore wanted to see what kind of character he would have to deal with. 'Now I have seen you, I have come to know you very well,' Theodosios told Andronikos in a rueful tone that was at once picked up by the latter's paranoia. From then on Andronikos sought every opportunity to humiliate the head of the Church.

By the spring of 1182 Andronikos was in de facto control of Constantinople, having moved Alexios and his mother Maria into the Mangana buildings. He kept up an elaborate pretence of doing obeisance to the emperor, with all the attendant hypocritical humility. Andronikos' paranoia reached new heights; a ragged beggar who was found wandering near the palace in the middle of the night was accused of being a sorcerer and publicly burned without trial. In this he was backed by the mass of people, whom he could charm effortlessly through his superb acting skills. Almost everyone was convinced he had young Alexios' best interests at heart by beefing up the imperial security detail. However, many of the nobility who could see through this crude façade tasted the ruthless side of his character. There were secret trials and eye-gougings; even a high-born supporter might enjoy one of Andronikos' banquets one night and then within a matter of hours find himself cast into a dungeon and eyeless, simply because he had gained some past fame and hence might possibly become a rival for the throne.

It got worse. Manuel's daughter Maria, who had tried to stir up the Church and people against her mother, was herself too near the throne for Andronikos' liking. A poisoned wine cup killed her and her husband, Renier of Montferrat, eliminating any threat from that quarter. In the summer of 1183 Andronikos sought the approval of the Holy Synod to wed his illegitimate daughter Irene to Alexios; the priests argued over the legitimacy of such a union, but gave way after receiving heavy bribes. Only Patriarch Theodosios stoutly resisted, but seeing that he could get nowhere and risked Andronikos' deadly wrath, he resigned his post and went to live as a hermit on an island. He was replaced by a pliant tool who could be expected to place the Church under Andronikos' thumb.

It remained for one last great theatrical performance to place Andronikos on the throne. That was to suggest to Alexios that he ought to have a co-emperor, sweetening the pill with exaggerated kindness. One day he took Alexios on his shoulders, like a father, and carried him ceremoniously to Sancta Sophia and back, to show the people that the young emperor had a protector. The nature of this 'protection' was soon revealed. The regent Maria was brought to trial on charges of conspiracy and banished to a convent. Andronikos had by now made himself thoroughly hated by the military aristocracy, and the Angeli got together a movement to topple him. The conspirators included the Admiral Kontostephanos. The movement was betrayed and shattered; Kontostephanos and his four sons were blinded, along with many others. Worse was to come.

Before being sent off to a convent, Maria had unwisely asked her brother-in-law, King Béla III of Hungary, to invade the Empire. Perhaps as a result, she was confined without food in a cramped dungeon to suffer abuse by the guards. Andronikos decided to eliminate her as a traitor and asked his eldest son Manuel and brother-in-law to do the wicked deed; both, to their credit, refused.

This unexpected reply struck Andronikos like a thunderbolt. He continually twisted the hairs of his beard around his fingers, his eyes were filled with fire, and shaking his head up and down [lamented] that he did not have friends who delighted in blood and were eager to commit murder at the nod of his head.

In the end a trusted eunuch carried out the execution. And typically, Andronikos arranged it with a sadistic twist, forcing Alexios to sign his own mother's death warrant. She was strangled with a bowstring. We are not told of Alexios' own reaction or feelings, but he was by no means a happy youth. That was apparent when both met at the Blachernai Palace after Andronikos formally elevated himself to co-emperor to great public rejoicing. 'With soul unwilling', the young emperor agreed to what was in essence a coup. But his feelings can be imagined when, the following day, Andronikos was crowned in Sancta Sophia and Alexios demoted to second in rank! The lame excuse was that 'it was not proper for a beardless child who had not yet reached maturity to take precedence in the proclamations over the grey-haired Andronikos'.

The usurper had every reason to feel satisfied as he left the cathedral on horseback escorted by a powerful bodyguard. The implacably hostile Choniates adds that at one point, probably because of fatigue (or perhaps fear of assassination) 'the old man was unable to contain the excreta of his bowels and defecated in his breeches'. Ensconced in the palace, Andronikos called his advisers together and quoted from Homer: 'Better the aged eagle than the fledgling lark.' The message was clear—there was no room any longer for Alexios. At first the advisers thought that the emperor would be merely deposed and relegated to private life. But what Andronikos meant became brutally apparent that same night, 24 September 1183; what went through the mind of poor Alexios II, just 13, the great-grandson of the fabled Alexios I and carrier of his name, can only be imagined as the bowstring tightened around his neck.

Andronikos' infamy did not stop with that regicide. When Alexios' body was brought to him he kicked it in the ribs, mocking and insulting his late parents as he did so. He ordered one of the ears pierced and hung from it a waxen replica of Andronikos' signet ring. Then he had the body put in a lead casket and thrown into the sea from a fishing boat, as the two officials charged with the task sang and danced while doing it. Alexios' head had been removed and was stuffed into a hole somewhere in Constantinople. Nor was that all. In a crudely symbolic act of political and sexual conquest combined, the 64-year-old Andronikos actually wed the 11-year-old Princess Agnes who had been Alexios' promised wife, with the blessings of the pliable patriarch. The marriage, we are told, may even have been consummated. A more bizarre and sordid beginning to the reign of Andronikos I Komnenos could scarcely be imagined.

One of Byzantium's cruellest rulers now began his reign. It was to be a mercifully short but exceptionally bloody one. He quickly alienated the clergy on whom his rise had depended and made plans to deal harshly with the military aristocracy from which he now was a hated outcast. He feared a military revolt, and with good reason. One of them erupted in Nikaia; Andronikos sped there with his general, Alexios Branas, a veteran of the campaigns in Serbia. Heading the revolt were Isaac Angelos, a great-grandson of Alexios I, and Theodore Kantakouzenos of another distinguished noble family, who fortified Nikaia. Andronikos' first tentative assaults on the walls were driven back and his siege engines put out of action. To counter this he had Isaac's mother Euphrosyne seized in Constantinople and brought to the battlefield where the terrified woman was tied to the business end of one of the emperor's battering rams; if it were used she would be squashed. The defenders shot back carefully at the attackers, managing to miss Euphrosyne. That night they torched the battering ram and saved her by pulling her up the walls by a rope.

After that coup the defenders lined the walls and 'poured down abuse on Andronikos, calling him butcher, bloodthirsty dog, rotten old man, undying evil... and every other obscene thing and name'. As Andronikos circled the city looking for a weak spot Kantakouzenos impulsively flung open a gate and charged the emperor at full speed, his lance levelled. But his horse stumbled, sending him flying head over heels and hitting his head hard on the ground. As he lay dazed Andronikos' troops cut him to pieces. With Kantakouzenos gone, Isaac Angelos found himself the leader of the defenders of Nikaia. But he seems to have temporarily lost his nerve; perhaps his forces were heavily outnumbered by those of the emperor. In agreement with the chief clergyman of Nikaia he rode out to Andronikos to seek peace. Andronikos could hardly believe his eyes; here was his main rival surrendering abjectly. He sent Isaac back to the capital and went on to besiege Brusa, another focus of revolt. In a matter of days the city was taken, its defenders killed and all their property seized. Many of the victims were hung from their own grapevines and left to rot in the sun.

Having thoroughly terrorized the Asian provinces of Byzantium, Andronikos returned to Constantinople. He still retained some popularity, as part of his savage nature was employed to root out corruption and what a later era would call white-collar crime in the state mechanism, and many of his victims no doubt deserved what they got. His threats to senior civil servants, laced with Old Testament-style thunder, were spine-chilling:

> [He] who disobeys my command shall be suspended from the mast of a ship, and should the roaring waves have swept it away, on a hilltop near the sea, he shall be fastened to a huge upright beam hewed from the nearby mountains, so that he may be clearly visible to all those sailing the boundless seas.

That was just one of the milder warnings. Yet he had his beneficent side. Anyone, however poor, who came to Andronikos with accusations of malfeasance in high places would be assured of a sympathetic hearing. Many influential men thus accused, to save their lives, would donate large amounts to the state, which benefited the treasury, and in turn the economy, which enjoyed a boom. He lavishly restored religious monuments and rebuilt the capital's underground aqueducts at great expense. But whatever popularity remained was rapidly swindling as evidence of his brutality mounted. He can be considered a twelfth-century Stalin. In the summer of 1184 he was actually a very frightened man; when during a horse race in the Hippodrome the railing of the emperor's box collapsed killing half a dozen spectators, he fled the box in panic, fearing a lynching by the incensed mob. His advisers suggested that he go back and display some public courage, which he did, but fled again into the palace before the games were over.

By now Isaac Angelos seems to have recovered his spirit and resolved on toppling Andronikos. But Constantinople and its environs were too dangerous for that, so he had sailed to Cyprus and set himself up as governor by means of forged imperial documents. If we are to credit Choniates, Angelos took many pages out of Andronikos' book. He terrorized the Cypriots with mass killings, robbed well-to-do households of their wealth and became a sexual predator. News of this soon got back to the emperor, whose first reaction was one of alarm lest Angelos employ his dubious talents against him. In order to discourage any of Angelos' kin and supporters in the capital, which included some members of the Doukas family, he had two leading Doukai arraigned on charges of treason. One of them had been employed to gouge out the eyes and mutilate the emperor's opponents; now he found himself on the receiving end of imperial punishment. On Ascension Day 1184, as Andronikos watched from an upper window of the Mangana Palace, one of the emperor's henchmen threw a stone 'the size of his hand' at the two condemned men; it was the signal for a mob of others, urged on by threats, to follow suit. Both men, barely alive, were carried away in blankets to meet their end by impalement.

The shock to the citizens of Constantinople was profound. Until that day most were prepared to give Andronikos some credit for being a strong, if irrational, ruler as long as it was the aristocracy that suffered rather than themselves. The Ascension Day atrocity, committed in the view of all, served as a wake-up call. But events were also moving in the West. Norman Sicily was under the rule of William II (the Good), in whose court resided a young man claiming to be Alexios II. This youth, almost certainly an impostor, implored William to use his military power to help overthrow the tyrant in Constantinople. Pressing the same request was a genuine member of the Komnenes who had gone to Sicily and was promising in return some Byzantine lands in south Italy. William, incensed at what he heard, assembled a large force of mercenaries and ships at Messina—up to 80,000 men in all—and placed them under the command of Richard of Acerra. At this point he seems to have forgotten about the pseudo-Alexios and begun to dream of himself on the Byzantine throne. In June 1185 Richard sailed unopposed across the Adriatic and took Dyrrachion without a fight; from there he proceeded by land across north Greece to Thessalonike while sending the navy around the Peloponnese. The army invested the port city, the second in importance after Constantinople, on 6 August, the navy arriving about a week later.

Heading the defence of Thessalonike was David Komnenos, a distant relative of the emperor, with orders to resist and repulse the attackers at all costs. There could have been few men less fitted for the task. 'More effeminate than a woman and more cowardly than the deer,' David Komnenos did absolutely nothing to repel the attackers, merely riding around on a mule and hiding under an arch to shelter from falling masonry. In short order Thessalonike surrendered, thanks to a unit of German imperial mercenaries who were bribed to open the western gates. Most likely having been fed lurid tales of the Byzantine emperor's inhumanity, the Normans and Sicilians embarked on an orgy of slaughter, rape and looting; up to 7,000 ordinary people, including children, were slain either in their homes or in the churches to which they had fled for sanctuary. The houses were simply appropriated. The invaders used the holy Orthodox icons for firewood and urinated on the floors of the churches. The survivors, treated with unbelievable humiliation, found themselves short of food as 80,000 Normans and Sicilians devoured everything available. The heaps of dead stank in the August heat. The resulting epidemic, aggravated by excessive winebibbing by the victors, carried off about 3,000 of them in a grim natural vengeance. Eventually the more level-headed commanders of the expedition restored some kind of order.

Ever since the days of the First Crusade, the Catholic Latins had made themselves heartily disliked by the Byzantine Greeks. Choniates, who may have witnessed the carnage in Thessalonike, expresses the common unflattering view:

> Between us and them the greatest gulf of disagreement has been fixed...
> Overweening in their pretentious display of straightforwardness, the
> Latins would stare up and down at us and behold with curiosity the gen-
> tleness and lowliness of our demeanour, and we, looking grimly upon
> their superciliousness, boastfulness, and pompousness, with the drivel
> from their noses held in the air... grit our teeth, secure in the power of
> Christ, who gives the faithful the power to tread on serpents.

It's an attitude gulf between East and West that persists to this day, and no one could know at the time that within twenty years Constantinople itself would suffer a far more devastating crime at the hands of West Europeans. The sack of Thessalonike was merely one more sad confirmation that any lingering hopes by idealists of reuniting the two split halves of the Roman Empire were now well and truly doomed. The Italians, it seemed, were no longer the descendants of the ancient Romans but a new, alien and aggressive race, a bigger menace even than the Muslims.

For the second time in a matter of months, the people of Constantinople were stunned. First was the shocking stoning of the two Doukas men, and now came the news of the mass butchery at Thessalonike. Andronikos himself never let up his savagery; the particularly gruesome burning of a young noble named Mamalos in the Hippodrome, when he tried repeatedly to flee the flames in panic, thoroughly alienated whatever spectators there were. The news from Thessalonike sobered him somewhat. He despatched his second son John to Philippopolis, but John preferred hunting to military action and turned out to be useless. Another general, Theodore Choumnos, approached Thessalonike but his army, which already must have suffered low morale, backed off at the sight of the occupiers, who now made preparations to march on Constantinople itself, with the pretender Alexios in tow.

Andronikos toured the walls of the capital, ordering repairs where necessary and demolishing all houses on the outside of the wall to clear a defensive space. Some 100 ships were stationed along the shore and inside the Golden Horn. Relatives of David Komnenos were thrown into jail. The emperor put on a brave face when couriers brought reports of the Sicilians' unstoppable progress, proclaiming publicly that he would spear them like wild boars. But few in the fearful city believed him. The monster had now been unmasked for what he was. Any single day in which he did not condemn anyone to death he considered a day wasted. He would find time for pleasure trips into the countryside, accompanied by a bevy of prostitutes to satisfy his lust stoked by various kinds of aphrodisiacs. Members of the Varangian Guard would accompany him on his return from such outings, and at night he would sleep soundly in the palace, guarded by a watchdog that 'would jump up and bark loud and long at the slightest sound'.

Andronikos needed all the protection he could get. His terrible exterior masked a desperate fear. He knew that opposition to him was sprouting everywhere, like a many-headed Hydra. 'If it is ordained that Andronikos shall be dragged down to the halls of Hades,' he told his assembled advisers on one occasion, 'they shall go first to prepare the way.' In late September 1185 he drew up a decree ordering the mass execution of all his opponents in prison and their families, stipulating the exact manner of death for each one. But far from making him feel more secure, the opposite occurred. His eldest son Manuel flatly refused to have anything to do with the ghastly decree.

According to Choniates, the emperor seems to have had a form of conscience after all, as he suspected that 'the Divinity had abandoned him for having killed the nobility in so many ways' and imagined that the Sicilian invasion might be a concrete sign of divine vengeance on him. To ward it off, he took refuge in wizards and divinations. In one session he asked who his successor would be; according to the story, the 'demon' replied in the form of a Greek S (C) imposed on an I. The emperor, accurately as it turned out, surmised that the letters stood for Isaac Angelos. He hid his concern beneath a contemptuous smile and said he didn't believe a word. Yet on 11 September he ordered Angelos arrested, dragged from his home by his hair and beard if need be. He certainly did not count on what would follow.

Isaac had no intention of going quietly. When the arresting official arrived at his house, he grabbed his sword, jumped onto his horse and charged the official. As the latter turned tail, Isaac caught up with him and felled him with a devastating sword blow straight down through the head, cleaving it in two like a melon. Another blow sliced off the ear of one of the hapless official's escort, and the rest fled. News of the incident flew through the city, but Isaac seems to have been uncertain about what to do next. He rode to Sancta Sophia to get to the pulpit from where murderers traditionally confessed their crimes. By now thousands of people had arrived at the cathedral to see what fate would befall Isaac who was joined by his uncle, John Doukas. Both expected to be arrested at any moment, but took heart from the crowd displaying its support. All night they remained inside Sancta Sophia by torchlight while the supporters stayed with them and attracted more as the night progressed.

When Andronikos heard about Isaac's deed he was in a royal apartment some distance from the city. He was worried enough to issue a promise that whoever supported Isaac would not be punished. The crowd around Sancta Sophia was naturally unconvinced; as dawn broke on 12 September they surged through Constantinople, seizing what weapons they could, breaking open the jails and boosting their numbers. At the same time in the great church, someone took down what was called the Crown of Constantine—a ceremonial part of the decoration of the high altar—and offered it to Isaac. Horrified, he refused, fearing that such a premature gesture of *lèse-majesté* would cost him his head. The elderly Doukas, with indecent haste, offered his own bald head 'that shone brighter than a full moon'. It was plain that Doukas was using the commotion to promote his own aim for the throne. But the crowd had other ideas. One elderly emperor, Andronikos, had been enough; they didn't need another decrepit one, especially John Doukas, 'with a beard parting in the middle and tapering at the ends.' Reluctantly Isaac submitted to the atypical coronation, assisted by an equally reluctant Patriarch Basil Kamateros.

Andronikos rode to the main palace, where the ominous rumble of the advancing mob reached his ears. He prepared his staff to resist, but most were demoralized and only a few heeded his orders. Impetuously he seized a bow and began shooting arrows at the now-visible crowd from the battlements on the palace tower; but he soon realized the futility of that and sent a messenger to the rebels (for that is what they by now had become) offering to abdicate in favour of his son Manuel. The rebels' reply was to heap insults on him. When they broke down a palace gate Andronikos fled through the palace towards the shore, on the way casting off his royal adornments and donning 'a barbarian cap that tapered to a point like a pyramid'. Thus partly disguised, he seized his impossibly young wife Agnes and his mistress Maraptike and boarded the royal ship which sailed up the Bosporus with the intention of seeking refuge among the Russians.

Isaac entered the palace flanked by his thousands of supporters to be pro-claimed emperor as Isaac II Angelos. Thus simply the great Komnene dynasty, which had begun with the vigorous Isaac I and reached its apogee with Alexios I and his son and grandson, came to an unexpected end. This finale was accompanied by scenes of mass looting in the palace, which Isaac was powerless to prevent. The imperial treasury lost huge sums, the armoury a great deal of its weaponry. Not even the palace chapels were spared; mobs in full rage rarely have spiritual scruples. Presently, we are given to understand, Isaac managed to restore some order. Presumably to enable repairs to be made to the main palace, he moved to the Blachernai Palace up the Golden Horn, where good news awaited him: the hated Andronikos had been captured and was on his way back, bound hand and foot.

The fleeing Andronikos had been unlucky in the weather. Barely had his boat reached the northern mouth of the Bosporus than strong winds blew it onto the European shore. There his pursuers caught up with him. On the boat trip back he composed a touching lament on his predicament, hoping vainly to create some sympathy among his captors which he might exploit for an escape. We are told that his prepubescent wife and mature mistress joined in the lament, though we can never be sure with what degree of sincerity. Even the most hostile sources concede that Andronikos had some good qualities, including an amazing ability to charm. But the captors remained unmoved. In Constantinople he was thrown into the Tower of Anemas, named after the handsome rebel who had caught the attention of Anna Komnene some eighty years before. With shackles on his feet and two heavy chains around his neck, he was led before Isaac. In the new emperor's presence he was slapped and kicked, and his beard, hair and teeth pulled out; many of the fiercest attackers were women whose husbands he had put to death. Someone brought an axe and hacked off his right hand.

Andronikos spent the next few days in jail, unfed and untreated. Then one of his eyes was gouged out and he was put on the hump of a scrawny camel to be paraded through the crowded main marketplace. Dressed in rags and looking like 'a leafless and withered old stump', he suffered the ferocious abuse of the mob. Had this wretch been the universally-feared emperor only a few days before? People threw human and cow dung in his face; others stabbed his ribs with spits; stones flew at him from all directions; a prostitute, we are told, emptied a pot of hot water over his head. When he arrived in the Hippodrome, the scene of every public event of any importance, he was taken off the camel and hoisted up feet first to hang between two columns.

Throughout this horrific ordeal he retained a certain dignity, answering the incessant physical and verbal attacks with a feeble, 'Why do you further abuse the broken reed?' The words made no impression at all on the crazed crowd; indeed, they may have inflamed it more. His private parts were beaten and lacerated.

He extended the stump of his right arm in anguish and lifted it to his mouth; to some it seemed as if he was drinking the blood still oozing from the wound. At last a soldier drove his sword into Andronikos' neck, slashing down into the abdomen, ending his suffering. At about the same time two Italian or Frankish soldiers hacked into the cleft of the dead man's buttocks, vying to see who cut could deeper. This perished, horribly, the last of the Komnene dynasty that had ruled Byzantium for a total of 106 years.

What remained of Andronikos hung lifeless between the columns for several days and was then thrown into one of the Hippodrome's rubbish bins reserved for dead animals. From there some kindly souls removed the body and carried it to a poor district of the capital where it appears to have lain in the open for a considerable time and in public view, as emperor Isaac had forbidden a Christian burial. Choniates retains a shred of sympathy for this complex man, whom he calls a combination of saint and devil, and avers that he would have equalled the best of the Komnene rulers 'had he mitigated the intensity of his cruelty'. If he had stuck to his admirable practice of enforcing social and economic justice he might well have continued the Komnene dynasty for a long time to come.

The dreadful manner of Andronikos I's death recalls that of the Emperor Phokas in 610, similarly done to death by a mob and by some accounts cut up for dog food. The question has been raised why an Empire based ultimately on Christianity, and ostensibly representing a higher sphere of governance than had been usual in pagan societies, would be prone to such violence in removing an emperor who was still, in theory, the vicegerent of God on earth? Guerdan's interpretation is that an emperor was expected to be noble enough to fulfil that exalted mission; if he fell short or resorted to repressive cruelties, then it was assumed that divine grace had abandoned him. In that case the offending ruler was deemed to have sinned grievously in representing God, and to deserve especially severe punishment. Writes Guerdan: 'The greater the divinity of the institutions, one might say, the less human the punishments' for high-level impiety.

Chapter 14

Twilight in Trebizond

While the Komnene dynasty was coming to its messy end, the Norman and Sicilian army under Baldwin (no relation to the Frankish rulers in Outremer) was marching on the capital from Thessalonike, no doubt kept well apprised of the tumultuous happenings. They were less than 200 miles from Constantinople when Baldwin received an offer of a truce from Isaac. The Norman general, infused with a sense of superiority that made him imagine he was Alexander the Great reincarnated, spurned it. The result probably came as a surprise even to the new emperor: after appointing the capable Alexios Branas to command all the imperial armies, he scoured the Empire for troops. With Andronikos gone, morale in the ranks soared. For too long the Byzantines had gone down to defeat at the hands of arrogant Latins; fired by the new patriotism, Branas' force, 'no longer having any commerce with fear, burned with desire to fall upon [the invaders], as an eagle falls upon a feeble bird.'

Branas struck at Mosynopolis (the modern Greek town of Komotini) and the lax Sicilians didn't know what hit them. They barely were able to put up a fight against the Byzantine onslaught, reeling all the way back to Amphipolis, a distance of some 150 miles. Baldwin sued for peace but the Greeks didn't trust him and made a second surprise attack on his force—apparently spontaneously and without orders—in early November 1185, when the autumn rains began to swell the rivers. The Sicilians were again routed, many perishing as they tried to escape across the swollen Strymon River. Baldwin and Richard of Acerra, and the pretender Alexios, were taken prisoner. The survivors of their army withdrew to Thessalonike, where a vengeful populace rose up to decimate them. Only a few made it over the snow-bound Balkan mountain passes to Dyrrachion. Back at home Isaac was lionized as a 'liberating and tyrant-killing god'.

The house of Angeli, of which Isaac was the founder, was fated to last less than twenty years. On the domestic front Isaac II reversed many of Andronikos' policies; unfortunately, these included the previous emperor's ferocious decrees against corruption which had the merit of considerably cleaning up Byzantine public and commercial life. Bribery and tax evasion again became common, at the expense of the army and navy which were allowed to decline. Heavy taxation in the provinces continued, sowing the seeds of persistent discontent. Though he was no longer in his prime, Isaac campaigned in the Balkans but was unable to prevent the growth of Bulgaria and Serbia as realms independent of Byzantium; Eastern Europe, it seemed, was coming of age. But the event that really caused a stir was the news in October 1187 that the Muslims under the fabled Salah ad-Din (Saladin) had taken Jerusalem, eliminating the 88-year-old Frankish kingdom.

The news didn't quite have the dramatic impact in Constantinople as it had it the West. In Byzantine Greek eyes, even though the Franks and Latins in the Middle East were fellow Christians, they did not cease to be heretics in the Orthodox mind. Many a Greek in those days (not to mention the centuries to come) would be hard put to say who was a bigger enemy of the faith, the Catholics or the Muslims. It had been the Greek Orthodox community of Jerusalem, chafing under the obligation to attend alien Latin rituals, that had been prepared to open the gates of Jerusalem to Saladin, who at least would allow them to worship as they pleased. It was no doubt in this spirit that Isaac sent his congratulations to Saladin, who willingly granted his request that Jerusalem's holy places revert to the Greek Orthodox Church.

The fall of Jerusalem triggered the Third Crusade, which saw luminaries such as Richard I of England, Philip II Augustus of France and Frederick I Barbarossa of the Holy Roman Empire take up cross and sword and trek eastwards. Of these monarchs it was Frederick who elected to march overland through the Byzantine Empire with an army of more than 100,000 men. When the German Crusaders occupied Philippopolis and appeared to be intent on proceeding to Constantinople, Isaac panicked. In late 1189 Frederick sent envoys to discuss how the army could cross into Asia; the emperor jailed them, probably intending to use them as hostages for the Crusaders' good behaviour. It had precisely the opposite effect, infuriating Frederick. Isaac relented, and in the ensuing negotiations he got Frederick to take his troops across by the Dardanelles instead of the Bosporus. In June 1190 Frederick Barbarossa drowned trying to cross a swollen stream in what is now south-east Turkey.

Yet the die was cast for the Angeli, who were fated to become the victims of Latin aggression. In the spring of 1195, while Barbarossa's son Henry VI was planning his own crusade and sending intimidating letters to Byzantium, Isaac was deposed and replaced by his elder brother Alexios Angelos, for reasons that remain obscure; quite likely Alexios simply believed that on the grounds of age alone he was better qualified for the throne than Isaac, who was blinded for good measure. So far had the erstwhile 'liberating and tyrant-killing god' fallen from grace. Alexios III was apparently devoid of any governing talents and Henry VI correctly saw him as a pushover. The German ruler bullied Alexios into raising a tax to pay the German mercenaries, the infamous *alamanikon*, that was supplemented by selling the precious ornaments on the royal tombs. Henry then arranged the marriage of Alexios' niece Irene to his own brother, Philip of Swabia, on the grounds of an unconfirmed rumour that Isaac had previously designated them as his heirs. But Henry's ascendancy did not last long. In September 1197 he died of a fever; most of his nobles returned to Germany to deal with civil strife that had broken out there, leaving the rank and file of the Crusaders unprotected. Unsurprisingly, they fled en masse.

Alexios III, sensing his weakness, responded to an overture by Pope Innocent III, the driving force behind the Third Crusade, for a possible reunion of the eastern and western churches. But with the great majority of Greeks dead against such a reconciliation, the overtures got nowhere except to make Alexios even more unpopular. In 1201 the son of the deposed Isaac, yet another Alexios, escaped from his prison cell and to Germany, where Philip of Swabia and his wife (Alexios' sister) welcomed him. This gave Philip an idea: he introduced Alexios to Boniface of Montferrat, who was preparing a crusade. Why not kill two birds with one stone by diverting to Constantinople on the way, toppling Alexios III and replacing him with his namesake nephew, who could become a trusted ally of Germany? Thus was born the idea of the Fourth Crusade.

The precise origins and motives of the Fourth Crusade are still disputed by historians, and we cannot go into them here. Suffice it to say that Constantinople, far from being an incidental destination, turned out to be the actual one. The driving force behind the crusade was the octogenarian doge of Venice, Enrico Dandolo, whose eyes were on the capital of the 'schismatic Greeks'. He certainly remembered the massacre of the Venetians of Constantinople twenty years before, and might be forgiven for burning with revenge. The Latins, ignorant of history, viewed the Byzantines as less than half-hearted crusaders anyway. On 8 November 1202 Dandolo led 480 galleys out of the harbour of Venice. With him was Alexios III's nephew and namesake whom the Venetians wished to impose as emperor. In June 1203 the fleet arrived off Constantinople; the troops gazed stupefied at the great city and the sheer impression of strength it gave, while the Byzantines gazed back in similar wonder. But the impressive skyline of the city was just a façade, as Byzantium by now had no navy to speak of. Isaac II had short-sightedly granted all the Empire's shipbuilding to Venice as part of the reparations for the Venetian massacre. Now there was nothing with which to fight a hostile Venetian fleet.

The attack on Constantinople got underway in earnest in July 1203. Though Alexios III's axe-swinging Anglo-Saxons and Scandinavians in the Varangian Guard did some damage, they were heavily outnumbered and had to fall back. Alexios fled under cover of darkness, leaving behind most of his family. Dandolo, by now the master of the situation, installed the imperial nephew as Alexios IV, to rule jointly with his blinded father, the ex-Isaac II. Then a fire lit by the attackers spread to engulf large parts of the city; it was attributed in part to the impatience of the Crusaders who wanted to get on to the Holy Land. But Dandolo had other ideas, and they were nothing less than the elimination of the Byzantine Empire and its replacement by an all-powerful Latin realm ruling the whole east Mediterranean.

With political tensions thickening, and with the Latins looking on approvingly, the Senate, clergy and a mass of people gathered in Sancta Sophia to declare Alexios IV deposed after some six months of rule. The news was given to the young emperor who was roused in the middle of the night by his Protovestiarios Alexios Doukas. He was bundled out of a palace side door wrapped up in a cloak—straight into the hands of his enemies, who lost little time in wringing his neck with the bowstring. Doukas then made his way to the cathedral, frowning under his thick dark eyebrows, where he was acclaimed Alexios V. This came as a nasty surprise to the Venetians, who were alarmed at the thought of a Doukas on the throne; the family was renowned for its pedigree, having so far produced two emperors, and for that reason could not be expected to be pliable. Dandolo took his decision: Constantinople would have to be taken by storm.

The attack began on 9 April 1204. Alexios V bravely resisted with what forces he had, but rather than suffer the indignity of being captured by the Latins, he escaped the city and fled to Thrace. What followed was one of the worst atrocities in history. Another fire destroyed, in Choniates' words, 'more houses than can be found in the three greatest cities of France.' Choniates himself witnessed horrors that he could not believe could be committed by fellow Christians. Sancta Sophia was thoroughly sacked of its centuries-old treasures. The holy icons, 'the body and blood of the Saviour,' were smashed, the great altar chopped to bits. Horses and mules were brought into the church to carry off the piles of loot, and when the heavy-laden beasts slipped on the marble floor, their enraged owners ran them through with swords, 'fouling the Church with blood and ordure.'

A common harlot was enthroned in the Patriarch's chair, to hurl insults at Jesus Christ; and she sang bawdy songs, and danced immodestly in the holy place.

It was not the Catholic Venetians, to their credit, who committed most of these atrocities but the less devout French and Flemings in the crusader army. Yet the Italians looted as eagerly as the rest, and for three days, 'in the streets, houses and churches there could be heard only cries and lamentations.' At a single blow, the mistress of the world had been beaten into a sad shadow of herself. The loss of monetary and cultural treasure was incalculable.

With the Byzantine imperial house vacant, Dandolo imagined himself to be a reincarnation of an early Roman emperor. But cannily realizing that he was too old himself to actively rule, he set up a Frenchman, Count Baldwin of Flanders and Hainault, as Baldwin I of the Latin Empire of Constantinople. The Latin occupation—still remembered bitterly by the Greeks as the 'Francocracy'—lasted fifty-seven dreary years with hardly any achievement to its credit. In 1261 the

Paleologos family recaptured the city, chasing its terrified last Latin emperor, Baldwin II, through the streets.

The gruesome overthrow and end of Andronikos in 1185 was naturally not the best time for the Komnene house, but that didn't mean it was about to lie low. 'In times of disaster,' writes Sir Steven Runciman in his history of the Crusades, 'the Greek spirit shows itself at its most courageous and energetic.' By 1204 Andronikos' elder son Manuel—who had displayed some nobility of spirit when he refused to accede to his father's plan to exterminate the aristocracy—had two grown sons of his own, Alexios and David. As Manuel had married Princess Rusudan of Georgia, the boys were sent for safety to the Georgian court. The Komnenes had never been reconciled to the Angeli, whom they regarded as jumped-up usurpers. In the chaos preceding the fall of Constantinople to the Crusaders the brothers made their move. The nearest free Byzantine territory was Trebizond to the west, situated on the south shore of the Black Sea. Trebizond was a wealthy city and province on the trade route between Persia and the Mediterranean. Thanks to its protected position between the sea and the Pontic Alps, plus the silver mines in its hinterland, it had managed to resist constant threats by the Seljuk Turks. After 1204 Trebizond was one of three independent Byzantine states, something like Byzantine governments-in-exile, after Nikaia and Epiros in north-west Greece.

Though Nikaia was nearer to Constantinople and de facto the Byzantine successor-state, Trebizond was the natural choice for the Komnenes; Queen Thamar of Georgia helped them seize Trebizond—presumably with the aid of some armed force—where in April 1204, at about the time the Fourth Crusaders were making their final assault on Constantinople, the 22-year-old Alexios was crowned Alexios I of the diminutive Empire of Trebizond. Thus began the rule of what became known as the Grand Komnenes—not as illustrious as the Constantinople Komnene of the eleventh and twelfth centuries, to be sure, but belonging to the same lineage and equally determined to uphold Orthodox Christendom from its foes in the east and west. Historians have debated whether Alexios and David actually hoped to recover Constantinople or were simply administering a buffer state to protect Georgia from the Seljuk Turks. The truth is probably a bit of both. As the brothers only learned of the taking of Constantinople some time after Alexios' coronation, the latter motive was probably more prominent.

Resistance to the Latins quickly crystallized in Nikaia, where Theodore Laskaris, who had married into the Komnenes, was acclaimed the legitimate emperor of Byzantium in opposition to the Latin puppet emperors in Constantinople. Away to the west in Epiros, another member of the wider clan, Michael Komnenos Doukas, threw his hat in the ring for the hopeful recovery of the capital. While Nikaia was where the action was, so to speak, Trebizond struggled on, surviving by trade with the Venetians and Genoese. The Italians, however, never ceased to regard Trebizond as a serious rival. As the local Trapezuntine ladies were considered especially attractive, with their large eyes, luscious dark hair and generous curves, some of the higher-born ones were used as brides with which to form alliances with neighbouring powers, including the Turks.

The Grand Komnene dynasty of Trebizond lasted more than 250 years and comprised twenty-one emperors, including two women. True to family tradition, they include four Alexii, four Johns, three Manuels and two Androniki—all, confusingly for the student of Byzantine history, counting from one. There's also an Anna Komnene. They have enough of a history to feed a separate book-length study which would be of little interest to a non-specialist, so our survey will necessarily be brief. David Komnenos began campaigning westwards in about 1206, to try and join up with the government-in-exile in Nikaia—or perhaps sideline it as a rival. He almost made it, seizing the key coastal cities of Sinope (now Sinop) and Herakleia Pontika (Karadeniz Ereğli), but lost his life in the attempt. Theodore Laskaris struck back, reclaiming the territory as far as Sinope, which itself was overrun by the Turks in 1214. Succeeding Alexios I in 1222 was Andronikos I Gidos, who seems to have been a general in Laskaris' service and one of just two Trapezuntine emperors not belonging to the Komnenes proper but marrying into the clan. Perhaps as a reward for fending off an attack by the Seljuks, Gidos received the hand of Alexios' daughter; Alexios' eldest son John for some reason was passed over. His successor John I Axuch Komnenos (1235–1238), made way for Alexios' second son Manuel I Komnenos. In his twenty-five-year rule Manuel proved himself worthy of his distinguished family name by capably leading the army and stabilizing the currency by the establishment of a new silver coinage. It was towards the end of his reign that news arrived of the triumphant recapture of Constantinople by Michael VIII Paleologos operating out of Nikaia. The Byzantine Empire was whole again—though very much reduced in territory and power. What, then was to become of the Komnenes of Trebizond?

It was a timely question as, three years before the recovery of Constantinople, the Mongols had sacked Baghdad, the seat of the decaying Abbasid caliphate. A new Asiatic power was at the gates, of concern to both the Seljuks and the Byzantines. But the Mongol seizure of Baghdad had one unexpected bonus for Trebizond as it shifted vital trade via the fabled Silk Road away from the Middle East and to the Black Sea region. The Grand Komnenes presumably made a deal with the Mongol Ilkhanate, as in the late thirteenth century Trebizond grew in wealth and prestige, its fame spreading to Western Europe. Marco Polo, the Italian traveller, set out for Asia from Trebizond and called there on his way back. Domestically, the doctrinal and political issues prevalent in Constantinople played out in Trebizond as well; one of them was whether to reconcile the eastern and western churches.

This controversy could have played a role in the toppling of George Komnenos, the sixth of the Grand Komnenes, by the nobility in 1280 while he was vacationing in the mountains.

The Grand Komnenes so far had not given up their claim of being the legitimate rulers of all Byzantium; the present (and last) ruling house at Constantinople, the Paleologi, were regarded as interlopers just as much as the Angeli had been. The logical grounds for such a claim were dubious—after all, had not the original Komnenes been just such a family of military usurpers? Most likely the pretence was kept up as a matter of domestic prestige, as during the reign of Manuel's son John II (1280–1297), fences with Constantinople were mended and the rulers of Trebizond quietly dropped their formal title of 'Byzantine emperors'. To seal the deal, John married a daughter of the real emperor, Michael VIII. Trebizond was gaining in prosperity and influence, and there were probably many there who dreamed of eventually overtaking the old Byzantine capital.

The thirty-three-year reign of Alexios II (1297–1330) brought problems for Trebizond. As the city prospered it incurred the rivalry of Genoa, which twice, in 1310 and 1319, attacked the outskirts. Away in Rome, Pope John XXII thought he would try and convert Alexios to Catholicism, but in 1330 bubonic plague carried off the emperor before the doctrinal blandishments could take effect. His successor Andronikos III reigned two years before succumbing to the same disease. This inaugurated an unsettled period. First Andronikos' successor, the 8-year-old Manuel II, was done to death after eight months of rule; we see here reproduced the old cycle of power and decadence that was so much a feature of past Byzantine history, with noble personages and achievements giving way to second generations of villainy and discord. Ordering the boy's death was Basil Komnenos, the younger son of Alexios II, who reigned from 1332 to 1340 and in that time managed to make the name of Komnenos hated almost as much as it had been under Andronikos I of Constantinople.

In April 1240 Basil's second wife, a member of the Paleologi, had him poisoned and elevated herself to the throne. She lasted fifteen months, as Trebizond came under attack from Turcoman tribes from central Asia. At this point another Anna Komnene makes her appearance in history, but she was to prove nowhere as capable and strong-minded as her illustrious twelfth–century namesake. This Anna Komnene was a daughter of Alexios II and is reported to have arrived in Trebizond with three Byzantine warships. She reigned for fourteen months as a puppet of the Trapezuntine Senate and the upper classes until unseated in September 1342 by a popular revolt led by John III Komnenos, apparently with the backing of Constantinople. Anna was strangled for her pains, and John, a weak and dissolute man, ruled with the aid of the Genoese. One by one, all the sins of old Byzantium were reviving in the city that wanted to be its successor.

Succeeding John was not a son but his father Michael, who in a burst of confusion in the previous year had reigned for a single day, only to be deposed. This
time he lasted five years, but with precious little to show for it except murderous
attacks by Genoese troops and the appearance of the Black Death plague, both
of which probably contributed to his public unpopularity. Stability returned in
December 1349, with the accession of a son of Basil, Alexios III. He is described
as tall, fair and good-looking, a lover of the good life and having boundless energy,
and may well have been compared to Byzantium's original Alexios I Komnenos.
He displayed some of the strength and resolve of the early Komnenes, as well as
their courage—he narrowly escaped being killed in a battle with the Turcomans
in 1355. In a remarkable forty-one-year reign Alexios III built up a strong central
administration with money exacted from greedy and recalcitrant nobles, some of
whom he had no compunctions in executing. The small area of the Trapezuntine
Empire no doubt made his task easier.

The start of the fifteenth century coincided with the tenth year of the respected
Manuel III Komnenos. His reign saw a reprieve for the Greeks, who for some
time had been facing a new Turkish threat in the form of the Ottomans. In 1402
the Ottoman Sultan Bayezid I was trounced by the Mongol warlord Timurlane at
Ankara and carried off in chains. But any popularity the Grand Komnenes may
have enjoyed thanks to Alexios III and Manuel III (who had gratefully allied himself with Timurlane) was frittered away by the latter's son Alexios IV (1417–1429)
who is suspected of having his father murdered. This Alexios married a daughter
of Byzantine Emperor John VIII, apparently to buttress diplomatic ties in the face
of a resurgent Ottoman threat. Two more daughters went to Muslim potentates
opposed to the Ottomans. Otherwise, little can be said for this callous character,
who was almost certainly done away with by his successor John IV. John's thirty-
one-year reign was marked by the great tragedy of the fall of Constantinople to the
Ottomans on 29 May 1453—the final and irrevocable end to the Roman Empire
in all its incarnations.

The conqueror of Constantinople, Sultan Mehmet II, now turned his attention
to this remaining Greek rump state at Trebizond, the elimination of which would
secure him control of all Asia Minor before the planned incursions into Europe.
More than a decade before, Sultan Murad I had attempted an amphibious landing
on Trebizond, but was defeated by rough seas. As a preliminary move Mehmet
demanded tribute from John IV, who gallantly refused. But John died in 1460,
to be replaced by his 4-year-old nephew. A relative, David Komnenos, seized the
opportunity to take the reins.

David had soaring ambitions such as assuming the role of crusader-in-chief to
eventually take back Jerusalem. He contacted the main powers of Europe to see if
he could get them to cooperate, but the crusading spirit had long ago sputtered

out; the European powers had other issues to worry and fight about. David, apparently overconfident in the little real military power he had, like his late brother refused Mehmet's demand for tribute. The sultan gathered his forces at Brusa and marched along the north coast of Anatolia. Sinope quickly capitulated, as did an independent Muslim province to the south-east. This enabled Mehmet to encircle Trebizond; after futile resistance lasting a month, the city surrendered on 15 August 1461. As the last of the Grand Komnenes took the road of exile, the last flickering light of what had been the mighty Byzantine Empire was snuffed out.

And the Komnenes themselves? For two years David Komnenos lived in comfortable circumstances near Adrianople with his three sons, under the watchful eye of the Turkish masters. Whether he was involved in some intrigue, or whether Mehmet simply didn't trust him to keep quiet, is not known; but all four were arrested in 1463 and thrown into Constantinople's Beyoğlu jail, where they were beheaded. David's daughter Anna was consigned to the sultan's harem. Another daughter, we are told, escaped by marrying into the Georgian noble house of Gurieli. And from that point all traces of the Komnenes of Byzantium disappear.

The name is still around. It's well-known in modern Greece; the Athens telephone directory lists well over 100 entries under Komnenos. Of course, it's impossible to tell whether any of these modern Komnenes have any blood connection with the old Byzantine dynasty. There are also plenty of Doukai and Paleologi, not to mention Choniates and Kontostephani and Angeli, enough to make it obvious to even the most cynical observer that if only in these names, Christian Byzantium lives on in the minds and hearts of the Greeks in south-east Europe.

Bibliographical Note

As I mentioned in the Preface, I have preferred to summarize all reference notes and attributions in this separate section rather than list them all by chapter. Whether I have done well or ill the reader will decide.

In the past fifty or so years the literature on Byzantium has grown dramatically, lifting the subject from its erstwhile status as a black sheep of mediaeval studies to a front-line subject. For a general excellently-written modern overview of Byzantium, the best recourse is John Julius Norwich's three-volume *Byzantium* (Penguin, London, 1988–1995), which not only does a great job of encapsulating eleven centuries of a gripping story into a digestible whole, but provides us with striking insights and interpretations worthy of being quoted in works such as this one. In my view Lord Norwich is fully the equal of older authorities on Byzantium such as A.A. Vasiliev, whose *History of the Byzantine Empire 324–1453* appeared in 1952 and set the standard for all subsequent works. *The Cambridge History of the Byzantine Empire*, edited by J. Shepard (Cambridge University Press, 2008), and *A History of Byzantium* by Timothy E. Gregory (Second Edition, Walden, Mass. and Oxford, Wiley-Blackwell, 2010) include the fruits of more recent scholarship.

Earlier one-volume books on Byzantium vary greatly in scope and style; some may be said to be journalistic in style (i.e. oversimplified and sensationalized) but nonetheless they contain useful nuggets. One of the best and earliest was Steven Runciman's wonderfully readable inaugural opus on Byzantium, titled simply *Byzantine Civilization* (Edward Arnold, London, 1933). C.W.C. Oman's *The Byzantine Empire* (T. Fisher Unwin Ltd, London, 1922) must have sparked many a twentieth-century interest in Byzantium in an era when the subject was still disparaged in the popular mind. A remarkable and vividly-written French work, *Byzantium: Its Triumphs and Tragedy*, by René Guerdan and translated from the French by D.L.B. Hartley (Allen & Unwin, London, 1956), brings the whole subject to theatrical life, though it is marred by several glaring inaccuracies. Unfortunately, all three books have long been out of print and can only be found through a diligent library search.

French scholarship boasts a considerable corpus of work on Byzantium. Charles Diehl, the doyen of French Byzantinists, came out with his defining *Histoire de l'Empire Byzantin* in 1918, at a time when the Ottoman Empire was on the eve of extinction and Europe and America were experiencing a new interest in the fate of ex-Byzantine lands such as Greece, Bulgaria, Turkey and Syria. In later years Diehl's *Byzantium:Greatness and Decline*, translated by N. Walford (Rutgers University Press, Brunswick, NJ, 1957) buttressed the knowledge of Byzantium in America. A more recent French authority is Helene Ahrweiler, who has pioneered studies in Byzantine political ideology. One of her latest works, *Why Byzantium?* (Metaichmio, Athens, 2012, in Greek only), has been useful to me for the more philosophical points of this book.

For a study of the Komnene dynasty the range of sources has to be narrowed and deepened. The period is rich in contemporary and detailed accounts of the eleventh and twelfth centuries. For Alexios I Komnenos the prime source is the *Alexiad* of his daughter Anna Komnene, translated from Greek by E.R.A. Sewter (Revised edition, Penguin Classics, London, 2009). All the unattributed quotes I use for the reign of Alexios I are from this work. It must, however, be used very carefully; Anna, while refreshingly candid and descriptive, nonetheless has an agenda, and that is to sanctify her father and justify her own devotion to him. This agenda sometimes leads her to hush up or minimize events that would take some of the sheen off that admittedly larger-than-life monarch. Fortunately, Peter Frankopan, a Cambridge scholar, guides us through some of these shoals in a series of detailed notes at the end.

Anna Komnene herself has been the subject of several studies, some of them from a moderately feminist standpoint. One of the most comprehensive is *Anna Komnene and her Times* (Garland, New York and London, 2000) a collection of monographs edited by Thalia Gouma-Peterson. In Greece, George Mintsis, a historian and political scientist, published *The "Erotic" Anna Komnene* (Stamoulis, Thessaloniki, 2005), which purports to analyse Anna's work through its supposed sexual-repression subtext but adds little to the study of the Komnene era as a whole. One of the most valuable aspects of Anna's work is the Greek perspective she provides on the First Crusaders, a perspective rather different from the self-righteous version that until recently was prevalent in the West. For this book Sir Steven Runciman's three-volume *The Crusades* (Penguin, London, 1991) has been a valuable companion and reference.

Michael Psellos, whose remarkable life and career saw the beginning of the Komnene dynasty, has left us his *Chronographia*, available in English in Penguin Classics as *Fourteen Byzantine Rulers* (translated and with an introduction by E.R.A. Sewter, 1966). Psellos' perceptive insights into the exercise of power are what give the book its immense value.

For the Komnenes after Alexios I, Niketas Choniates is the writer to turn to. Though other contemporaries such as Ioannes Zonaras and Ioannes Kinnamos also recorded events, Choniates is the most detailed. Again, any unattributed quotes in this text for the reigns of John II, Manuel I, Alexios II and Andronikos I are from

Choniates' inimitable *Annals*. A twelfth-century treasure, they have been rendered into lively English by Professor Harry Magoulias in *O City of Byzantium: The Annals of Niketas Choniates* (Wayne State University Press, Detroit, 1984). The *Annals* read almost like a Byzantine news magazine, where politics and scandals endlessly succeed one another, with Choniates not hesitating to pass devastating judgements where he sees they are merited.

For the chapter on the Scandinavians, Russians and Anglo-Saxons serving in the imperial Varangian Guard, I am heavily indebted to *The Viking Road to Byzantium* by H.R. Ellis Davidson (George Allen & Unwin, London, 1976). Apart from the occasional scholarly monograph, this may well be the sole full-length work on this little-known yet fascinating subject. Finally, the Grand Komnenes of Trebizond, another subject usually relegated to the obscurer alcoves of history, is brought back into the light in a reprint of William Miller's *Trebizond: The Last Greek Empire of the Byzantine Era, 1204–1461*, first published in 1922 but reprinted in 1969 (Argonaut, Chicago, 1969). As this book was in its final stages of writing, Professor Sergei Karpov of Moscow Lomonosov State University acquainted me with his monumental *History of the Empire of Trebizond*, which is at present available only in Russian and Greek.

The House of Komnene Family Tree

KOMNENE FAMILY TREE **(EMPERORS UNDERLINED)**

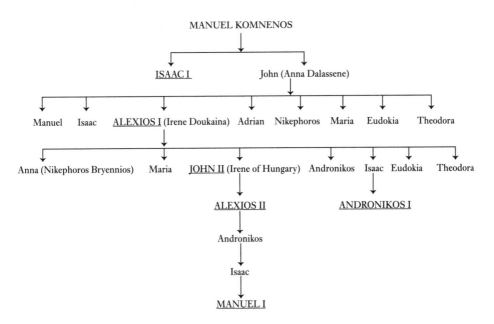

Index of Names

As is usual in works dealing with ancient or mediaeval history, the index is ordered by first rather than family names, e.g. 'Alexios I Komnenos' rather than 'Komnenos, Alexios I,' except for references to more recent persons such as writers, e.g. 'Runciman, S.'